AKSUM AND NUBIA

AKSUM AND NUBIA

Warfare, Commerce, and Political Fictions in Ancient Northeast Africa

by

George Hatke

New York University Press
and
Institute for the Study of the Ancient World
2013

Gentium Plus font provided by SIL International; Estrangelo Edessa font provided by Beth Marduto.

At the time of publication, the full-text of this work was available at: http://dlib.nyu.edu/awdl/isaw/hatke2013-aksum-and-nubia/ .

Library of Congress Cataloging-in-Publication Data

Hatke, George, 1978-
Aksum and Nubia : warfare, commerce, and political fictions in ancient Northeast Africa / George Hatke.
p. cm.
Includes bibliographical references and indexes.
ISBN 0-8147-6066-X (alk. paper)
1. Aksum (Ethiopia)--History--To 1500. 2. Nubia--History--To 1500. 3. Aksum (Ethiopia)--Relations--Nubia. 4. Nubia--Relations--Ethiopia--Aksum. I. Title.
DT390.A88H38 2013
939.78--dc23
2012040344

ISBN

ISBN 978-0-8147-6066-6 (cloth)
ISBN 978-0-8147-6278-3 (ebook)
ISBN 978-0-8147-6283-7 (ebook)

In memory of James Henry Breasted (1865-1935),

a historian of the Nile Valley through whose work I first became interested in history

Preface

This book began as a paper presented at the thirtieth annual conference of the Sudan Studies Association, held at Ohio State University May 13-15, 2011.[1] Having defended my doctoral dissertation on Aksumite relations with Ḥimyar at Princeton University some months earlier,[2] I approached the topic of Aksumite relations with Nubia with the aim of fleshing out the history of Aksum's foreign policy vis-à-vis regions to the west of Ethiopia. What I discovered is that, while the documentation for Aksumite contact with the middle Nile Valley was nowhere near as abundant as that available for its contact with South Arabia, there was still a great deal to be said on the subject of Aksumite-Nubian interaction—so much so, indeed, that it soon became clear that an article-length work could not adequately treat all the available evidence. During my two-year appointment as a post-doctoral fellow at the Institute for the Study of the Ancient World at New York University (2011-2013) I expanded upon what was already a lengthy paper, the result of which is the present monograph.

As the scope of this monograph is relatively narrow both chronologically and geographically I have sought to reach as wide an audience as possible by framing my thesis on Aksumite-Nubian interaction within the broader context of pre-industrial inter-polity relations, without presuming any prior knowledge of either Ethiopia or Nubia on the part of my readers. The intended audience includes anyone, scholar and layman alike, with an interest in African history or Late Antiquity. For my part, I approach the subject as a historian of the Red Sea region in ancient and medieval times with a background in Near Eastern Studies and a competence in several Semitic languages. It is not solely for these reasons, however, that I present in this volume a history of Aksumite relations with Nubia rather than a history of Nubian relations with Aksum. However one approaches the study of contact between Ethiopia and the middle Nile Valley in antiquity, the fact remains that the relevant written sources were almost without

[1] The working title of the paper was "Aksum and Nubia: Battles, Merchants, and Political Fictions in Ancient Northeast Africa."
[2] Hatke 2011.

exception produced by Ethiopians, rather than Nubians. Regarding the use of primary texts in direct quotation, all translations of sources in Geʻez, Syriac, and Arabic are my own. To these direct quotations I append the original text in transliteration and reserve the use of the original script only in isolated cases for the purpose of clarifying the phonology of certain words and proper names. For sources in Greek I rely on translations, while still incorporating the original Greek text wherever possible for the benefit of those readers with a background in Classics.

I would like to express my sincerest gratitude to the many people who helped make this book a reality. Among these I thank Roger Bagnall, Giovanni Ruffini, Glen Bowersock, and my peer reviewers for their thorough reading of the manuscript and their invaluable advice and suggestions. I also thank Richard Lobban and Jay Spaulding for reading and commenting on a preliminary draft of the paper I presented at the 2011 conference of the Sudan Studies Association. For assistance with technical matters ranging from layout to publication I thank Sebastian Heath. For the maps I am indebted to Jeffrey Becker and the Ancient World Mapping Center of the University of North Carolina. Any remaining errors in this book are my own. Last but not least I thank Alden Young, through whom I first learned of the Sudan Studies Association conference, and who encouraged me to present a paper there.

Contents

Preface 7

1. Introduction 11

1.1. Before Aksum and Kush 14

1.2. The First Millennium BCE: A Turning Point in State Formation 18

2. The Question of Aksumite Trade with Nubia 25

3. The Third Century CE: *Monumentum Adulitanum II* (RIE 277) 37

3.1. Cosmas Indicopleustes at Adulis 38

3.2. Dating *Monumentum Adulitanum II* 41

3.3. Aksumite Expansion in Northeast Africa 44

3.3.1. Aksum and Rome's Southern Frontier 48

3.3.2. Aksum and "Ethiopia" 52

3.3.3. Sasu: A Scribal Error for Kush? 53

3.3.4. Aksum's Northern and Western Frontiers in the Third Century 57

4. The Fourth Century CE: Aksum in Nubia 67

4.1. Ousanas and Kush: RIE 186 67

4.2. Aksum Invades Kush: Two Greek Inscriptions from Meroë 71

4.2.1. Dating RIE 286 and SNM 24841 75

4.2.2. The Political Implications of the First Aksumite Invasion of Kush 78

4.3. Trouble on the Western Front? A Possible Clue in RIE 186 80

4.4. The Noba: A New Force to be Reckoned With 82

4.5. ʻĒzānā's Nubian War 85

4.5.1. The Greek Account: RIE 271 86

4.5.2. The Vocalized Geʻez Account: RIE 189 99

4.5.2.1. The Haughty Noba 101

4.5.2.2. Pillaging the Towns of the Noba 106

4.5.2.3. The Attack on Kush 114

4.5.2.4. Tallying Up the Spoils of War 122

4.5.3. A Third Account of the Nubian War: RIE 190 129

4.6. Assessing the Impact of Aksum on Nubia in the Fourth Century 135

4.6.1. The Archaeological Evidence 136

4.6.2. The Graeco-Roman Textual Evidence 140

4.6.3. The Fall of Kush: Was Aksum to Blame? 143

5. After Kush: Aksum and Nubia in the Sixth Century CE 149
5.1. Kālēb and Nubia: RIE 191 150
5.2. The Nobades and Blemmyes: Would-be Mercenaries of Aksum? 158
5.3. Longinus' Mission and the Aksumite Presence in Alodia 161
5.4. Into the Middle Ages: *Ḥaḍānī* Dāne'ēl and Aksum's Western Neighbors 163
6. Conclusion 167
Bibliography 173
Maps 200
Map 1. Northeast Africa in the third century CE 200
Map 2. Northeast Africa in the fourth century CE 201
Map 3. Northeast Africa in the sixth century CE 202
Index 203

1. Introduction

The Ethiopian kingdom of Aksum[3] and the Nubian kingdom of Kush were two of the great African civilizations of antiquity. Both were expansionist polities linked to the outside world through long-distance trade and have left rich records of their respective histories in the form of monuments and inscriptions. Aksum dominated the northern highlands of Ethiopia from at least the turn of the Common Era down to the seventh century, Kush the middle Nile Valley as far south as the lower Blue Nile from the early ninth century BCE to the mid-fourth century CE. Thanks to these inscriptions, as well as to references in Graeco-Roman literature and foreign imports that have survived in the archaeological record, it is possible to reconstruct a fairly detailed history of how Aksum and Kush interacted with the outside world. Recent scholarship views foreign influences as playing a "continuing but fluctuating role" in Nubia,[4] an observation which applies equally to Aksum and which has the benefit of acknowledging northeast Africa's ties to the outside world without giving undue weight to the impact of foreign contacts, whether political, economic, or cultural, as agents of change. Unfortunately there is relatively little evidence of Aksumite contact with Kush. No mention of Aksum has yet been found in Kushite inscriptions, and though we find references to Nubia and its peoples in inscriptions of the Aksumite kings Ousanas (c. 310-330 CE) and 'Ēzānā (c. 330-370 CE), such epigraphic material has long suffered from misinterpretation, in addition to which the extent and nature of

[3] It is certainly true that the ancient kingdom of Aksum encompassed not only northern Ethiopia but also much of what is now Eritrea. By referring to Aksum as an Ethiopian polity the author does not wish to imply that modern Eritreans have any less claim to the Aksumite legacy than modern Ethiopians. Rather, Ethiopia is simply employed in the present context as shorthand for the northern Horn of Africa, including the area of present-day Ethiopia and Eritrea but excluding Djibouti and Somalia, much as one might classify the Harappan civilization as Indian, even though it was based in the Indus Valley of today's Pakistan.

[4] Connah 2001: 63. This perspective is to a large extent a reaction to earlier diffusionist theories about Nubian, particularly Kushite, influence on the rest of Africa. On Kushite civilization as an amalgam of different influences, rather than a center of cultural diffusion across Africa, see Haycock 1971: 30.

Aksumite-Kushite relations outside this fourth-century timeframe remain obscure.

To the extent that conflict between the two kingdoms occurred, there seems to have been an imbalance of military power, for while what textual evidence does survive from the reigns of Ousanas and ʻĒzānā records that the Aksumites invaded Nubia on two occasions, there is little evidence of Kushite military activities to the east of the Nile Valley. A far greater threat to Aksum than Kush was the Noba, a Nubian-speaking group already ensconced in Kush, who attacked Aksum's western frontier in the fourth century CE. Overall, however, Nubia was never as important to Aksum geopolitically as Arabia. Despite the evidence of Aksumite military activities in Nubia, Aksum was always more interested in its Arabian neighbors across the Red Sea, and is known to have occupied much of present-day Yemen in the third century and again in the sixth under the leadership of the great warrior-king Kālēb (c. 510-540 CE). By contrast, no full-scale occupation of Nubia was ever attempted by the Aksumites. Nevertheless, the fact that Aksum was victorious in its confrontations with Nubia in the fourth century provided fertile grounds for developing the political fiction of rule over Nubia, a political fiction maintained by later Aksumite kings. It is no surprise, then, to find Kālēb and his son and successor Waʻzeb (c. 540-560 CE) laying claim to Kush and the Noba in their royal titles, side by side with their parallel claims to vast tracts of territory in South Arabia.

The present study contends that the reasons for the seemingly weak ties between Aksum and Nubia can be explained by the geographical orientation of the Ethiopian Highlands and the middle Nile Valley. This is hardly reason to assume rigid geographical determinism, however, since Aksumite records of war with Nubia indicate quite clearly that the middle Nile Valley, though not as important to Aksum either politically or economically as South Arabia, was still by no means insignificant strategically to the Ethiopian kingdom. It will be argued that the main cause for conflict between Kush and Aksum in the fourth century had less to do with political or economic rivalry at the highest level, than with the security of the frontier region that separated them. Documentation for this conflict is provided by a series of Aksumite inscriptions in Greek and Ge'ez from the reigns of Ousanas and 'Ēzānā. Following the fourth century we no longer have the benefit of such documentation of Aksumite-Nubian relations. Indeed there is no evidence at all for Aksumite relations with Nubia in the fifth century, after the fall of Kush. In the sixth century it becomes possible to pick up the trail once more, since it is at that time that we find archaeological and literary evidence of contact between Aksum and the Nubian kingdom of Alodia. While this study makes no attempt to substantially rewrite the history of Aksumite-Nubian contact, it is hoped that it can at least clarify what we can and cannot say about relations between the two regions, as well as draw attention to the need for further archaeological research in the still understudied area between the Nile Valley and the Ethiopian Highlands.

The layout of this monograph is as follows. Chapter 2 focuses on the period between the first and third centuries CE and argues that, as far as long-distance trade is concerned, the economies of Kush and Aksum operated not very differently but independently of each other. That of Kush was intimately bound to the Nile Valley, which constituted not only the agricultural base of the Kushite state but also the main route—indeed the only regularly used route—linking Nubia to Egypt. Aksum, however, depended on agriculture in the Ethiopian Highlands but, while several tributaries of the Nile, most notably the Blue Nile, originate in these highlands, Aksum's main outlet to the outside world was the Red Sea. In no way, then, can Aksum be classified as a civilization of the Nile Valley. During the period in question the region between Kush and Aksum remained a nebulous one, occupied by peoples with some cultural ties to Ethiopia but, as far as we can tell, of little significance as a crossroads for Kushite-Aksumite interaction. Chapter 3 focuses on Aksumite expansion towards the west and north, based on the testimony of *Monumentum Adulitanum II* (RIE 277), a third-century Aksumite inscription erected at Adulis which, though now lost, was copied in the sixth century by Cosmas Indicopleustes. It will be argued that, in the course of the military campaigns described in *Monumentum Adulitanum II*, the Aksumite army pushed as far north as the southeastern frontier of Roman Egypt and as far west as the modern Sudanese-Ethiopian borderlands, Kush was left in peace. Since the economy of third-century Kush does not seem to have depended very heavily—if at all—on either the Eastern Desert between the Nile Valley and the Red Sea or the Sudanese-Ethiopian borderlands, whatever territorial gains Aksum made at this time seem to have had no direct impact on Kush. With Chapter 4 we come to the first hard evidence of conflict between Aksum and Kush in the form of several Aksumite inscriptions in Greek and Ge'ez, some from the town of Aksum and some from Meroë, all of which describe Aksumite military campaigns in Nubia. The case will be made that two such campaigns took place, the first in the reign of Ousanas and the second in the reign of 'Ēzānā. While Ousanas' campaign seems to have reached Meroë, and thus involved the Kushite state directly, the second campaign, waged by 'Ēzānā, focused on curbing the power of the Noba, a people who threatened Aksum's western frontier. Based on chronological details and Christological formulae in the Greek record of 'Ēzānā's campaign (RIE 271), it is possible to date the second Aksumite invasion of Nubia to 360. But in neither case did the Aksumites succeed in holding onto Nubia for long, and in fact the long-standing thesis that the kingdom of Kush was brought to an end by 'Ēzānā's invasion is open to serious question. Nevertheless, the political fiction of Aksumite rule of Kush persisted into the sixth century, as will be discussed in detail in Chapter 5. This chapter also examines the evidence, preserved in Syriac by John of Ephesus and supported in part by limited archaeological evidence, for sporadic Aksumite contact with post-Kushite Nubia. It will be argued that at no time in the sixth century, much less later, did Aksum exercise any political control in Nubia. But before embarking on this study of Aksumite-Nubian relations over a five-century period it is fitting to begin with a brief survey of the evidence of Ethiopian-Nubian contact before the first century CE, a topic with which the remainder of this introductory chapter is concerned.

1.1 Before Aksum and Kush

Commercial contact between the Nile Valley and the Horn of Africa pre-dates the earliest written records. Already in Late Predynastic times (c. 4000-3000 BCE) Egypt imported obsidian, whose nearest sources are in Ethiopia and Eritrea.[5] That the northern Horn of Africa was the source for at least some of this obsidian is evident from a fragment of a vessel from Abydos which was made of obsidian from the northern Rift Valley of Ethiopia.[6] The discovery of obsidian fragments in the course of excavations in the Gash (al-Qāsh) Delta of the eastern Sudan and in Nubia indicates that the middle Nile Valley and the desert to the east was also part of this network of trade.[7] Initially much of the obsidian from the Horn of Africa probably reached Egypt through middlemen in the eastern Sudan, for it was only with the shift from reed or papyrus to wooden boats around the mid-fourth millennium BCE and the introduction of the sail c. 3100 BCE that the Egyptians would have acquired the ability to sail over long distances in the Red Sea[8] and thus reach the northern Horn directly. There are also hints of indirect connections between the Nile Valley and the Indian Ocean by way of the Red Sea and the northern Horn of Africa from an early date. It is probable that the humped zebu (*Bos indicus*), a domesticate of Indian origin which began spreading westward c. 3000 BCE and is attested in an early second millennium BCE context at Laga Oda in Eritrea,[9] reached the Nile Valley via the Horn.[10] That Asian broomcorn millet (*Panicum miliaceum*), attested in

[5] Zarins 1990: 532-5; Inizan and Francaviglia 2002; Mitchell 2005: 80; Boivin and Fuller 2009: 130-1; Khalidi 2009: 283.

[6] Roy 2011: 264.

[7] Zarins 1990: 533; Phillips 2003a: 439-40. As no obsidian material has been found in Predynastic contexts at Elephantine on the northern frontier of Nubia, it is unlikely that the obsidian found in Egypt came from Nubia by way of the Nile (Roy 2011: 264). A Red Sea route is more likely. On Predynastic maritime trade, see Ward 2006: 126. Predynastic Egyptian pottery found in the eastern Sudan (Fattovich 1995: 72) may be related to this trade.

[8] Boivin et al. 2009: 260, 261.

[9] Mitchell 2005: 81, 83.

[10] A pottery figurine of a humped zebu from Zilum in northeastern Nigeria, dating from c. 600-400 BCE (Magnavita 2006: 71-3, 78), provides what may be a *terminus ante quem* for the zebu's diffusion from the Horn into Nubia, as Nubia would have been the likeliest intermediate stage along the route of diffusion from the Red Sea coast to the Lake Chad basin. The zebu is depicted in Egyptian art as early as c. 2000-1500 BCE (Boivin and Fuller 2009: 159), indicating that the initial stage of the animal's diffusion from the Horn to the Nile Valley must have taken place by that time. One should be careful not to read too much into the diffusion of the humped zebu to the western end of the Indian Ocean, however, as this process probably involved only a

Yemen as early as c. 2000 BCE, appears in Sudanese Nubia by c. 1700 BCE[11] also suggests that Nubia felt the impact of Afro-Arabian trade to a limited degree. Indirect evidence for the maintenance of trade ties between Nubia and the northern Horn is provided by references in Egyptian inscriptions from the late third millennium BCE to incense obtained from Nubia,[12] which could only have come from regions further to the southeast, where trees producing aromatic gum are found.[13] Nubian use of incense imported from the Horn of Africa is implied by the incense burners produced by the A-Group culture (c. 3700-2800 BCE), some of which contain residue of burnt substances which, though not yet subjected to chemical analysis, are likely derived from aromatic materials.[14] To the Egyptians, the incense-producing region par excellence was the land of Punt, most likely located along the coast of present-day Sudan and Eritrea.[15] Archaeological evidence for a Bronze-Age trade network linking Nubia with the Horn has been detected in pottery from the Gash Delta, based upon which some scholars have suggested that Nubia exerted a cultural influence on regions to the east of the Nile through the mediation of the Kerma and C-Group cultures (c. 2500-1500 BCE).[16] In addition to indications in Egyptian inscriptions that the Puntites traded with their neighbors to the west and north,[17] evidence for Nubian involvement in Egyptian trade with Punt has recently come to light at Marsā Gawāsīs, the Red Sea port from which the Egyptians sailed to Punt, at which Nubian sherds of C-Group and Kerma type

limited number of zebu (Boivin et al. 2009: 267) and involved a significant interbreeding of African taurine and Indian zebu stocks (Fuller et al. 2011: 547).

[11] Boivin et al. 2009: 266; Fuller et al. 2011: 547.

[12] Grimal 1992: 87.

[13] Resinous material has been found at several Predynastic Egyptian sites, and while not all of it has been fully analyzed, it is quite possible that much of it reached Egypt via Nubia (Roy 2011: 252). If so, the northern Horn of Africa is the likeliest source, as Nubia lacks trees producing aromatic gums.

[14] Boivin and Fuller 2009: 138.

[15] Kitchen 1990: 173. Arguments for locating Punt in South Arabia or Somalia, also famous in antiquity as sources of aromatic gums, are not supported by the evidence (Kitchen 2004: 28-30).

[16] Fattovich 1995: 72; Manzo 1997: 79-83; Phillips 2003a: 437; Mitchell 2005: 79-80.

[17] Kitchen 1990: 174-7.

have been found.[18] At the site of Kerma itself, believed by many scholars to have been the capital of a kingdom called Kush in Egyptian inscriptions,[19] a fragmentary painting of a royal tomb chapel from c. 1700 BCE depicts a sailed vessel suggestive of an ocean-going boat, together with stilted huts entered by ladders similar in form to the Puntite houses depicted in reliefs from the reign of Ḥātshepsūt (c. 1479-1458 BCE).[20] It is possible, then, that this painting reflects earlier contact between Kerma and Punt. Nubian relations with the Horn were not without political significance, as the coterminous emergence of what may have been a complex chiefdom or proto-state based at Maḥall Teglinos in the eastern Sudan, which is known to have traded with both Ethiopia and Nubia, has also been suspected,[21] thus raising the possibility that economic relations between Nubia and the Horn led to secondary state development in the borderlands between the two regions. The political effects of Nubian relations with the Horn are also reflected in an inscription from the tomb of one Sobeknakht, governor of al-Kāb in Upper Egypt c. 1575-1550 BCE, which states that the Kushites of Upper Nubia forged an alliance with the Medjayū tribes of the Eastern Desert and the Puntites and that all three groups together invaded Egypt.[22] Thus, whether through trade or politics it is clear that the peoples of Nubia and the northern Horn of Africa were in contact in late prehistory and throughout the Bronze Age. Despite this economic and political ferment, the evidence for contact between Ethiopia and Nubia becomes much scarcer in later times, during which an acceleration in social and political development in northeast Africa gave rise to a new kingdom of Kush in Nubia as well as the kingdom of Di'mat in northern Ethiopia and Eritrea.[23]

[18] Manzo 2010.
[19] Kendall 1997.
[20] Boivin and Fuller 2009: 140.
[21] Fattovich 1995: 72-3; al-Nūr 2004.
[22] Davies 2003.
[23] Phillipson (2009a: 266-8) notes that inscriptions mentioning Di'mat (*D'mt*) are very few, numbering only six as of 2008, and on this basis questions whether Di'mat was the only Pre-Aksumite state in the northern Horn of Africa, or was even the name of a state at all. It is true that there are Pre-Aksumite inscriptions, including royal inscriptions, which do not mention Di'mat, though it need not follow from this that these inscriptions are to be associated with a separate (and apparently nameless!) polity. Indeed Manzo

1.2. The First Millennium BCE: A Turning Point in State Formation

The early first millennium BCE marks a turning point in the history of both Nubia and the Horn of Africa. Sometime around the beginning of the ninth century BCE a powerful Nubian state arose at Napata (c. 400 km north of Khartoum),[24] the written history of which we can follow with reasonable confidence from the reign of its King Alara (=Ary?), who ruled c. 785-765 BCE.[25] The kingdom based at Napata was known both locally and abroad as Kush. That this kingdom bears the name given to Upper Nubia in earlier Egyptian inscriptions likely reflects the continuity of toponyms in the middle Nile Valley rather than the lineal descent of the Napatan dynasty from the older kingdom of Kush.[26] Even after its capital shifted 200 km south to Meroë c. 250 BCE, the Nubian kingdom continued to be called Kush (Meroitic *Qes*), and it was by this name, in the form *Kāsū*, that it was known to the Aksumites. To the southeast of Nubia, Semitic-speaking peoples from the Arabian Peninsula had begun settling in the northern highlands of today's Ethiopia and Eritrea sometime before the turn of the first millennium BCE[27] and there intermingled with the indigenous

(2009: 299-300) suggests that the "uniformity of the Pre-Aksumite decorum system over a large geographical area" resulted from the implementation of a planned program aimed at the construction and communication of a unitary state identity of Di'mat. Thus with due caution, and for lack of any better term, the name Di'mat will be retained in this study as the name for the first state in Ethiopia.

[24] A longer chronology, stretching back to c. 1000 BCE, has been proposed by Morkot 2000: 140-4, though the prevailing opinion among scholars is that the era of the preliterate rulers of the Napatan dynasty extends for six reigns up to King Alara (c. 785-765 BCE), in which case the inception of the dynasty can be placed no earlier than c. 885 BCE (Zibelius-Chen 2006: 284).

[25] Morkot 2000: 147-50, 156-7.

[26] Fattovich 1995: 69.

[27] Archaeological evidence of the diffusion of southern Levantine material culture to Yemen during the fourth and third millennia BCE (Buffa 2007: 271-7, 278-9) may provide a context for the migration of pre-literate Semitic-speakers to South Arabia. This connection was proposed some years ago by Knauf (1988), who argued for the settlement of western Arabia by Semitic-speakers from the Levant after c. 2000 BCE, based also on archaeological evidence as well as on similarities between Canaanite and Arabian toponyms. Although Marrassini (2003: 146) suggests that some Semitic-speakers had begun moving across the Red Sea from Arabia to the Horn of Africa as early as the third millennium BCE, implying an earlier date for the presence of Semitic-speakers in Arabia than that proposed by Knauf, archaeological evidence of Bronze Age contact between South Arabia and

Cushitic-speaking agro-pastoralists.[28] Then around the eighth century BCE the cultural impact of Saba', a kingdom based in northwestern Yemen,[29] made itself felt in the northern Horn of Africa, where the South Arabian system of writing (*musnad*), the Sabaean language and pantheon, and the South Arabian style of art and architecture were adopted by the elite of the local kingdom of Di'mat.[30] Our knowledge of Di'mat's history, based as it is on a handful of brief inscriptions, is considerably more fragmentary than that of Kushite history, and we possess nothing like a coherent narrative. Absolute dates for the rise and fall of Di'mat are difficult to determine on the basis of the epigraphic evidence but,[31] while an approximate timeframe of c. 700-

the Horn of Africa suggests that interaction was relatively limited during the third millennium BCE but increased during the following millennium (Buffa 2007: 261-71, 278).

[28] On the archaeological remains of these indigenous agro-pastoralists, see Finneran 2007: 67-108. Based on a study of Semitic and Cushitic vocabulary relating to agriculture and livestock, it has been argued that, while the indigenous Cushitic-speaking peoples of Ethiopia did practice agriculture, most agricultural technology, including the plough, was introduced by Semites from South Arabia (Marrassini 2003).

[29] Better known to the west as Sheba, by which Saba' is known in the Hebrew Old Testament.

[30] Robin and Maigret 1998. While the South Arabian, specifically Sabaean, influence is, on account of its prominence in monumental culture, more visible than the local, archaeological evidence indicates that indigenous traditions prevailed at the popular level (Finneran 2007: 138-9, 144-5; Fattovich 2009; Manzo 2009; Phillipson 2009a). At the same time, many recent studies, by treating Sabaean influence in the northern Horn of Africa as a superficial phenomenon, overlook the more deeply-rooted impact of Semitic speech, which was diffused into the region by way of South Arabia. Given the internal diversity of Ethiosemitic, and particularly the distinctiveness of the Gurage group, the diffusion of Semitic to the Horn of Africa is likely to have been not only a long but also a very complex process (Boivin et al. 2009: 271). A recent study gives an estimate of c. 2850 YBP for the origin of Ethiosemitic, corresponding roughly with the probable date of initial Sabaean settlement in the Horn of Africa (Kitchen et al. 2009: 2709), but fails to take into consideration the significant disparity between Ancient South Arabian and Ethiosemitic. Given the lexical and morphological differences between the two, it is clear that Sabaic cannot be regarded as the ancestor of all Semitic languages spoken in the Horn of Africa (Appleyard 1996: 207-8; cf. Robin and Maigret 1998: 792-3). This being the case, there is every reason to believe that the first stage of Semitic settlement in the Horn of Africa predates Sabaean influence, perhaps by several centuries.

[31] Kitchen's attempt to do just this is premised on his assumption that Di'mat was actually ruled from South Arabia (Kitchen 1994: I: 115-17), a theory which is entirely without support (Finneran 2007: 144).

400 BCE for Di'mat has been proposed in light of ceramic evidence,[32] such epigraphic material as exists suggests that those Di'matite kings attested in inscriptions reigned over a shorter period than this, most likely between the end of the eighth century BCE and the beginning of the sixth.[33] Excavations at Yehā in northern Ethiopia, where early material showing cultural links with South Arabia has come to light, also suggest that the upper end of the timeframe for Di'mat can be extended into the eighth century BCE.[34]

Much as the Kushite elite modeled their art, architecture, and religious and ceremonial life on Egyptian prototypes, to the point of erecting inscriptions in the Egyptian language and building pyramids over the tombs of their rulers,[35] the elite of Di'mat emulated the high culture of Saba' and to that end built temples based on South Arabian prototypes and erected inscriptions in the Sabaic language.[36] In both cases foreign influence was to an extent diffused by expatriate communities, represented in Di'mat by merchants and artisans hailing from Saba'[37] and in Nubia by Egyptian civil servants who took up residence during the period of pharaonic occupation in the New Kingdom (c. 1539-1077 BCE).[38] Yet the Egyptians in Nubia and the Sabaeans in Ethiopia always remained few in number[39] and the cultural

[32] Finneran, loc. cit.: 119-20. These dates correspond roughly with the combined Yehā I and Yehā II phases proposed by Fattovich 2009: 281-2, who is, however, wary of designating Pre-Aksumite culture as "Di'mat" (ibid.: 287). It is true that graffiti from the Qōḥaytō Plateau in Eritrea exhibit numerous similarities with the early forms of the *musnad* script found at Durayb-Yalā, Hajar bin Humayd, and Jabal Balaq, dating from the beginning of the first millennium BCE (Ricci 1994), though these graffiti, even if correctly dated, need not be related to Di'mat and may in fact have been left by Sabaean merchants—or by Sabaicized Ethiopians—before the rise of Di'mat.

[33] Robin and Maigret 1998: 783. The comparative rarity of references to Di'mat in inscriptions also suggests that it was a short-lived polity (Manzo 2009: 300).

[34] Robin and Maigret: 778; Manzo 2009: 292.

[35] Welsby 1996: 73-7, 91-2, 100-13, 115-22, 178-9, 189.

[36] Robin and Maigret 1998; Finneran 2007: 120, 121-2, 130, 134-7, 145; Manzo 2009: 299-300.

[37] Robin and Maigret 1998: 782, 789, 790; Finneran 2007: 122, 144; Phillipson 2009a: 267.

[38] Morkot 2000: 75.

[39] Kitchen et al. 2009: 2709; Finneran 2007: 144; Morkot 2000: 81-3.

influence of both seems to have been mediated to a large degree through locals.[40] To this it should be added that Saba' never actually ruled Ethiopia as Egypt did Nubia.[41] Furthermore, the internalization of foreign influences in no way hindered independent cultural innovation on the part of the Nubians and the Ethiopians as time went on.[42] Nowhere is this more apparent than in the development by both peoples of new scripts for the purpose of writing local languages. Thus from the late second century BCE on the Kushites wrote in Meroitic, a language of unknown, though probably Nilo-Saharan, origin using first a simplified form of hieroglyphics and, somewhat later, a cursive script,[43] while the Ethiopians, following the rise of the Aksumite state between c. 150 BCE and the turn of the Common Era, came to write in Ge'ez, an Ethiosemitic language using a cursive script (*fidal*) based on the *musnad* script of South Arabia.[44] Even so, links with the past were maintained as Kushite kings, portrayed wearing Egyptian attire, continued to be buried beneath pyramids until the very end of their kingdom around the mid-fourth century, much as Aksumite kings paid

[40] Thus the inscriptions from the period of the Di'mat kingdom display at times certain local idiosyncrasies in morphology and vocabulary (Drewes 1980; Robin and Maigret 1998: 784-7; Finneran 2007: 120, 121-2; Phillipson 2009a: 265), indicating that the authors were in many cases Ethiopians, not expatriate Sabaeans. In the case of Nubia, Egyptian influence was mediated through the children of the local Nubian elite who were educated in Egypt (Morkot 2000: 81-7). On the complexities of ethnic identity in Nubia under Egyptian rule, see Smith 2003.

[41] Finneran 2007: 144. The reference to Saba' (*S^1b'*) in the titles of some Di'matite rulers has been taken as evidence of a close union between Di'mat and Saba', if not the tutelage of the latter (Robin and Maigret 1998: 788), though it is more probable that, since *S^1b'* can refer to both the kingdom of Saba' and the Sabaean people, it was used in royal titles in reference to the Sabaean expatriate community in Di'mat. This scenario is also (cautiously) suggested by Phillipson 2009a: 267.

[42] In the Ethiopian context, the culture of the Proto-Aksumite period (c. 400-150 BCE) owes nothing to South Arabia and is instead African in character (Finneran 2007: 141-4). On Nubianizing trends in religion and art during later phases of Kushite history, see Welsby 1996: 77-9, 181-5; Edwards 2004: 179, 181.

[43] On the Nilo-Saharan, specifically East Sudanic, origins of Meroitic, see Rilly 2007: 471-87; idem 2009: 2. On the history and use of Meroitic in Nubia, see Welsby 1996: 189-95; Edwards 2004: 176-79; Rilly 2007.

[44] Schneider 1983; Frantsouzoff 2006.

homage to South Arabian culture in the fourth and sixth centuries CE by erecting inscriptions in Ge'ez using the *musnad* script.

The early first millennium BCE, then, marks the stage at which the elites of both Nubia and Ethiopia settled decisively on their chief route of contact with the outside world: Kush with Egypt via the Nile Valley, Di'mat with South Arabia via the Red Sea.[45] This development was in due course to have political effects, for the Kushite elite not only adopted the culture of pharaonic Egypt but actually invaded Egypt in the mid- to late eighth century BCE[46] and ruled the country as its Twenty-fifth Dynasty until 663 BCE, when they were driven out by the Assyrians.[47] Di'mat never ruled South Arabia, though its kings claimed dominion over the expatriate Sabaean community of Ethiopia as well as the indigenous people.[48] Yet Di'mat's successor, the kingdom of Aksum, would indeed occupy the Tihāma of western Yemen in the third century CE,[49] and all of South Arabia in the reign of King Kālēb (c. 510-540 CE).[50] By contrast, Kush and its Ethiopian neighbors, developing as they did along increasingly different trajectories, appear to have left little evidence of direct contact with each other for most of the first millennium BCE.[51] In Tomb 12 at Yehā, an alabaster vessel has

[45] This might explain why, as noted by Manzo (2009: 300), South Arabian cultural elements were favored over those of Nubia in Pre-Aksumite Ethiopia.

[46] Although the Kushite king Ka<u>sh</u>ta, who came to the Nubian throne c. 760 BCE, managed to establish control as far north as the Aswān region (Grimal 1992: 335), probably c. 755-750 BCE (Török 1997: 145), it was not until the reign of his son and successor Piye (c. 753-723 BCE) and even more so that of the latter's brother <u>Sh</u>abaqo (c. 722-707 BCE) that the Kushites achieved control of all of Egypt (Welsby 1996: 63). Given that the establishment of Kushite rule in Egypt was a long process, it is difficult to assign a precise date to its inception.

[47] Although Kushite rule in Egypt came to an end in 663 BCE, official documents in Thebes continued to be dated according to the regnal years of the Kushite king Tanwetamani as late as 656 BCE (Grimal 1992: 352; Török 1997: 187). This, however, reflects nothing more than the political fiction of continued Kushite rule in Egypt.

[48] See above, n. 41.

[49] On the epigraphic sources relating to Aksumite relations with South Arabia in the third century, see Robin 1989.

[50] Kālēb's invasions of South Arabia are treated in detail by Hatke 2011.

[51] Fattovich (2004: 74) believes that Kushite military campaigns against the Tigrayan Highlands precipitated Di'mat's decline, though there is no evidence that the Kushite army was ever active in that region. For his part,

come to light which has been compared with vessels from royal Kushite cemeteries dating between the eighth and seventh centuries BCE,[52] suggesting ties between Di'mat and the Nile Valley. Such ties do not, however, appear to have been very important,[53] and to date no material with demonstrable links to Di'mat has come to light in Nubia. Even in the Gash region Pre-Aksumite-style pottery is limited to a handful of isolated finds,[54] and what few objects of Nile Valley origin have been discovered in Ethiopia in Pre-Aksumite times seem to post-date Di'mat's floruit. Among these are a few bell-shaped cups from Yehā and Ḥaweltī in northern Ethiopia, dating from the mid-first millennium BCE, which are paralleled by Kushite vessels from the same period.[55] From the period c. 400-150 BCE date two blue faïence amulets representing Egyptian deities, one the god Ptaḥ, the other the head of the goddess Ḥatḥor, both discovered in a deposit of ritual objects at Ḥaweltī.[56] A tiny figurine of carnelian from Matarā in Eritrea and an uninscribed amulet from Aksum also seem to be Nile Valley imports.[57] A Kushite origin for these objects is quite possible, though an Egyptian origin cannot be dismissed, particularly in light of a renewed Egyptian interest in the Red Sea region during the Ptolemaic era (305-30 BCE).[58]

Finneran (2007: 143) believes that the use of model axes as grave goods, as well as a possible instance of a human sacrificial burial at Bēta Gīyōrgīs, can be compared with similar funerary practices in Nubia, and can thus be regarded as evidence of a cultural exchange between the two regions. Such cultural traits as these, however, are too vague and are encountered over too wide an area to support Finneran's hypothesis. Cultural links between Ethiopia and Nubia have also been seen in a stone sphinx from 'Ādī Gramaten in Eritrea (Manzo 2009: 295, 296 [Fig. 4]), recalling the sphinx motif found on other Pre-Aksumite objects (Finneran 2007: 136). But since the sphinx is a common a motif throughout the Near East, and since the sphinxes depicted in Kushite art are too different in style from their Pre-Aksumite counterparts, any direct link between Ethiopia and Nubia in this case seems unlikely.

52 Fattovich 1990: 14; idem 2009: 282.

53 As Fattovich (2009: 284) points out, very few ceramics from Yehā are comparable in style to Kushite pottery.

54 Finneran 2007: 114; Fattovich 2009: 283, 285.

55 Fattovich 1990: 14; idem 2009: 284.

56 De Contenson 1963: 48.

57 Chittick 1982: 51.

58 The Ptolemies are known to have sent several elephant-hunting expeditions to the Horn of Africa (Raschke 1978: 946-8 [n. 1185-1186]; Casson 1993). The inscription of Ptolemy III (246-222 BCE) discovered at Adulis in

The discovery of a large number of Ptolemaic beads in Tomb 6 at the Ona Enda 'Abbāy Zawgē site at Bēta Gīyōrgīs near Aksum suggests as much.[59] More clearly Nubian in origin are four bronze vessels found at 'Ādī Galamō to the west of Ḥaweltī, one of which is engraved with images of lotus flowers and frogs and another embossed with a line of cattle.[60] These motifs are common in late Kushite art, the closest parallels to the frog and lotus decoration dating from the first- to third-century CE.[61] Similarly, the line of cattle is closely related to the decoration on a bronze bowl from Karanog in Egyptian Nubia, dating from roughly the same period.[62] Given its chronological context, the 'Ādī Galamō material reflects Kushite trade with Aksum rather than with Aksum's predecessors. With this we enter the Aksumite period with which this study is primarily concerned.

the sixth century CE (§3.1) could well have been erected in the course of one of the Ptolemaic expeditions to the southern Red Sea. A votive stele of Ptolemaic date, first discovered by the Scottish traveler James Bruce at Aksum in 1770 and presented in 1955 to the National Museum of Scotland (Phillips 1997: 449), may also be a relic of Ptolemaic contact with the Horn.

[59] Finneran 2007: 143.

[60] Leclant 1961: 392.

[61] Kirwan 1960: 172; Chittick 1982: 51.

[62] For this image, see Connah 2001: 51 (Fig. 2.11).

2. The Question of Aksumite Trade with Nubia

Though excavations at the hill of Bēta Gīyōrgīs indicate that the district of Aksum, the town after which the kingdom took its name, was occupied at least as early as the fourth century BCE,[63] it was not until the first century CE that the kingdom of Aksum was first mentioned by Graeco-Roman authors. That it attracted the attention of the Mediterranean world at this time is undoubtedly the result of the increase in western trade with India via the Red Sea following the conquest of Egypt by Augustus in 30 BCE, a development which brought Ethiopia into commercial contact with the Roman Empire. Though the Ptolemaic kings of Egypt had sent numerous expeditions as far south as Somalia in search of elephants for use in warfare,[64] their contact with the indigenous peoples of the Horn of Africa remained limited, that with India even more so.[65] With the establishment of regular trade with the Red Sea and Indian Ocean under the Julio-Claudian dynasty (27 BCE-68 CE), however, Graeco-Roman authors began to show much greater interest in the commerce of the Horn of Africa.[66] Chief among these authors was an anonymous merchant from Egypt whose *Periplus of the Erythraean Sea*, written in Greek sometime in the mid-first century CE as a guide to fellow traders, provides a wealth of information on the commerce of the Red Sea and the western Indian Ocean.[67] Given Ethiopia's close ties to the Graeco-Roman world even at this early date, it is no surprise to learn from the *Periplus* that the

[63] Fattovich 2004: 74.
[64] Casson 1993.
[65] Sidebotham 1986: 7-12.
[66] Ibid.: 13-47, 116-41. On the new pattern of seafaring, based on sailing in open water with the monsoon winds, which began c. 120-100 BCE and facilitated the growth of Indian Ocean trade, see Curtin 1984: 96-100. That Roman trade with the Indian Ocean world greatly exceeded that of the Ptolemies probably has much to do with the fact that the population of the Roman Empire, estimated at approximately fifty to sixty million, was far greater than that of Ptolemaic Egypt, which was probably no more than seven to eight million (Sidebotham 1996: 289).
[67] Casson 1989. On the Egyptian origin of the anonymous author of the *Periplus*, see ibid.: 7; Seland 2010: 14.

Ethiopian king of the day, one Zoskales,[68] was proficient in reading and writing Greek.[69] That later Aksumite kings erected inscriptions in Greek[70] demonstrates that Zoskales was by no means an exceptional case in this regard. Though the author of the *Periplus* does not specifically refer to Zoskales as a king of Aksum and mentions him instead in the context of the commerce of Adulis, he calls Aksum (Ἀξωμίτης) a "metropolis" (μητρόπολις) but refers to Adulis as simply "a fair-sized village" (κώμη σύμμετρος).[71] This strongly suggests that Aksum, not Adulis, was the political center of Ethiopia by this time. In addition, Zoskales is described in the text as the only ruler of the region between Ptolemaïs Theron on the Sudanese coast[72] and "the rest of Barabaria" (=northern Somalia).[73] In this the testimony of the *Periplus* is mirrored in the archaeological record, which has yet to yield evidence for the existence of any state other than Aksum in the Horn of Africa during this period. Finally, given that the coastal plain of Eritrea is only about 40-60 km wide and is largely unsuitable for agriculture, any state as large as Zoskales' realm would have to have been based in the more fertile highlands in which Aksum was located.[74]

The archaeological record similarly substantiates the *Periplus*' description of extensive commerce between Ethiopia and the Roman world by way of the Red Sea.[75] While similar evidence exists for Kushite trade with the Mediterranean world,[76] such trade seems to have reached Nubia almost exclusively by way of the Nile Valley. To date the only place on the Red Sea coast where possible evidence of a

[68] The oft-repeated identification of Zoskales with the Za-Haqelē of late medieval Ethiopian king-lists is unlikely given that the earliest of these lists post-date the *Periplus* by well over a thousand years (cf. Casson 1989: 109).

[69] *Periplus* 5:2.21-2.

[70] Bernard 2000.

[71] *Periplus* 4:2.6.

[72] Casson 1989: 100-1; but see Bukharin 2011.

[73] On the location of "Barbaria" see Beaucamp in *Martyrium Arethae* 2007: 262 (n. 178).

[74] Seland 2010: 38. Seland (ibid.) may well be correct that Zoskales maintained different places of residence throughout his realm and periodically spent time at each, as did many kings throughout history, including medieval Ethiopian kings.

[75] For an assessment of this trade, based primarily on pottery evidence, see Manzo 2005.

[76] Raschke 1978: 869-70 (n. 900); Török 1989: 61, 117-50.

Kushite connection has come to light is the Roman port of Berenike, where a quantity of the cotton textiles have been unearthed, some fifty percent of which are woven from the S-spun yarn typical of Kushite cottons.[77] Most of these textiles, however, are likely to have come not from the Kushite heartland but from Qaṣr Ibrīm in Egyptian Nubia, where between sixty and seventy percent of textiles during the first four centuries CE are of cotton, and where cotton seems in fact to have been cultivated.[78] Given Qaṣr Ibrīm's location on the border of Roman Egypt, it is likely that the town's exportation of cotton reflects a Roman demand for cotton textiles rather than Kushite activities in the Red Sea region. There is certainly no reason to assume that there was a market for Kushite cottons anywhere further afield than Berenike.[79] That the rest of Africa's Red Sea coast, including the portion of coast occupied by Aksum, has yet to produce a single object of Kushite origin[80] reinforces this point. Significantly, the Kushites, unlike the Aksumites, had no Red Sea ports of their own.[81] By contrast, Aksumite pottery and coins have come to light not only on the northern Eritrean coast and its hinterland[82] but also at Berenike and some 300 km further north at Quṣayr al-Qadīm (Myos Hormos).[83] During the sixth century CE, Aksum also traded extensively with 'Aqaba (Ayla), whose distinctive pottery has been found at Aksum, Adulis, and off the Dahlak archipelago;[84] sixth-century textual sources likewise allude to trade between 'Aqaba and the Aksumite realm.[85] By way of the Red Sea the Aksumites maintained direct contact with the Indian Ocean. Already in the first century CE Zoskales was importing iron and steel from

[77] Wild et al. 2005: 145.

[78] Ibid. On ties between Lower Nubia and the Red Sea, see Raschke 1978: 868-9 (n. 899).

[79] India, for example, produced plenty cotton textiles of its own, and it is probable that most if not all of the cotton textiles at Berenike woven with Z-spun yarn are of Indian origin (Gradel et al. [in press]: 17; but see Wild et al. 2005: 146).

[80] Welsby 1996: 62; cf. Manzo 2004: 77.

[81] On Aksumite port facilities, see Peacock and Blue 2007.

[82] Ibid.

[83] Tomber 2005: 100; Sidebotham et al. 2008: 182; Sidebotham 2011: 75, 185, 231, 248-9, 275, 277, 280.

[84] Hatke 2011: 236.

[85] Ibid.: 265.

northwest India,[86] while material evidence of the growth of Aksumite trade in the Indian Ocean in later centuries survives in the form of Aksumite pottery at Qāni' in Yemen[87] and Kāmrej in Gujerat;[88] Aksumite coins in Yemen, India, and Sri Lanka;[89] Aksumite inscriptions in Yemen;[90] and Aksumite graffiti in Soqotra.[91] Of Indian material which has come to light in the Aksumite realm, terracotta plaques of Buddhist origin from Ḥaweltī,[92] an Indian seal from Adulis,[93] and a cache of second- to third-century CE coins minted by the Kuṣāṇa dynasty of northwestern India, found at Dabra Dāmō in northern Ethiopia,[94] may be noted. To be sure, the discovery of Kushite pottery of first- to third-century CE date at Tabot,[95] located in the desert roughly halfway between Barbara and Sawākin, indicates that Kush did trade with the peoples of the Eastern Desert. Yet this, like the apparent exportation of Kushite cotton textiles to Berenike, is a far cry from active participation in Red Sea trade,[96] which explains why the

[86] *Periplus* 6:3.1.
[87] Sedov 1996: 22; idem 2007: 85.
[88] Tomber 2005.
[89] Munro-Hay 1989a; Metlich 2006: 102-3.
[90] Hatke 2011: 355-84.
[91] Robin and Gorea 2002: 427-8.
[92] Raschke 1978: 966 (n. 1258).
[93] Chatterji 1968: 52-3.
[94] Kobishchanov 1979: 58. On the dates of the kings who minted these coins, see Falk 2001; idem 2004.
[95] Magid 2004: 157, 159, 163.
[96] Cowrie shells (*Monetaria moneta*) have been found at Meroë and can only have come from the Red Sea or Indian Ocean (Carter and Foley 1980: 303), though it is impossible to tell whether these reached the town directly or came by way of intermediaries in the Eastern Desert, such as the Beja/Blemmyes. In the past, scholars were wont to see Indian influence on Kush, and cited as evidence to that effect the depiction of the Kushite god Apedemak with three heads and two pairs of arms in a relief of early first-century CE date at Naq'a (Arkell 1961: 166; Adams 1977: 318 [Fig. 51], 331). While this image invites comparison with Indian depictions of Hindu deities, the fact that multi-headed and multi-armed deities are not depicted in Indian art before c. 500 CE (Shinnie 1978: 253) makes the theory of Indian influence on Kushite depictions of Apedemak quite untenable (cf. Haycock 1971: 29; Raschke 1978: 966 [n. 1258]). That Apedemak is portrayed in this manner seems in fact to represent a Kushite artist's attempt to depict Apedemak from several angles at once (Welsby 1996: 181-2). A related theory that cotton cultivation was introduced to Kush from India (Arkell 1961: 166; Adams 1977: 331) is also without basis (Gradel et al. *in press*), and there are

anonymous author of the *Periplus*, concerned as he is with maritime rather than overland trade, passes over Nubia with scarcely a mention. Only once in his description of the Red Sea coast between Berenike and Adulis does he allude to a region "in the parts towards the west."[97] The text, preserved in a single manuscript (Codex Palatinus Graecus 398, fols. 40v-54v),[98] is defective at this point, with a blank space that would accommodate eight to nine letters, though the tentative reconstruction of "a metropolis called Meroë" (μητρόπολις λεγομένη Μερόη) has found favor with most scholars.[99] But even if we accept such a reconstruction for the sake of argument, this tangential allusion to Meroë serves only to highlight that Kush was peripheral to the Red Sea arena to which Aksum belonged, particularly when one compares it with the *Periplus*' much fuller description of Adulis and the details it provides regarding the routes into the interior of the Ethiopian Highlands.[100] Thus we find once again that Nubia and Ethiopia interacted with the outside world primarily through two separate routes. Not only did Nubia look northwards down the Nile Valley for its source of foreign cultural models, but it also relied on the Nile Valley as its main link to the commerce of the Roman world. On the other hand Ethiopia, having adopted many aspects of Sabaean culture as well as Semitic speech by virtue of its orientation towards the Red Sea, continued to maintain its most significant foreign trade relations via that route during the Roman period.[101] The paucity of Aksumite material that has come to light in Nubia[102] suggests that the middle Nile Valley had far less to offer Aksum than the maritime world of the Red Sea and Indian Ocean.

no grounds for supposing that the Nubian (Nobiin) word for cotton, *koshmaag*, is derived from the Sanskrit *karpā'sa*, as recently suggested by Fuller (2008: 19).

[97] *Periplus* 2:1.11.

[98] The manuscript itself is of tenth-century date. A fourteenth- to fifteenth-century copy of this manuscript (BM Add. 19391, fols. 9r-12r) contains all of the errors of the former and has no independent authority (Casson 1989: 5).

[99] Ibid.: 100.

[100] *Periplus* 4:1.19-6:3.7.

[101] Phillipson 1998: 65, 70; Peacock and Blue 2007; Hatke 2011: 32-4, 237-43, 265-8.

[102] See §4.2; §4.6.1; §5.1.

Given the expansion of international trade during the Roman period it is perhaps surprising that Aksum and Kush did not grow closer during this period, but in fact it was precisely because of the growth of international trade that contact between the two kingdoms remained minimal. In the Bronze Age, Nubians and Ethiopians had interacted to a larger extent than they did in later periods for the simple fact that foreign trade did not yet exist on the scale it would achieve during the Roman period. Already in the early first millennium BCE Nubia and Ethiopia had begun to grow apart with the rise of a Kushite state based in the middle Nile Valley that looked towards Egypt and a kingdom of Di'mat based in the northern Ethiopian Highlands that looked towards South Arabia. This process of divergence was then further accelerated by the rise of the Roman Empire and the development of regular and more extensive intercontinental trade, as a result of which the Nubians and Ethiopians came to know of a wider world that promised far more than commercial and cultural exchanges with each other ever could.

This being the case, what exactly did Ethiopian-Nubian relations look like c. 100 BCE-200 CE? To begin with, Aksum and Kush were separated by the grasslands of the eastern Buṭāna and the Gash Delta, the latter region being inhabited by the Early Ḥājiz Group (c. 500 BCE-200 CE), whose closest cultural links were with Ethiopia rather than Nubia.[103] The extent and nature of Kushite activities in this region remain uncertain. At Jabal Qaylī in the western Buṭāna, a relief of the Kushite king Shorakaror dating from the mid-first century CE may commemorate military operations in that region in view of the depiction of naked enemies falling before the king;[104] but with nothing more than the king's name in the accompanying inscription it is unknown who these enemies might have been.[105] More suggestive of Kushite conflict with a specific region in the Sudanese-Ethiopian borderlands is an inscription of late first-century BCE date from

[103] Edwards 1989: 37.
[104] *Fontes Historiae Nubiorum III* 1998: 908-12.
[105] Kirwan (1960: 171) believes that the fallen foes are Aksumite, though there is no evidence of Aksumite military activities as far west as the Buṭāna during this period. Indeed, since the triumph of the ruler over his enemies is a standard, if not stereotypical, image in Kushite art, it is not impossible that Shorakaror's monument is symbolic, rather than historical, in nature.

Temple 250 at Meroë, first excavated by Garstang in 1909-10.[106] On the east façade of the pylon towers of the temple's central court building is depicted a row of bound prisoners whose bodies are covered by large cartouches.[107] On the south tower, the cartouches are inscribed with names in Meroitic hieroglyphs, while on the north tower the cartouches are left blank.[108] Judging from analogous representations on Egyptian temples, these figures symbolize conquered peoples.[109] Of the seventeen figures traceable at the time of Garstang's excavations, only nine were well enough preserved for their names to be made out. One of these names, Teseni, suggests the name of Tasanay, a town located in western Eritrea on the Gash River.[110] If this identification is correct, it would indicate that, by the first century BCE, Kush laid claim to a region in close proximity to the nascent Aksumite state. It could be that such a claim was based on a Kushite attack on western Eritrea or perhaps on the dispatch of diplomatic gifts from that region to win the good-will of Kush—though interpreted by the Kushites as tribute.[111] If the Kushites did in fact make a show of force on Ethiopia's western frontier on this occasion, they made no further attempts to annex that region, for no Kushite sites have been found east of the Buṭāna. Indeed

[106] This so-called "Sun Temple" is more properly a temple dedicated to the union of the gods Amūn and Rēʿ (Török 2002: 219-20). Though the first temple at the site is supposed to have been erected in the late seventh to early sixth century BCE, the inscriptions and reliefs with which we are presently concerned can be dated to the late first century BCE based on a sunk relief depiction of Prince Akiñidad (ibid.: 213, 215). This individual is known from epigraphic evidence to have played a role in the Kushite attack on the Roman frontier in 25 BCE (Török 1997: 451-2; Zibelius-Chen 2006: 299), which gives us an approximate timeframe for the reliefs from Temple 250 at Meroë.

[107] Török 2002: 220.

[108] Ibid.

[109] Griffith 1911: 58-9 (pl. XXXIV).

[110] Al-Nūr 2004. Griffith (1911: 59) compares another name from the southern tower, Awir, with several toponyms in the Red Sea region, among them Aua, mentioned in *Monumentum Adulitanum II*, though this is connection seems far-fetched.

[111] An analogous situation is the dispatch by autonomous Aegean peoples of diplomatic gifts to Egypt during the New Kingdom (1539-1075 BCE), depicted in Egyptian tombs as the offering of tribute. One is reminded as well of the Chinese habit of referring to goods brought by foreign merchants and diplomats as "tribute."

it is probable that the ʻAṭbara River lay outside Kush's jurisdiction,[112] in which case it is unlikely that any Kushite show of force as far east as Eritrea ever led to the establishment of permanent rule there.

Since Aksum and Kush are not known to have taken steps to fortify their respective frontiers against each other, the question arises as to what extent Aksum and Kush maintained peaceful trade relations. As we have seen there is little material evidence of commercial exchanges between Nubia and Ethiopia during the first millennium BCE, even though this period saw the rise and expansion of both Kush and Diʻmat, a parallel development which might be thought to have facilitated such exchanges. In a study of the foreign trade of Aksum, Manzo draws attention to pottery found in Tomb 2 at Ona Enda ʻAbbāy Zawgē, the impressed decoration of which is similar to specimens from Soba and Jabal Moya in the central Sudan, produced until the first century CE, or perhaps as late as the third.[113] The degree to which the latter two sites were incorporated within the Kushite state is uncertain, however.[114] Manzo also suggests that fragments of glass vessels discovered in Early Aksumite assemblages (c. 50 BCE-150 CE) are Kushite on the grounds that their colors (blue, red, pink, and white) are atypical of those found in the Mediterranean region,[115] though there is, in fact, evidence for the production of glass in these colors in Roman Egypt.[116] A beaker from Ona Enda ʻAbbāy Zawgē, decorated with rocker impressions on a smooth surface, black on the interior and reddish-brown on the exterior, is identified by Fattovich and Bard with Kushite ware dating between the third century BCE and the fourth century CE.[117] A Kushite origin has also been suggested for a conical bronze seal from the same site.[118] Lastly, a find at Aksum which is characteristic of the later phases of Kush is a half-portion of a thumb-ring or "archer's loose" in black and white stone, probably diorite.[119] A device used to protect the thumb while holding the

[112] Manzo 2004: 77.
[113] Idem 2005: 56; Chittick 1982: 52.
[114] Welsby 1996: 140.
[115] Manzo 2005: 56.
[116] Whitehouse 1997; Rehren 2001.
[117] Fattovich and Bard 2001: 9, 19.
[118] Ibid.: 11.
[119] Chittick 1982: 52.

bowstring and maximize shooting range, the thumb-ring is attested at many sites in Nubia.[120] The example from Aksum was, unfortunately, discovered in a much disturbed deposit,[121] making it a difficult object to date, a problem all the more acute in that the thumb-ring was widely used in Nubia during post-Kushite times.[122] Due caution is also in order given the widespread find-spots of such thumb-rings, some of which lie well beyond the known sphere of Kushite trade.[123] Thus, although some commercial interaction between Kush and Aksum did take place, it is not impossible that thumb-rings continued to circulate as curiosities well after the Kushite period, which calls into question the reliability of the thumb-ring from Aksum as evidence of Kushite trade with Ethiopia.[124] Considering the relative proximity of Kush and Aksum, the objects cited above constitute a surprisingly small amount of material, particularly when compared with the abundant Roman material (pottery, glassware, and to a lesser extent metalwork) imported by the two kingdoms independently of each other. Whether or not the original text of the *Periplus* actually referred to Meroë, it is significant that this source never explicitly refers to Aksumite trade with Nubia. Thus, while it is certainly possible that Zoskales maintained trade ties with the Nubian region to the west of Ptolemaïs Theron, the fact remains that the *Periplus* says nothing of such trade, and it may be that what commerce took place involved nothing more than small-scale commercial transactions with local agro-pastoralists of the sort who left their distinctive Eastern Desert Ware at sites like Tabot in the eastern Sudan.[125]

[120] Welsby 1996: 42.
[121] Chittick 1982: 52.
[122] Ibid.; Welsby 1996: 42.
[123] Trigger 1969: 26 (n. 12); cf. Raschke 1978: 874-5 (n. 917).
[124] Commenting on the discovery of one such thumb-ring in the Daju Hills of South Dārfūr, believed to be of Kushite origin, Trigger (1969: 26 [n. 12]) compares the circulation of Native American arrowheads in modern North America.
[125] Magid 2004: 164; Manzo 2004: 79, 80. Though found at sites in Nubia as well as in the Eastern Desert (Barnard 2008: 416-17), Eastern Desert Ware vessels differ in technology, shape, and decoration from pottery produced by permanent inhabitants of the Nile Valley, in addition to which preliminary analyses of the fabric of more than 140 Eastern Desert Ware vessels indicates that this type of pottery was made in several regions, all of them most likely outside the Nile Valley (ibid.: 418-19). On Eastern Desert Ware in the context

Presumably the Kushite south, with its more plentiful resources and greater proximity to Aksum, would have been a greater attraction for Aksumite merchants than regions further north. Since some of the foreign pottery from Ona Enda ʻAbbāy Zawgē has similarities with wares produced in the central Sudan, Aksumite contact with the southern frontier of Kush is quite likely. One must not, however, give too much weight to this meager data, particularly when what has long interpreted as literary evidence of Aksumite trade with this region is questionable. The alleged evidence in question is a passage in the *Periplus*, in which we are told that the city of Aksum received "all the ivory from beyond the Nile through what is called Kyeneion."[126] Many scholars have identified this toponym with the town of Sinnār on the Blue Nile in the Sudan,[127] at which Kushite material and bronze vessels imported from Roman Egypt have been found.[128] Fragments of worked ivory at Aksum,[129] as well as an entire elephant tusk at Adulis,[130] are likely representative of Kyeneion's ivory trade. However, while excavation of a storeroom in the palace of Queen Amani<u>sh</u>a<u>kh</u>eto at Wād ban Naqʻa, dating from around the turn of the Common Era, has revealed a quantity of elephant tusks[131] suggesting a parallel Kushite trade in ivory, there is no evidence that the Aksumites sought their ivory from regions as distant as Sinnār. Casson argues that the "Nile" in the passage from the *Periplus* cited above does not refer to the river commonly known as such, particularly given that ancient authors were poorly informed about the upper waters of the Nile and seem to have incorrectly regarded various rivers in Ethiopia as part of it.[132] He makes a case instead for identifying the *Periplus*' "Nile" with the Tekkazē River,[133] noting that in an inscription left by a third-century Aksumite king (*Monumentum Adulitanum II*=RIE 277), a reference to conquests

of Aksumite expansion to the north during the third century CE, see §3.3.1.
[126] *Periplus* 4:2.9-10.
[127] For references to the relevant literature, see Casson 1989: 107.
[128] Dixon 1963; Welsby 1996: 140; Török 1997: 137; Hintze 2000: 52.
[129] Connah 2001: 96 (Fig. 3.10), 97.
[130] Anfray 1981: 377.
[131] Raschke 1978: 905 (n. 1005).
[132] Casson 1989: 107.
[133] The same hypothesis was earlier put forward by Chittick 1982: 50.

"beyond the Nile" occurs in a context which only suits the Takkazē.[134] In light of this, Casson suggests that Kyeneion could be present-day Welkitē in central Ethiopia.[135] He proposes another possible candidate for Kyeneion—and one much closer to the city of Aksum—on the basis of an alternative identification of the "Nile" with the Marab, citing Conti Rossini, who suggests equating Kyeneion with Qōḥayn in northeastern Eritrea.[136] This hypothesis is especially attractive in that the modern name is a good fit for ancient Kyeneion, in addition to which elephants were still seen during the late nineteenth century around the headwaters of the Baraka, just to the north of Qōḥayn.[137] If, therefore, the Aksumites looked no further for their ivory than the Ethiopian Highlands, then the case for regular Aksumite trade with Kush, at least in ivory, is further weakened. Such marginal items as the Sudanese pottery found at Ona Enda 'Abbāy Zawgē may well reflect small-scale trade between Aksum and communities living on the periphery of the Kushite "state, but not trade for the purpose of acquiring the sort of luxury items that attracted the attention of foreign commentators like the author of the *Periplus*.

[134] Casson 1989: 107.
[135] Ibid.
[136] Ibid.: 107-8.
[137] Ibid.: 108.

3. The Third Century CE: *Monumentum Adulitanum II* (RIE 277)

Having examined the evidence for contact between Aksum and Kush during the first two centuries of the Common Era, one is left with the impression that the two kingdoms, though closely tied to the commerce of the outside world, had little interest in maintaining intensive trade ties with each other. While it cannot be doubted that Aksum and Kush maintained trade ties, it is difficult to determine what sort of items they might have traded. Livestock is one possibility, particularly given the moister climate in the southern regions of Kush. For their part, the Kushites may have engaged in small-scale trade with pastoralists to the north of Aksum, witness the Kushite pottery at Tabot. By the third century, much of the Eastern Desert, as well as the nebulous area between southern Kush and the Ethiopian Highlands, came to be annexed by Aksum. For our knowledge of this new development we are indebted to a Nestorian Christian merchant who visited Ethiopia in 518.[138] This merchant is known only by the name Cosmas Indicopleustes, literally "Cosmas who has traveled to India," bestowed on him in later centuries in reference to his travels in Ethiopia, long referred to by Graeco-Roman authors as "India."[139] The *Christian Topography* authored by this merchant was intended as a defense of the flat-earth theory in the face of the contention by "pagan" geographers that the earth was round. Ironically, it is as "evidence" marshaled in support of his bizarre claim that the earth was shaped like the Tabernacle of Moses that Cosmas incorporates a good deal of useful information on the Horn of Africa which, when examined on its own terms, and in isolation from Cosmas' cosmological theories, is of great value to historians. Not only does Cosmas describe Aksumite trade, but he also preserves a record of a series of campaigns mounted by a third-century Aksumite king which, were it not for the *Christian Topography*, might well have been lost forever. As a result of these campaigns Aksumite rule was extended, albeit briefly, throughout the Eastern Desert as far as Roman Egypt and

[138] On the date of Cosmas' journey, see Hatke 2011: 79-80.
[139] On the identification of Ethiopia with India, see Mayerson 1993. There is no evidence that Cosmas visited South Asia (Frézouls 1989: 442-3, 458-9).

over a sizeable portion of the western coast of Arabia as far north as the Gulf of ʻAqaba (see Map 1). The effects of this development on Kush, however, are less clear.

3.1. Cosmas Indicopleustes at Adulis

When visiting Adulis, Cosmas and a fellow merchant named Mênas were commissioned by the town's governor to record two Greek inscriptions,[140] the first recording the Asiatic campaigns of Ptolemy III (246-222 BCE),[141] the second the campaigns of a king of Aksum.[142] The

[140] *Top. Chr.* 2.56.
[141] Ibid.: 2.58-9.
[142] Ibid.: 2.60-3. The case has occasionally—though never successfully—been made that the anonymous king who erected *Monumentum Adulitanum II* was not an Aksumite. Theories that the king hailed from South Arabia (Drewes 1962: 106-7; Beeston 1980) can be easily dismissed for two reasons. Firstly, *Monumentum Adulitanum II* is in Greek, and while two South Arabian merchants named Hāni' and Zayd'īl are known to have left a brief bilingual Greek-Minaic inscription on the island of Delos (Robin 1991: 61 [Fig. 17], 62; Maraqten 1994: 162-3), no royal South Arabian inscriptions in Greek have ever come to light. By contrast, several Aksumite kings left inscriptions in Greek (Bernard 2000). Secondly, most of the battles recorded in *Monumentum Adulitanum II* took place on the African continent, which suits the inscription's attribution to an Aksumite king; but since no South Arabian king at any point in history is known to have waged war in Africa, attributing *Monumentum Adulitanum II* to a ruler from South Arabia is quite out of the question. More recently it has been argued that *Monumentum Adulitanum II* was erected by a king of the Red Sea littoral of Eritrea (Fauvelle-Aymar 2009). Quite apart from the implausibility that a polity based in this region would have had the resources and manpower to wage long-distance military campaigns against the Ethiopian Highlands and much of the western coast of the Arabian Peninsula like those described in the inscription, the argument against the Aksumite origin of *Monumentum Adulitanum II* suffers from the emphasis which Fauvelle-Aymar (ibid.: 143) places on the identification of the Gaze people (Γάζη ἔθνος) with the Aksumites. Since *Monumentum Adulitanum II* records the king's campaign against these people, the king, so Fauvelle-Aymar contends, cannot easily have been an Aksumite himself. As Fauvelle-Aymar (ibid.) correctly points out, one of the eleventh-century scholia added to the text of the *Christian Topography* identifies the Gaze with the Aksumites and notes that the Ethiopians were still called Agaze. However, it must not be forgotten that, since the scholia are not integral parts of the original text of the *Christian Topography*, they may well reflect later traditions regarding Ethiopia and its peoples. In her addition of the text, Wolska-Conus (in *Top. Chr.* 1968: I: 78) suggests that Cosmas is not the author of the scholia but cautions, "[p]eut-être faut-il mettre à part les annotations qui accompagnent les inscriptions axoumites, très discutées par les spécialistes, sur lesquelles il est difficile de porter un jugement." To be sure, *'Agʿāzī* (literally, "the free ones") is a name

two texts are known today as *Monumentum Adulitanum I* and *II* respectively. As preserved in Cosmas' treatise, *Monumentum Adulitanum II*, also known as RIE 277, does not include the Aksumite king's name, possibly because the opening part of the inscription in which it would have appeared had been damaged by the time of Cosmas' visit and could no longer be read. It does not help matters that Cosmas, when writing his *Christian Topography* some twenty-five years after his visit to Ethiopia, confused the identification of the two inscriptions from

by which Ethiopians have called themselves during the Middle Ages, while what seems to be a related epithet, *Yg‘ḏy*^{n}, is applied to King Rābiḥ of Di‘mat and his son Liman (Sima 2003: 144) during the Pre-Aksumite period. Nevertheless there is no reason to assume that the Aksumites regularly used *'Ag‘āzī* as a generic name for themselves, given that this name is nowhere attested in Aksumite inscriptions (ibid.: 144-5). Although [*'Ag*]*‘āzə*[*yān*] has been read in a fragmentary sixth-century Ge‘ez inscription from Ẓafār in Yemen, that text is too badly damaged to provide any indication as to who was meant by this name (ibid.). For all we know, these putative **'Ag‘āzəyān* were mercenaries from the Ethiopian Highlands recruited by the Aksumites. 'Abrehā, a general of the sixth-century Aksumite king Kālēb who seized power in Ḥimyar at some point between 531 and 547, bears a title that has been interpreted as "the *'Ag‘āzī* king" (*mlk*^{n} *'g‘zy*^{n}) in his famous Dam Inscription from Mārib in Yemen (CIH 541). But as Sima (ibid.) points out the meaning of this title is enigmatic in that 'Abrehā was at this time no longer an Aksumite general but rather an autonomous ruler of Ḥimyar. In addition, the reference to 'Abrehā as *'Ag‘āzī* need not imply that the Aksumites were regularly known by this name, particularly given that 'Abrehā began his career as a slave of a Roman citizen at Adulis (Procopius, *De Bell. Pers.* 1.20.4-5), in which case he may not have been Aksumite at all but might instead have been taken into bondage from one of Aksum's African vassals. Even this assumes that the reading *mlk*^{n} *'g‘zy*^{n} in CIH 541 is in fact correct; as Müller (2010: 111 [n. 5]) notes in his edition of the text, an alternative reading *'l‘zyn* is also possible. 'Abrehā's title might in that case be reconstructed as **malik*$^{\bar{a}n}$ *'Əlla-‘Ūzāyān*, "the King 'Ella-‘Ūzāyān," with no connection to the *'Ag‘āzī* at all. Since, therefore, the case for associating the Aksumites with the name *'Ag‘āzī* is extremely dubious, the identification of the Gaze people of *Monumentum Adulitanum II* with the Aksumites is best rejected, at least insofar as Aksum's third-century history is concerned. It is perfectly plausible that *'Ag‘āzī*, though originally a name for a single group in the Ethiopian Highlands, was adopted by Ethiopians in later centuries as a generic name for themselves, much as the name "Ethiopian" itself, originally a designation for Nubians, was appropriated by the Aksumites in the mid-fourth century (see §3.3.2). But even if, for the sake of argument, the Aksumites adopted *'Ag‘āzī* as a term of self-identification as early as the sixth century, it need not follow that the people thus designated in the third-century *Monumentum Adulitanum II* were Aksumites. In short, there is no basis for Fauvelle-Aymar's identification of the Gaze people with the Aksumites, and his theory that the king who erected *Monumentum*

Adulis and placed his transcriptions of them back to back, without any break to indicate that they were separate inscriptions. Regarding Cosmas' confusion of the two inscriptions, his claim at one point in the *Christian Topography* that the Ptolemaic inscription was carved on a δίφρος,[143] usually translated as "throne," is undoubtedly wrong, as this description is at odds what we know about Ptolemaic inscriptions. On the other hand it was common practice for Aksumite kings to erect stelae as parts of symbolic thrones to commemorate military victories. Indeed the anonymous Aksumite king who erected *Monumentum Adulitanum II* claims at the conclusion of the inscription to have set up just such a throne to Ares at Adulis in the twenty-seventh year of his reign.[144] In his own inscriptions the fourth-century Aksumite king 'Ēzānā also claims to have erected thrones at the conclusion of military victories.[145] But then, only a few paragraphs after erroneously attributing the throne-inscription to Ptolemy III, Cosmas corrects his mistake, noting that the Ptolemaic inscription was carved on a stele[146] and thus implying that the stele on which the text of *Monumentum Adulitanum II* was inscribed was indeed part of a symbolic stone throne. Though Cosmas believed that both inscriptions were erected by Ptolemy III, *Monumentum Adulitanum II* bears all the characteristics of a royal Aksumite inscription, and was undoubtedly recognized as such by Kālēb, the king of Aksum who requested copies of both texts from

Adulitanum II, by virtue of his having made war on the Gaze, was not an Aksumite can be safely dismissed. As for Fauvelle-Aymar's hypothesis that the inscription was erected by a king of Africa's Red Sea littoral around the end of the first century BCE or the turn of the Common Era (Fauvelle-Aymar 2009: 145), this too is easily rejected on grounds of the references in *Monumentum Adulitanum II* to military operations in Arabia. Since no African kingdom other than Aksum is known to have invaded Arabia, much less during the period posited by Fauvelle-Aymar, attributing the inscription to a polity based on the narrow coastal strip of Eritrea is extremely dubious. As Finneran (2007: 165) points out, the palace excavated at Adulis is similar enough in form with Aksumite palaces excavated elsewhere to indicate a standardized layout for all palaces, and thus the existence of a centralized state organization based at Aksum, which in turn controlled Adulis.

[143] *Top. Chr.* 2.54.6-18.

[144] Ibid.: 2.63.8-12.

[145] RIE 188:24; RIE 189:39 (Bernard et al. 1991: 260, 264). *Manbar*, the Ge'ez word for throne used in 'Ēzānā's inscriptions, seems to correspond with the word δίφρος used in *Monumentum Adulitanum II*.

[146] *Top. Chr.* 2.58-9.

the governor of Adulis just as he was about to send his army against the Ḥimyarites of South Arabia in 518.[147] Since the ruler who erected *Monumentum Adulitanum II* records his conquest of a large portion of Arabia's Red Sea coast in the inscription, Kālēb may well have appreciated the text for its propaganda value as a document validating Aksum's irredentist claims to Arabia.[148]

3.2. Dating Monumentum Adulitanum II

Though *Monumentum Adulitanum II* is primarily concerned with Aksumite military operations in northeast Africa, its references to similar operations in western Arabia are relevant for the present study in that they provide evidence for a relative date of the inscription and substantiate the case for the authenticity of the text as preserved by Cosmas. According to the copy of the text preserved by Cosmas in his *Christian Topography*, the Aksumites annexed the entire Red Sea coast of Arabia from the port of Leuke Kome in the north to the land of the Sabaeans in the south, i.e. from the Gulf of 'Aqaba to the northern border of modern Yemen.[149] In the process they brought to submission the kings of the Arabitae and the Kinaidokolpitae, two peoples who lived along the coast of the northern Tihāma, and imposed tribute upon them.[150] Indicative of the authenticity of Cosmas' copy of *Monumentum Adulitanum II* is the fact that a parallel account of Aksumite warfare on the opposite side of the Red Sea survives in a fragmentary Greek inscription (RIE 269) found at Aksum by Littmann's

[147] Ibid.: 2.56.1-7.

[148] On Kālēb's irredentist claims to Arabia, see Hatke 2011: 154-60.

[149] *Top. Chr.* 2.62.4-9. Despite a great deal of speculation as to its exact location, Leuke Kome is in all likelihood to be identified with 'Aynūna in northwestern Saudi Arabia (28º 5' 8" N/35º 11' 13" E) (Hackl et al. 2003: 565-6). On archaeological remains from the region of Wādī 'Aynūna, see Rihani 2004: 371-2; Sidebotham 2011: 175. Regarding the Sabaeans of South Arabia, *Monumentum Adulitanum II* says nothing of the Aksumite king having made war on them, which would imply that his campaigns took him only as far as the northern borders of the kingdom of Saba' but not beyond. It is quite possible that the anonymous king who erected *Monumentum Adulitanum II* did not make war on the Sabaeans was because western Yemen was already under Aksumite control.

[150] *Top. Chr.* 2.62.4-9. On the identification of the Kinaidokolpitae, see Cuvigny and Robin 1996. The identification of the Arabitae is a bit more problematic, as this group, despite its name, does not seem to be coterminous with the Arabs. On this issue, see Hatke 2011: 40-1.

team at the turn of the twentieth century.[151] Of the eight lines of text that remain, the third reads "and the region beyond the sea" (καὶ τὸ πέρα τῆς θαλάσ[σης]).[152] Given the Ethiopian provenance of the inscription, "beyond the sea" can only refer to Arabia, particularly in light of the comparable statement in *Monumentum Adulitanum II* that the Arabitae and Kinaidokolpitae lived "across the Red Sea" (πέραν δὲ τῆς Ἐρυθρᾶς θαλάσσης οἰκοῦντας).[153] If Littmann is correct in his reconstruction of Line 7 of RIE 269 as [τ]ὸ πεζικ[ὸν], "the infantry," it would appear that military operations were involved. It is quite possible, in fact, that RIE 269 from Aksum records the same Arabian campaign recorded in *Monumetum Adulitanum II* from Adulis, in which case there is every reason to assume that Cosmas' is a faithful copy of an authentic Aksumite inscription, albeit one that preserves a different version of the events recorded in RIE 269.

Determining the date of *Monumentum Adulitanum II* is made difficult by the lack of a royal name in Cosmas' transcription, as well as in RIE 269 from Aksum, with which *Monumentum Adulitanum II* is probably contemporary. It is quite clear, though, that the military campaigns recorded in both can only have taken place before 'Ēzānā's conversion to Christianity in the mid-fourth century,[154] for in the concluding portion of *Monumentum Adulitanum II* as well as in RIE 269 the king renders thanks to Ares, known from other inscriptions as the Greek deity with whom the Aksumites identified their god Maḥrem,[155] and whom this king, like others who ruled during Aksum's pre-Christian period, regarded as his progenitor.[156] The mention of an Arabian campaign in *Monumentum Adulitanum II* is also of importance in that it allows us to narrow the timeframe of the events described in the inscription. From South Arabian inscriptions we know that Aksum was politically involved in South Arabia c. 200-270, during which time

[151] Littmann 1913: 2-3. For a French translation of, and commentary on, RIE 269, see Bernard 2000: 3-4.

[152] Littmann 1913: 2.

[153] *Fontes Historiae Nubiorum III* 1998: 950 (Greek text), 951-2 (English translation). The similarity between the passage in *Monumentum Adulitanum II* and Line 3 of RIE 269 is noted by Littmann (1913: 3).

[154] On 'Ēzānā's conversion to Christianity, see §4.5.1.

[155] Höfner 1965: 560.

[156] Ibid.: 559; Brakmann 1994: 37.

the kingdom alternately formed alliances with and fought against both Saba' and Ḥimyar depending on the political climate of the day, established a governor (Sabaic *'qb*=Ge'ez *'aqābī*) at Najrān, stationed garrisons in the Tihāma, and at one point even occupied the region around the Ḥimyarite capital of Ẓafār for seven months.[157] This seventy-year period is the likeliest timeframe for the Arabian campaign documented in *Monumentum Adulitanum II*, and thus for the African campaigns also recorded in the inscription. For the purposes of the present study it need not concern us whether the king who erected *Monumentum Adulitanum II* is to be identified with Gadarā,[158] an Aksumite king mentioned by name in several third-century South Arabian inscriptions, or with Sembrouthes, another third-century Aksumite king who erected an inscription in Greek at Daqqī Maḥārī in Eritrea (RIE 275) in the twenty-fourth year of his reign.[159] What is important is that after the Ḥimyarites annexed Saba' in the 270s and crushed the last pockets of resistance in the eastern Ḥaḍramawt in the 320s,[160] they established political supremacy in South Arabia, with the result that no further Aksumite military operations in Arabia are recorded until Kālēb's first invasion of Ḥimyar in 518.[161] Although the Ḥimyarite king Karib'īl Watar Yuhan'im (c. 312-316) is known to have maintained diplomatic relations with Aksum,[162] there is no question of a fourth-century Aksumite occupation of Arabia's Red Sea coast of the sort described in *Monumentum Adulitanum II*. Indeed a South Arabian inscription ('Abadān 1) recording the campaigns launched by the Ḥimyarite king Tha'rān Yuhan'im (c. 324-375)[163] to extend Ḥimyar's control to the west, east, and north makes no mention of conflict with the Aksumites even in the Tihāma,[164] the region of South Arabia nearest to Ethiopia, and the one in which Aksumite influence in the

[157] On Aksumite military activities in South Arabian during the third century, see Robin 1989.

[158] As argued by Robin in Cuvigny and Robin 1996: 710-11.

[159] As argued by Fiaccadori 2004.

[160] Robin 2005: 140-5. On the somewhat earlier Ḥimyarite conquest of the western Ḥaḍramawt, see ibid.: 136-40.

[161] On this invasion, see Hatke 2011: 119-76.

[162] Al-Iryānī 1973: 147 ff.; Hatke 2011: 60-1.

[163] Tha'rān 'Ayfa' and Dhamar'alay 'Ayfa', though referred to as "kings" in 'Abadān 1, seem to have been simply members of the royal family rather than actual rulers (Robin and Gajda 1994: 133).

third century had been the strongest. In all likelihood, then, *Monumentum Adulitanum II* describes the political conditions of the Red Sea region before the Ḥimyarites gained full control of the Red Sea coast of Arabia in the fourth century. Moreover, since Sabaean and Ḥimyarite records alike indicate Aksum's political and military influence in South Arabia c. 200-270, there is little doubt that *Monumentum Adulitanum II* can be assigned to somewhere within this seventy-year period.

3.3. Aksumite Expansion in Northeast Africa

Much though one would hope for a more precise date, the rough timeframe of c. 200-270 for the events described in *Monumentum Adulitanum II* has great significance for our understanding of Aksumite expansion in northeast Africa. A third-century date for the inscription means that Kush was still in existence when Aksum was expanding its borders, as is clear from epigraphic and archaeological evidence. The latest reference to a Kushite ruler by name in external sources, a demotic graffito from Philae mentioning King Teqorideamani, dates from c. 253, but since there are at least seven royal tombs at Meroë that postdate Teqorideamani's burial (Bagrawiyya North 28), Kush must have endured in some form into the fourth century.[165] That ʿĒzānā encountered Kushites in the course of his Nubian campaign in the mid-fourth century supports this hypothesis,[166] though it is not clear whether Kush was still a united kingdom at that time. Insofar as the places and peoples mentioned in *Monumentum Adulitanum II* can be identified, the main theater of military operations on Aksum's African front in the third century was the Ethiopian Highlands.[167] In addition to campaigns in that region, the king who erected *Monumentum Adulitanum II* claims to have also subdued the population to the north of the highlands, an act whose possible impact on the Kushite state

[164] The details of the Ḥimyarite campaigns against the Tihāma are dealt with in ʿAbadān 1:5, 24-7 (Robin and Gajda 1994: 114, 115, 117, 118-19, 121, 124-5). On the chronology of this period of Ḥimyarite history, see Robin 2005.

[165] Török 1988: 33.

[166] See §4.5.2.3.

[167] For a tentative identification of the toponyms and ethnonyms attested in *Monumentum Adulitanum II*, see Huntingford 1989: 44-7; Bernard 2000: 35-40.

bears consideration. According to Cosmas' copy of the inscription the Aksumite king proclaims:

> Having subdued [the nations of] Atalmo and Beja and all the nations of the Tangaites together with them, who inhabit the region up to the border of Egypt, I had a land route made from the places in my kingdom all the way to Egypt.
>
> (Ἀταλμῶ καὶ Βεγὰ καὶ τὰ σὺν αὐτοῖς ἔθνη πάντα Ταγγαϊτῶν τὰ μέχρι τῶν τῆς Αἰγύπτου ὁρίων οἰκοῦντα ὑποτάξας πεζεύεσθαι ἐποίησα τὴν ὁδὸν ἀπὸ τῶν τῆς ἐμῆς βασιλείας τόπων μέχρι Αἰγύπτου.)[168]

Of the peoples mentioned in this passage, the only group which can be identified without difficulty are the Beja, for they are well known from Aksumite inscriptions and medieval Arabic sources as a people dwelling to the north of the Ethiopian Highlands. Traditionally pastoralists, they speak Tu Beḍawiɛ, an Afro-Asiatic language of the Cushitic branch.[169] The Beja have long been identified with the Blemmyes (Greek Βλέμμυες/Βλέμυες),[170] a people mentioned in Graeco-Roman sources as early as the third century BCE,[171] whose name may in turn be cognate with the *Brhm/Blhm* known from Egyptian and Kushite records.[172] Aksumite inscriptions, to be sure, never use the term Blemmyes and instead employ Βεγὰ or Βουγαειτῶν in Greek and *Bəgā* in Ge'ez. However, while it has been suggested that the use of "Blemmye" as a broad category in Graeco-Roman parlance obscures the diversity of the ancient population of the Eastern Desert,[173] the identification of the Blemmyes with the Beja is confirmed

[168] Greek text and translation in *Fontes Historiae Nubiorum III* 1998: 950-1.
[169] Appleyard 2004; Bechhaus-Gerst 2004.
[170] Burstein 2008: 253, 256.
[171] Snowden 1970: 117, 128.
[172] Raschke 1978: 890 (n. 953); Winnicki 2009: 488-94.
[173] Barnard 2005; Burstein 2008. Burstein (loc. cit.) goes so far as to argue that the Blemmyes during Late Antiquity were for the most part sedentary folk based in the Nile Valley and cites textual evidence to that effect. Since, however, the Romans probably had more direct contact with Blemmyes in the Nile Valley than those out in the Eastern Desert, the textual evidence of Blemmyan settlement in the Nile Valley may be somewhat skewed. Also, it is not uncommon for an ethnic group to contain nomadic as well as sedentary

by medieval documents from Qaṣr Ibrīm in the which the Coptic term *Blēmous* is given as the equivalent of the Arabic *Buja.*[174] Similarly, Browne's study of Blemmyan names preserved on a Coptic ostracon from Ṣaqqāra has revealed their Beja origin.[175] In all likelihood, then, the Beja with whom the Aksumites fought are the same as—or at least closely related to—the Blemmyes who made numerous raids on the southern frontier of Roman Egypt beginning in the last third of the third century CE.[176] Since the mid-third century is roughly the period from which *Monumentum Adulitanum II* dates, it is not impossible that Aksumite punitive campaigns against the Beja were waged in response to a parallel southward expansion of the Eastern Desert's population towards Aksum's northern frontier. Plagues which broke out in Nubia at the turn of the third century and again c. 250-253, mentioned by Cassius Dio in his *Roman History*,[177] may have accelerated such population movements in the Eastern Desert, or at least weakened the ability of peoples on the desert frontiers of Aksum and Roman Egypt to resist the incursions of the Beja and other pastoralist groups like them. Well attested though the Beja/Blemmyes are in ancient sources, the

elements, and the Blemmyes of antiquity were probably no different. Burstein's argument, on the basis of a reference in Ammianus Marcellinus, that the people known to Roman authors as the Saracens (i.e., Arabs) dominated the Eastern Desert in Late Antiquity (ibid.: 258-9) is misleading. All the text in question says is that the Saracens territory extended as far as the Nile cataracts and the frontiers of the Blemmyes, an area encompassing only the northern part of the Eastern Desert. The case for Arab settlement in that area has recently been made, primarily on the basis of archaeological evidence, by Power (2007), who argues that in Late Antiquity as today the Wādī Ḥammāmāt marked the border between Arab and Beja domains (ibid.: 203). Curiously, Burstein (2008: 260) has no problem accepting that the Beja against whom the Aksumites fought were pastoralists based in the Eastern Desert.

174 Plumley and Adams 1974: 238.

175 Browne 2004.

176 *Fontes Historiae Nubiorum III* 1998: 1054; Lassányi 2008: 598. On earlier skirmishes between the Romans and the pastoral peoples of the Eastern Desert, see Raschke 1978: 890 (n. 953).

177 *Fontes Historiae Nubiorum III* 1998: 960-2, 996-7. The first plague is mentioned by Cassius Dio in his *Roman History*, the second by the twelfth-century Byzantine author, John Zonaras. Although the latter authority is very late, his reference to a plague originating in "Ethiopia" (i.e. Nubia) c. 250-253 is probably derived from one of the lost books of Cassius Dio (ibid.: 997).

Atalmo and Tangaites are not known from any source apart from *Monumentum Adulitanum II*. Nevertheless it would appear that the Beja, Atalmo, and Tangaites are related, for all three groups are classified together as nations whose territories extended as far as the borders of Egypt, in which case they can be located in the Eastern Desert. The name Tangaite has been compared with that of the region of Tāka in western Eritrea,[178] whose dominant population is Beja, along with minority groups like the Khasa,[179] who are mentioned in the records of 'Ēzānā's Nubian campaign of 360.[180] In scholia appended to Cosmas' text in two medieval manuscripts, Cod. Florentinus Laurentianus Plut. IX. 28 from the tenth century and Cod. Vaticanus Graeucus 699 from the eighth or ninth century, the Atalmo are glossed as Blemmyes and the Tangaites as Attabitē and Adras.[181] Although Attabitē and Adras, like the ethnonyms Atalmo and Tangaites, are unknown from external sources, such names as Attabitē, Adras, and Atalmo seem to preserve the element **Ad-* prefixed to the names of numerous Beja tribes living in present-day Sudan and Eritrea,[182] as well as tribes of the Banī 'Āmir, an ethnic group which now speaks Tigrē, an Ethiosemitic language, but which is of Beja origin and currently inhabits the Sudanese-Eritrean borderlands.[183] Whether or not one accepts Huntingford's claim that the Atalmo were the ancestors of the modern Ad Elman, a Beja tribe living in Eritrea,[184] it is probable that the Atalmo and Tangaites of *Monumentum Adulitanum II* are to be located within the Eastern Desert traditionally inhabited by the Beja. As this is a large area, a bit of explanation is required as to what the inscription means by "the border of Egypt."

[178] Fauvelle-Aymar 2009: 153.
[179] Smidt 2010: 821. On the region of Tāka during the Middle Ages, see Nibbi 1997: 305, 307.
[180] §4.5.1, §4.5.2.1.
[181] Huntingford 1989: 43. Regarding these scholia, due caution is of course in order. On the somewhat problematic authenticity of the scholia appended to the medieval manuscripts of Cosmas' *Christian Topography*, see §3.1.
[182] Tucker and Bryan 1956: 119-20.
[183] Ibid.: 133-4. On the dialect of Tigrē spoken by the Banī 'Āmir and the Beja influence on this dialect, see Morin 1996.
[184] Huntingford 1989: 46.

3.3.1. Aksum and Rome's Southern Frontier

Superficially, the passage from *Monumentum Adulitanum II* quoted above would seem to suggest that, in subduing the tribes all the way to the frontier of Roman Egypt, the Aksumite army would, by implication, have had to pass through Nubia. The trouble with the scenario of a third-century Aksumite invasion of Nubia is that no Nubian ethnic group is mentioned in the record of armed conflict preserved in *Monumentum Adulitanum II*, nor is conflict with Aksum hinted at in any of the graffiti from Lower Nubia recording diplomatic visits by Kushite envoys to Roman Egypt. There is also the problem of which particular "border of Egypt" *Monumentum Adulitanum II* refers to. In the Graeco-Roman parlance which would have informed the author of that inscription "Egypt" refers to the Egyptian Nile Valley, the desert to the east and west being regarded as separate regions.[185] Thus the "border of Egypt" of which *Monumentum Adulitanum II* speaks is to be located in the Nile Valley. The question is where. Throughout most of the third century the Dodekaschoinos region,[186] extending up the Nile from Syene (Aswān) to Hiera Sykaminos (Maḥarraqa), constituted the southernmost reach of Roman authority in the Nile Valley, as it had since Augustus annexed the region in 21/20 BCE.[187] Judging from a milestone found at Kalabsha in Egyptian Nubia bearing the names of Diocletian and of several tetrarchs who held office between 295 and 305 CE,[188] Rome remained in control of the Dodekaschoinos until the very end of the third century. This is supported by Procopius' statement that it was not until 298 that Diocletian withdrew the Roman frontier to Syene,[189] where he built a line of fortresses to guard

[185] Roger Bagnall, pers. comm.

[186] I.e., the land of the twelve *schoinoi*, a distance of about 75 mi (Adams 1977: 334).

[187] Török 2009: 442. On the Roman occupation of this region, see Raschke 1978: 866-6 (n. 898); Adams 1977: 340-4; Török 2009: 443 ff. Though firmly integrated into Roman Egypt, the Dodekaschoinos was administered on behalf of the Roman authorities by the local Nubian elite (Török 1997: 459).

[188] Lohwasser 2008: 576.

[189] *De Bell. Pers.* 1.19.28-35. On the historicity of this strategic move on the part of Diocletian, see Burstein 1998. Procopius claims that when Diocletian withdrew the Roman frontier to Syene, he filled the consequent political vacuum by settling the region with the Nobatae. Also known as the Nobades, the Nobatae were a Nubian-speaking group related to the Noba mentioned in fourth-century Aksumite inscriptions (see §4.4 ff). Török (1988: 31)

Egypt's new frontier.[190] A pilgrimage to Philae undertaken by the Kushite king Amaniyesebokhe, who ruled during this period, probably represents the beginning of direct Kushite rule in the Dodekaschoinos.[191] If c. 200-270 CE is accepted as a timeframe for *Monumentum Adulitanum II*, the Aksumite military expansion in the Eastern Desert described in that inscription can be assigned to the period in which Roman control still extended as far as Hiera Sykaminos, which would thus mark the "border of Egypt." But the Aksumites could hardly have pushed their frontier to this border by way of Nubia, for reasons already noted. In addition, archaeological, epigraphic, and literary sources give every indication that the Kushites maintained unbroken control of the region to the south of the Dodekaschoinos throughout the Roman period, including the period c. 200-270. This latter, southern part of Lower Nubia, called Akiñ/Akine in Meroitic texts, was administered on behalf of the royal house of Meroë by a high official known as the *peseto*, whose very title has been interpreted as "king's son" on the basis of Demotic and Greek calques.[192] While in normal circumstances it was a member of the higher priesthood of Lower Nubia who held this office, rather than a literal member of the royal family, the *peseto* was a representative of the Kushite king and seems to have facilitated the flow of trade goods from Roman Egypt to Upper Nubia.[193] Some holders of the office of *peseto* were even promoted to the rank of *pqr*, the exact significance of which is unclear, but which seems to have involved close contact with the royal family at Meroë.[194]

contests Procopius' statement, pointing out that "both epigraphic and archaeological sources attest a Meroiticisation of the Dodekaschoinos after the Roman withdrawal." This contention receives support from the lack of Meroitic inscriptions from before the third century, which suggests that the region had earlier been within the Roman sphere of influence (Haycock 1967: 112-13). But as far as ethnicity is concerned it is not impossible that the population of Lower Nubia at this time included at least some Nobatae who had adopted Kushite culture.

190 Lassányi 2008: 598.

191 Török 2009: 472-3.

192 Török 1997: 434; idem 2009: 497-8.

193 Török 1997: 434-5.

194 Török 2009: 496-7.

Clearly, then, Kush maintained firm, centralized control over Nubia as far as Hiera Sykaminos throughout the third century and does not appear to have been contested in this regard by any foreign power. Indeed the only territorial gains in Nubia during the third century were achieved not by Aksum but by Kush, which acquired the entire Dodekaschoinos upon the Roman withdrawal from that region under Diocletian. Thus we must look for some other way to explain the reference in *Monumentum Adulitanum II* to the expansion of the Aksumite state up to the border of Egypt. What is proposed in the present study is that the territory Aksum acquired in this way was Beja, rather than Nubian, land. Since the Aksumite king is reported in *Monumentum Adulitanum II* to have made war on the "nations" inhabiting the Eastern Desert as far as the borders of Egypt, it is evident that already by the third century Beja territory extended well to the north of Kush. Such Beja tribes as the 'Ababda and the Bisharīn have continued to reside in the desert of southeastern Egypt down to the present;[195] that their ancient ancestors at times pushed on to the Thebaid has long been known from the historical records of their raids on Upper Egypt during Roman times.[196] That the Eastern Desert tribes mentioned in *Monumentum Adulitanum II* ranged as far as southeastern Egypt is also supported by archaeological evidence from Berenike. Excavations at that site have revealed fragments of Eastern Desert Ware, associated with pastoral communities living in the desert between Nubia and the Red Sea from the late third to the sixth century CE,[197] who included groups like the Beja. Furthermore, strata at Berenike from the fourth to fifth centuries show a significant rise in ovicaprid bones combined with a drop in fish remains and Nile Valley commodities, a change in diet which also supports the hypothesis of the growing demographic influence of desert pastoralists at the port.[198] Although the settlement of these groups at Berenike does not seem to

[195] Sidebotham et al. 2008: 260-2.
[196] Snowden 1970: 136-40.
[197] Wendrich 1998: 249; Barnard 2002: 53; Manzo 2004: 79; Barnard 2008: 418 (who extends the period in which Eastern Desert Ware was used down to the beginning of the eighth century CE).
[198] Barnard 2002: 53.

have been accompanied by violence,[199] the fact that the Romans maintained a military presence at Berenike during the early third century[200] suggests that a need for proper defense was still felt at that time. The garrison then stationed at Berenike included soldiers from the Syrian city of Palmyra.[201] This garrison may not have been maintained for the entire third century, however, for a decline in the town's infrastructure and administration identified in the archaeological record for that period, and occasioned no doubt by the general political, social, and economic decline of the Roman Empire,[202] hints at neglect of Berenike as the third century wore on. It could be that, by subduing the tribes of the Eastern Desert and creating a direct overland route from the Ethiopian Highlands, as described in *Monumentum Adulitanum II*, the Aksumites sought to establish a measure of *de facto* order on Egypt's southeastern flank where the Romans could not. How this order was enforced is hard to say, though it need not have entailed anything more than the periodic collection of tribute from the Eastern Desert tribes who lived between the Ethiopian Highlands and the Nile Valley in Upper Egypt.[203] When one takes this broader perspective of Rome's southern frontier, the expansion of Aksum to the border of Egypt, as described in *Monumentum Adulitanum*

[199] At least, no trace of destruction has been uncovered in fourth- to fifth-century strata at Berenike.
[200] Sidebotham 2011: 260.
[201] Sidebotham et al. 2008: 354; Sidebotham 2011: 260.
[202] Lassányi 2008: 598; Sidebotham 2011: 259-60.
[203] If so, one should not expect to find evidence of intensive Aksumite activity, such as fortifications, in the archaeological record. To date only a meager quantity of Aksumite material has come to light at Berenike, most notably a coin of the Aksumite king Aphilas (c. 300-310) and some Aksumite sherds (Sidebotham 2011: 248, 277-8). It is not impossible that the road from Aksum to the Egyptian border described in *Monumentum Adulitanum II* was connected in some way with the route between Berenike and the Nile (cf. Fauvelle-Aymar 2009: 153). A Geʿez graffito left by one 'Abrehā Takla-'Aksūm in the Wādī Manīḥ along the road from Berenike to Coptos (Littmann and Meredith 1954) indicates direct Aksumite contact with Upper Egypt by way of Berenike. Given its reference to "the power of the Lord of the Highest Heaven" (*ḫayla 'əgzī'a samāya 'aryām*), this graffito most likely dates from no earlier than the mid-fourth century, when such phraseology, associated with an early stage of Ethiopian Christianity, first appears in Aksumite inscriptions (see §4.5.2). In that case the Wādī Manīḥ graffito would postdate *Monumentum Adulitanum II* by several decades if not an entire century and thus cannot be directly tied to the latter.

II, can be seen as the establishment of an Aksumite sphere of influence over not the middle Nile Valley but rather the Eastern Desert. This area would not have extended as far as Nubia which, given the great S-shaped bend in the middle Nile, lay much further west, but would instead have abutted Roman Egypt somewhere around Syene.

3.3.2. Aksum and "Ethiopia"

That Aksum's third-century expansion in Africa left Nubia untouched is also implied in the concluding portion of *Monumentum Adulitanum II*, in which the Aksumite king, after claiming that he had reduced the peoples along his frontier, states that his realm extended "on the west to the territory of Ethiopia and Sasu" (ἀπὸ δὲ δύσεως μέχρι τῶν τῆς Αἰθιοπίας καὶ Σάσου τόπων).[204] The "Ethiopia" alluded to here is clearly something quite different from the country now known by that name, as it is treated as a region bordering on, and therefore distinct from, the Aksumite realm. Somewhat confusingly for the modern-day student of African history, the Graeco-Roman world knew of Nubia as "Ethiopia,"[205] and it was not until the reign of ʿĒzānā (c. 330-370 CE) that the Aksumites appropriated the name "Ethiopians" for themselves. Thus in RIE 270*bis* ʿĒzānā styles himself "King of Aksum and Ḥimyar and Raydān and the Ethiopians and Sabaeans and Salḥē[n] and Ṣeyāmō and Kush and the Beja" (Βασιλεὺς 'Αξωμιτῶν καὶ 'Ομηριτῶν καὶ τοῦ 'Ραειδᾶν καὶ Αἰθιόπων καὶ Σαβαειτῶν καὶ τοῦ Σιλεῆ καὶ τοῦ Τιαμῶ καὶ Βουγαειτῶν καὶ τοῦ Κάσου).[206] That the "Ethiopians" are in this case the subjects of Aksum living in the Ethiopian Highlands is evident from the Geʿez version of this inscription, written in unvocalized *musnad* in RIE 185*bis* I and in unvocalized *fīdal* in RIE 185*bis* II, in which the equivalent of Αἰθιόποι is given as *Ḥbšt*^{m}[207] and *Ḥbśt*[208] (=**Ḥabashat*) respectively.[209] The latter term is applied to Ethiopians in Sabaic (*'ḥbs*^{2}=**'Aḥbāsh*) as well as in Arabic (*Ḥabasha*). This novel identification of the kingdom of Aksum as "Ethiopia" quickly

[204] *Fontes Historiae Nubiorum III* 1998: 951.
[205] Snowden 1970.
[206] RIE 270*bis*: 1-4 (*Fontes Historiae Nubiorum III* 1998: 1095 [Greek text], 1096 [English transl.]).
[207] RIE 185*bis* I: 2 (Bernard et al. 1991: 246).
[208] RIE 185*bis* II: 2-3 (Bernard et al. 1991: 247).
[209] Dihle 1965: 66.

gained currency in the Graeco-Roman world, for not long after ʻĒzānā's time the ecclesiastical historian Philostorgius (c. 368-439) became the first foreign author to call the Aksumites Ethiopians.[210] It is clear, then, that the fourth century marks the time at which the Aksumites first identified themselves with the Ethiopians of Graeco-Roman parlance and came to be identified as such by foreigners.[211] Since there is no indication that this was the case before ʻĒzānā's reign, it can reasonably be concluded that the "Ethiopia" to which *Monumentum Adulitanum II* refers is not to be sought within the borders of modern Ethiopia but is instead to be identified with the kingdom of Kush in Nubia. Yet the king who erected *Monumentum Adulitanum II* did not make any attempt to engage Kush, for he claims in the inscription to have merely extended the borders of his realm *up to* (μέχρι)—but not including—"Ethiopia." There was thus no Aksumite invasion of Kush at this time.

3.3.3. Sasu: A Scribal Error for Kush?

What then of Sasu, the other land which marked the western limit of the Aksumite king's realm according to *Monumentum Adulitanum II*? As this land is mentioned in the inscription in connection with "Ethiopia," a link with Nubia seems possible, all the more so in that the very name Sasu recalls *Kāsū*, by which Kush is known in Aksumite inscriptions. The theory that the Sasu in Cosmas' copy of *Monumentum Adulitanum II* is nothing more than a mistranscription of the name for Kush was first suggested at the end of the nineteenth century by Glaser, who identified the toponym with the Khartoum region.[212] A half century later, Wainwright, following Glaser's lead, hypothesized that Cosmas mistook the letter *kappa* for a *sigma* (thus *Κάσου>Σάσου), an error all the more understandable if the Nestorian merchant was

[210] Murray 1967: 80.
[211] Why this was done is a matter for speculation, though it may be that the Aksumites appropriated the Graeco-Roman name for Nubia after reducing the last kings of Meroë to vassal status. Since the term "Ethiopian" was applied by the Greeks and Romans to black Africans in general (Snowden 1970), ʻĒzānā may also have styled himself "King of the Ethiopians" in the Greek text of RIE 270*bis* as a means of announcing to Greek-speaking visitors to Aksum that his was *the* African kingdom par excellence.
[212] Glaser 1895: 146.

unfamiliar with the name "Kush" to begin with.[213] At the time when Wainwright was writing the only Aksumite references to Kush known to scholars were those attested in ʻĒzānā's inscription in vocalized Geʻez from Aksum (RIE 189). Thanks to the discovery of two Greek inscriptions of ʻĒzānā at Aksum (RIE 270*bis* and RIE 271) some decades later we know that the name Kush was written in Aksumite inscriptions in Greek in the forms Κάσου and Χάσω. The attestation of Κάσου in RIE 270*bis* might seem to give credence to the theory that the name Sasu is indeed a misreading of a Greek rendition of "Kush," and in this regard Wainwright is followed by Kirwan.[214] There are, however, two objections which can be made to this theory. Firstly, there is the matter of inconsistency in nomenclature. If the "Ethiopia" of *Monumentum Adulitanum II* is to be identified with Kush, as argued above,[215] why should Kush be referred to again in the same passage by a different name, *Κάσου (>Σάσου)? Secondly, emending Cosmas' Σάσου to Κάσου, and thus taking the reference to Sasu in *Monumentum Adulitanum II* as a reference to Kush, creates a serious problem when one considers the Adulis inscription in light of the full report on Ethiopia preserved in the *Christian Topography*. In an earlier part of his report Cosmas describes Aksumite trade with Sasu, saying that it was to this region that the Aksumite king sent a caravan every two years to bring back gold.[216] According to Cosmas these commercial expeditions were dispatched through the governor (ἄρχοντος) of the Agaw,[217] the Cushitic-speaking people who had for centuries dominated the northern and north-central highlands of Ethiopia.[218] How much of the Agaw region lay under the jurisdiction of Aksum's governor is uncertain,[219] though his influence may have been felt as far south as

[213] Wainwright 1942a: 55.
[214] Kirwan 1960: 171-2; idem 1994: 248.
[215] §3.3.2.
[216] *Top. Chr.* 2.51-2.52.
[217] Ibid.: 2.51.3-6.
[218] Ehret 2002: 128.
[219] If the Agaw are to be identified with the Ἀθαγαοὺς (=*Ad Agaw*) of *Monumentum Adulitanum II* (Bernard 2000: 36) and the Atagaw of one of ʻĒzānā's pre-Christian inscriptions from Aksum (RIE 187:7) (Bernard et al. 1991: 256), it would appear that some of the Agaw-speaking regions of the Ethiopian Highlands were incorporated into the Aksumite state at least as early as the third century, and certainly by the fourth, even if the Aksumites

Lake Ṭānā. A merchant first and foremost, Cosmas took a keen interest in commerce and sought out information about foreign lands and trade routes from fellow merchants whom he met in the course of his travels.[220] Though Cosmas never specifies his informants in his description of Aksumite trade with Sasu, the very fact that he gives Σάσου, rather than Κάσου, as the name of the gold-producing country can only mean that he heard the name pronounced Sasu. If so, Sasu cannot be dismissed as a mistranscription of the Greek name for Kush found in Aksumite inscriptions but must instead be regarded as a country quite distinct from Kush.

Regarding the location of Sasu, we are forced to rely solely on the *Christian Topography*, as the name occurs in no other source. Cosmas' claim that Sasu was located near the ocean at the opposite end of Africa[221] is clearly wrong and is no doubt the result of his misunderstanding of both the geographical extent of Sasu and the geography of Africa in general.[222] Cosmas describes Aksumite commerce with Sasu as what scholars have long designated as "silent" trade, whereby the people of Sasu would leave their gold and retreat, after which the Aksumite merchants would come forward and lay out beef, salt, and iron in exchange, both sides adding to the quantity of the products they had brought until a satisfactory trade had been reached.[223] Transactions were made in this way, says Cosmas, because the people of Sasu spoke languages different from those of the

had to undertake periodic punitive campaigns in 'Ēzānā's reign to enforce their suzerainty over the Agaw. On Aksumite relations with the Agaw, see Tadesse Tamrat 1988: 8-9.

[220] Thus, for example, Cosmas attributes his information on the Christian community of Dioskorides (Soqotra) to Greek-speaking inhabitants of the island whom he interviewed during his stay in Ethiopia (*Top. Chr.*: 3.65.1-13).

[221] Ibid.: 2.51.1-3. That Sasu and the incense-producing region along the coast of the Horn of Africa were viewed by Cosmas as being located at opposite ends of Ethiopia is made clear in his account of the geography of Africa (ibid.: 2.48.8-11).

[222] Judging from the information he provides in his *Christian Topography*, Cosmas was ignorant of the lands south of the "Cape of Spices" in Somalia (Frézouls 1989: 448-9). In fact, despite his having visited Ethiopia, he was poorly informed about the western frontiers of Aksum, hence his claim that the kingdom had a southwestern coast (ibid.).

[223] *Top. Chr.*: 2.52.1-9.

Aksumites and there were no available interpreters.[224] Such an account, and others like it,[225] must be treated with caution, not least because modern scholarship has cast doubt on similar descriptions of silent trade throughout history—all of which are based on second- or third-hand information.[226] In fact, many face-to-face commercial transactions are conducted using nonverbal signals[227] and in this way overcome the language barrier. Since a language barrier did exist, Sasu could only have been located well beyond the heartland of the Aksumite state, in a region where neither Semitic- nor Agaw-speakers proficient in the local languages could be found. According to Wainwright, the likeliest location of Sasu is the Fazogli region between the Blue Nile and the Sobat River, on the modern Sudanese-Ethiopian border, which he deduces on the basis of eighteenth- and nineteenth-century reports of gold deposits in the area, as well as reports of the Agaw obtaining this gold from locals.[228] At times iron was exchanged by the Agaw for this gold, much as it was for the gold of Sasu in Cosmas' time.[229] If one overlooks Wainwright's implicit assumption that Kush, by being identified with Sasu, extended as far east as this region—a hypothesis for which there is no support whatsoever—his location of Sasu in the Sudanese-Ethiopian borderlands has much to commend it. On account of its gold deposits[230] the Fazogli region has long attracted the interest of Ethiopia and would again be pulled into the latter's sphere of political influence in the early seventeenth

[224] Ibid.: 2.52.10-11. Both salt and iron retained an economic importance in early modern Ethiopia and to that end served as forms of currency (Pankhurst 1961: 261-5).

[225] A similar case of alleged "silent" trade at Hiera Sykaminos on the southern frontier of Roman Egypt is described by Philostratus c. 220 in his biographical novel of Apollonius of Tyana (*Fontes Historiae Nubiorum III* 1998: 962-4).

[226] Curtin 1984: 13. As Curtin quite rightly points out in reference to the implausibility of "silent" trade, "[t]o bargain with such elaborate avoidance, yet to assume that total strangers will act with honesty and good faith, calls for an unusual degree of cross-cultural understanding from both parties—and to believe it requires unusual credulity from the reader."

[227] Curtin, loc. cit.

[228] Wainwright 1942a: 53-5.

[229] Idem 1942b: 86-7.

[230] Arkell 1944.

century.[231] The Benēshangūl-Gūmez region somewhat further east, in the westernmost reaches of modern Ethiopia's Gojjam Province, also produces gold and is another possible candidate for Sasu.[232] The word *tagkhara* (ταγχάρα) which Cosmas gives as the indigenous name for the nuggets of gold obtained from Sasu[233] has been compared with a Ge'ez word for topaz, *tankar/tankarā*, which Leslau believes is of Agaw origin,[234] while in the Fazogli region itself the related term *tingalo* remained the typical word for gold nugget down to modern times.[235] In all likelihood, then, Sasu was located somewhere near the present-day border between the Sudan and Ethiopia, a historically Nilo-Saharan-speaking region[236] the languages of which, as Cosmas' account indicates, would have been quite foreign to the Semitic- and Cushitic-speakers of the Ethiopian Highlands. But while *Monumentum Adulitanum II* records an extension of Aksumite control to the borders of this region in the third century, there is no evidence that the Aksumites pushed further west into either Sasu or Kush at that time, only that the territory they annexed bordered both.

3.3.4. Aksum's Northern and Western Frontiers in the Third Century

Having examined the external evidence for the geography of the Aksumite frontier, we can conclude that, far from implying any confrontation with Nubia, *Monumentum Adulitanum II* alludes to nothing more than the extension of Aksumite rule during the third century to the eastern frontier of Kush. Despite the inscription's reference to "borders" it must be remembered that the frontiers of ancient states were often highly nebulous affairs which represented the limits of a ruler's tribute-paying domain rather than defined boundaries that can be easily traced on a map.[237] Thus one must not

[231] Pankhurst 1997: 369.
[232] Ibid.: 30.
[233] *Top. Chr.* 2.52.1-3.
[234] Leslau 1991: 577. For other etymologies, see Chittick 1982: 53 (n. 2). The derivation of *tagkhara* from the Persian *tanga* or the Baluchi *tango*, both meaning "gold" (ibid.) are highly improbable on philological as well as historical grounds.
[235] Wainwright 1942a: 56.
[236] Young 1999: 322.
[237] On the question of political "boundaries" in pre-colonial Africa, see Wright 1999.

imagine anything like a true "boundary" between Kush and Aksum. Rather, both kingdoms had their respective spheres of influence, the contours of which at any time depended on who paid tribute to whom —when tribute actually *was* paid. Insofar as we can speak of a Kushite frontier in the sense of an outermost limit of Kush's sphere of influence, it is known that Kush still occupied the western Buṭāna into the fourth century, and certainly throughout the third, for, in addition to archaeological evidence to that effect,[238] we find a Latin graffito at the Kushite site of Muṣawwarāt al-Ṣafrā' dating from the late third or early fourth century (SMBK inv. no. 9675=Ägyptisches Museum, inv. no. 1504) which records the visit of a Roman diplomat named Acutus.[239] This man had come all the way from the city of Rome itself to pay respects to the Kushite queen at Muṣawwarāt al-Ṣafrā', left unnamed.[240] If this graffito is representative of late Kushite control of the region of Muṣawwarāt al-Ṣafrā', then Kush not only held the western Buṭāna during roughly the same timeframe as that of *Monumentum Adulitanum II* but also maintained a political presence there which was significant enough to attract the attention of distant Rome. In light of this, it is most probable that the frontier between Aksum and "Ethiopia" to which *Monumentum Adulitanum II* refers lay somewhere in the Buṭāna, not the Nile Valley. Further south, the eastern borders of Fazogli and/or Benēshangūl-Gūmez, where Sasu was probably located, marked the limit of Aksumite expansion to the west, in which case the southern reaches of Kush in the lower Blue Nile Valley[241] would have remained unaffected. To summarize the extent of Aksum's African empire in the third century we can state with some confidence that to the north the Aksumite frontier extended as far as the desert of southeastern Egypt, where it abutted the east bank of the

[238] A small Graeco-Roman-style kiosk at Naq'a in the Buṭāna may date as late as the third century (Shinnie 1978: 253).
[239] Łajtar and van der Vliet 2006.
[240] Ibid. The sequence of pyramids at Meroë's Bagrawiyya North Cemetery ends with Bagrawiyya N 25, a tomb belonging to a queen (Zibelius-Chen 2006: 303)—the "Lady Queen" mentioned in the Latin graffito from Muṣawwarāt al-Ṣafrā' perhaps?
[241] On Kushite influence in this region, which seems to have extended as far south as Sinnār, see §2. On parallel Kushite influence in the lower White Nile valley, see Edwards 2004: 163.

Nile near the southern frontier of Roman Egypt. To the west, the frontier extended as far as the eastern Buṭāna, after which it curved around to the east towards the present-day Sudanese border with Ethiopia. This region annexed by Aksum in the third century was one in which neither Rome nor Kush had had any direct influence, which may explain the curious fact that the campaigns described in *Monumentum Adulitanum II* passed unnoticed in third-century Roman sources and, as far as we can tell, led to no military action against Aksum on the part of Kush.[242] As we know from the records of ʿĒzānā's campaigns against the Beja a century later,[243] the Eastern Desert tribes often posed a serious threat to the Aksumite state, comparable perhaps with that posed by the Oromo to Ethiopia during the sixteenth and seventeenth centuries.[244] Establishing a sphere of influence in the desert to the north of the Ethiopian Highlands would have been Aksum's way of both neutralizing this threat and allowing more efficient patrolling and regulation of desert traffic, hence the road which the anonymous king claims in *Monumentum Adulitanum II* to have constructed to link his realm with Egypt.

As it would in effect have bypassed Nubia, the implications of this road for Kush require further comment. That the Aksumites built

[242] Burstein (1998: 130) thinks that a reference to *Aethiops et Indus* in an anonymous panegyric in honor of Consantius Chlorus indicates Roman conflict with the Kushites and Aksumites in the 290s, though this is after the timeframe for *Monumentum Adulitanum II* proposed here. It is true, as Török (1988: 29) notes, that the Blemmyes are at times reckoned as "Indians," which may be the case in this panegyric, although other late antique texts distinguish between the two groups (Barnard 2005: 28, 34). Even if frictions arose between the Roman Empire and Aksum towards the end of the third century, there is no evidence that Aksumite expansion in the Eastern Desert as far as the Egyptian border was the cause. In his account of the conversion of Aksum to Christianity, Rufinus alludes to a disturbance in Roman relations with Ethiopia in the early fourth century (Rufinus, *Historia ecclesiastica* 10.9 [transl. Amidon 1997: 19-20]), though this seems to have involved Red Sea traffic, and was not the outcome of Aksumite military operations in the Eastern Desert which took place several decades earlier.

[243] The Geʿez records of these operations are RIE 185 I+II and RIE 185*bis* I+II (Bernard et al. 1991: 241-50); the Greek records are RIE 270 and RIE 270*bis* (*Fontes Historiae Nubiorum III* 1998: 1094-1100; Bernard 2000: 5-15). On these campaigns, see §4.5.2.4.

[244] Like the Beja, the Oromo are a Cushitic-speaking people, but one which threatened Ethiopia from the south rather than the north. On their history in Ethiopia, see Marcus 1994: 34 ff.

roads across their kingdom is confirmed by archaeological surveys of northern Eritrea, which have revealed traces of one such road on the Qōḥaytō Plateau.[245] The Aksumites' construction of a road all the way to the Egyptian border has suggested to some scholars that Aksum sought to undermine Kushite trade by establishing an alternative to the riverine route through which commerce passed between Nubia and Roman Egypt.[246] But, as has been argued above,[247] the two separate arteries of trade in ancient northeast Africa – one running the course of the Nile Valley and the other linking Ethiopia with the Red Sea – had coexisted quite independently of each other since at least the early first millennium BCE. At no point is there any indication that the Romans favored one route over the other in its trade with the peoples to the south of Egypt. Indeed, since Aksum had enjoyed unhindered access to the Red Sea by the first century CE, according to the *Periplus of the Erythraean Sea*, a parallel overland route linking Aksum with Egypt across the Eastern Desert would have been rather superfluous if its function had been exclusively economic. In this connection it should be noted that the construction of roads is mentioned in other Aksumite inscriptions, but with an emphasis on facilitating the flow of tribute from conquered regions rather than the stimulation of trade *per se*. Thus in RIE 186 from Aksum, dating, so it will be argued in the present study,[248] from the reign of Ousanas in the first quarter of the fourth century, we are told that the Aksumite king, having received the submission of the *Ḥmš*^{m} (=Ḥamasen?) region and the *Mṭn*^{m} people (=the Μετίνε of *Monumentum Adulitanum II*?),[249] made a road to facilitate the transport of tribute from the conquered peoples as well as provisions for his troops:

> [15.]And he laid out a road and administered(?) the la[16.]nd.
> And in safety he procured by way of the road whatever

[245] Eigner 2004: 115.

[246] Adams 1977: 385; Török 1988: 41-2; idem 1997: 475-6; Ehret 2002: 215; cf. Welsby 1996: 172. Writing of the invasion of Kush by the fourth-century Aksumite king ʿĒzānā, Arkell (1961: 171-2) similarly regards Aksum and Kush as trade rivals.

[247] See §1.2, §2.

[248] See §4.1.

[249] For tentative identifications of *Ḥmš*^{m} and *Mṭn*^{m} see Huntingford 1989: 52; Merid Wolde Aregay 2005: 161, 181 (n. 13).

tribute the district of Gab[17.]al[250] possessed, and with [it] food for men and women, [18.]and he sustained [his] four army divisions.

(*[15.]w-ṣyḥ[m] fnt[m] w-gbr[m] bḥ[16.]r[m] w-'mn[m] qbl[m] b-fnt[m] ḏ-b-dwl[m] Gb[17.]l[m] 'mẖ[m] w-msl[m] šbṭ[m] 'd[m] w-'nst[18.m] w-'šbṭ[m] l-'rb't[m] srwt[m]=*Wa-ṣēḥa fənōta wa-gabra bəḥēra. Wa-'əmūna qabbala ba-fənōt za-ba-dawala Gabal 'amməẖā wa-məslē[hū] śəbāṭa 'ed wa-'anəst wa-'aśbaṭa la-'arbā'tū sarāwīt.*)[251]

Although trade as well as tribute might have passed along this road, it is clear from RIE 186 that commerce was not the main purpose of the road laid out by Ousanas. The road from Aksum to the Egyptian border described in *Monumentum Adulitanum II* is likely to have also had some utility for merchants, which might explain the Roman pottery found at Tabot in the eastern Sudan, occupied during the period from which *Monumentum Adulitanum II* dates.[252] The distance between the city of Aksum and the Egyptian border was certainly not an insurmountable one, for according to Cosmas Indicopleustes and Procopius the journey from Aksum to the first Nile cataract could be made in just thirty days.[253] But in light of RIE 186 it would seem that the construction of roads by the Aksumites in the aftermath of military conquest was aimed at the transport of tribute and foodstuffs from vassal peoples,

[250] Probably to be identified with the Gabala, referred to in *Monumentum Adulitanum II* as a nation which, together with the Lasine and Zaa, lived on a mountain "seething with streams of hot water" (*Fontes Historiae Nubiorum III* 1998: 951). Huntingford (1989: 46) tentatively identifies Gabala with Gabalē, located near Enṭalō in Ethiopia's northern Tigray Province, though the reference to "streams of hot water" in *Monumentum Adulitanum II* suggests a local near geothermal springs. Although several such springs exist in central Ethiopia, those closest to Aksum are located in the Afar region to the southeast of Tigray. It is possible, then, that the Gabala of *Monumentum Adulitanum II* and—assuming they are one and the same people—the Gabal of RIE 186 are to be identified with the Gabala tribe of the upper Awash, mentioned in the chronicle of 'Amda Ṣeyōn (1314-1344) (Morin 2004: 153-4). Since the Awash Basin has a number of geothermal springs, locating Gabal(a) in this region would fit the reference to hot waters in *Monumentum Adulitanum II*.

[251] RIE 186: 15-18 (Bernard et al. 1991: 252).

[252] Magid 2004: 166.

[253] *Top. Chr.* 2.48.7; Procopius, *De Bell. Pers.* 1.19.27-8.

not luxury items from abroad.[254] The bones of cattle and ovicaprids, as well as the desiccated sheep and/or goat faeces, at Tabot[255] may hint at the site's use as a transit station for the transport of tribute to Aksum in the form of livestock. It is true that control of the Eastern Desert would have given the Aksumites access to valuable natural resources, though it is not clear what role these played in tipping the economic balance of northeast Africa in favor of Aksum. The territory of the Blemmyes was famous for its emerald mines, as reported by Olymiodorus of Thebes c. 423,[256] and according to Cosmas Indicopleustes, writing a century later, the Aksumites acquired these emeralds from the Blemmyes and exported them to India.[257] Eastern Desert Ware of fourth- to sixth-century date has come to light at several of the beryl mines in the Eastern Desert,[258] indicating Blemmyan activities there, and it is not impossible this trade was facilitated at least in part by the Aksumite road mentioned in *Monumentum Adulitanum II*. In and of itself, however, Aksum's gaining control of access to mines of precious stones could hardly have brought economic ruin upon Kush. Also located in the Eastern Desert are numerous gold mines, most notably those of the Wādī al-'Allāqī in southeastern Egypt, which were exploited since pharaonic times[259] and were, according to Ibn Ḥawqal (fl. 943-977), located on the borders of the Beja's territory (*fī ḥudūd il-Buja*).[260] It is dubious, however, whether gold-mining operations took place in this region during the period from which *Monumentum Adulitanum II* dates. Firstly, early Roman gold-mining operations in the Eastern Desert were concentrated well to the north of the Wādī al-'Allāqī,[261] while some gold mines, like those at Bi'r

[254] In her description of her journey up the Nile in the winter of 1873-4, the English novelist Amelia B. Edwards (1877: 303-4) mentions an encounter with an "Abyssinian caravan" in Lower Nubia, noting that the caravan included no fewer than seventy camels bearing what she estimated as 840 elephant tusks. She does not, however, give any information on the route by which this caravan reached Nubia.
[255] Manzo 2004: 79.
[256] *Fontes Historiae Nubiorum III* 1998: 1127; Raschke 1978: 678, 1063-4 (n. 1725).
[257] *Top. Chr.* 11.21.1-5.
[258] Barnard 2002: 53.
[259] Klemm et al. 2001.
[260] Ibn Ḥawqal 1938-9: I: 162.
[261] Sidebotham et al. 2008: 223-5.

Umm Fawākhir in the Wādī Ḥammāmāt, were only exploited between the fourth and sixth centuries CE,[262] after the Aksumite military campaigns described in *Monumentum Adulitanum II*. Mines, it should be noted, do fall out of use and in time might even be forgotten. Secondly, when one bears in mind that the Aksumite heartland was much further removed from these mines than Roman Egypt, and that Aksumite expansion to the border of Sasu would already have given Aksum relatively easy access to the gold of the Sudanese-Ethiopian borderlands, it seems unlikely that the Aksumites would have invested in extensive gold-mining operations in the Eastern Desert, particularly when there is no evidence that they were aware of the gold resources there. Thirdly, there is no evidence that the Kushites either controlled or exploited the gold mines of the Eastern Desert at the time of the Aksumite campaigns described in *Monumentum Adulitanum II*—or indeed at any point in their history with the exception of the Twenty-fifth Dynasty (c. 722-655 BCE)[263]—in which case Aksumite expansion into the Eastern Desert would hardly have had much of an adverse economic effect on Kush and is unlikely to have been conceived as a means to that end.[264] Quite apart from these points it must be borne in mind that Aksumite growth need not be related to Kushite decline, particularly when the theory of Kushite economic decline in the third century is far from proven. Excavations of the top strata at Meroë, dating from the third and fourth centuries, have revealed the continued importation of manufactured products from the Roman world, as well as Roman influence on the local material culture.[265] The

[262] Ibid.: 221-2.

[263] Welsby 1996: 169, 175. It may be significant in this regard that, apart from a single gold vessel, gold was not among the items seized by the Aksumites in the course of 'Ēzānā's Nubian campaign (§4.5.2.2).

[264] Even when Ptolemy II (285-246 BCE) conquered the Wādī al-'Allāqī (Török 1997: 426), thus opening the region up to gold-mining (Sidebotham et al. 2008: 217-24), there is no record of immediate conflict with the Kushites (Welsby 1996: 66). This could hardly have been the case had Kush exercised control over the gold-producing region of the Eastern Desert. In fact, what conflict did take place between Kush and Ptolemaic Egypt in the reigns of Ptolemy IV (221-203 BCE) and Ptolemy V (203-181 BCE) resulted not from disputes about control of the Eastern Desert's gold mines but from Kushite intervention in Egyptian affairs (ibid.: 67), particularly in the form of Kushite support to Upper Egyptian rebels (Török 1997: 427).

[265] Török 1988: 40.

expansion of Kushite settlement in the Dodekaschoinos following the withdrawal of Roman forces in Diocletian's reign, and with it the imposition of direct rule from Meroë, similarly belies claims that Kush was on the verge of collapse in the third century.[266]

Such economic interests as might have led to Aksumite expansion into the Eastern Desert may in fact have more to do with maritime than overland trade. Curiously, although Berenike's economic fortunes revived after the third century, only one or two of the ten forts defending the port's desert frontier still operated during that period, while several Late Roman settlements in the desert were left unfortified.[267] It could be that once Aksum established control over the Eastern Desert and its tribes as far as the frontier of Roman Egypt, Berenike's desert hinterland was no longer in need of fortifications on the scale of those of earlier centuries. A similar effort to establish and enforce the security of the lands bordering the Red Sea is mentioned in *Monumentum Adulitanum II* in connection with the Aksumite king's campaign against the Arabitae and Kinaidokolpitae of western Arabia. These two groups, according to the inscription, were required thereafter to pay tribute and make traveling safe by land and sea.[268] In light of this, subduing the tribes of the Eastern Desert can be seen as part and parcel of the same policy of establishing security on both sides of the Red Sea, the main difference being that the Aksumite road to Egypt had no counterpart in Arabia. Since the foreign trade of Kush did not take the Red Sea route, there is no reason to assume that Aksumite expansion into the Eastern Desert, as documented in *Monumentum Adulitanum II*, constituted an act of aggression against Kush. Far from attempting to harm Kushite commercial interests, Aksumite expansion northwards into the Eastern Desert and westwards towards Sasu and the borders of "Ethiopia" would seem to reflect instead the creation of buffer zones shielding both the Aksumite heartland and the Red Sea coast from attack and thereby facilitating the fbw of tribute. In such a situation the Aksumite frontier could take on great strategic importance, as we will see in the following chapter, where it will be argued that concern about the

[266] Haycock 1967: 113-17; Török 1997: 434-5; idem 2009: 496-7.
[267] Sidebotham 2011: 275.
[268] *Top. Chr.* 2.62.4-8.

security of the western frontier—not trade—was the main factor behind the Aksumite invasions of Nubia in the fourth century.

Before leaving the third century, however, it should be stressed that, despite the best intentions of the king who erected *Monumentum Adulitanum II*, the control of the Eastern Desert established by this ruler need not have been particularly stable or long-lived. The Blemmyes of the Eastern Desert were far from pacified by the Aksumites during the third century, and indeed would continue to threaten the frontiers of both Aksum and Roman Egypt for much of the fourth. This being the case, it would seem that the far-flung conquests recorded in *Monumentum Adulitanum II* were in fact quite ephemeral and would thus have hardly diverted Nubia's long-distance commerce to Aksum, as some have imagined. Part of the reason why Aksum would have had difficulty in holding onto the Eastern Desert for long was simple geography. Based as they were in the fertile Ethiopian Highlands, the Aksumites during the third century had little experience in governing desert regions like those inhabited by the Blemmyes, and their military operations in South Arabia seem to have for the most part avoided desert areas. Since no Aksumite king after the third century is known to have attempted to re-establish Aksumite control of the Eastern Desert in northeast Africa or the barren Ḥijāzī coast across the Red Sea, it is likely that the difficulties of governing large areas of desert inhabited by nomads outweighed any possible benefits.[269] If anything, the third century may be seen as a period of Aksumite experimentation in military expansion, with the inevitability of success in some areas and failure in others. Thus some ventures, like the occupation of South Arabia, would be resumed in later centuries, while others, like extending Aksumite control all the way to the border of Roman Egypt, were not. During the fourth century, the most

[269] The only Ethiopian king of antiquity who is known to have engaged in long-distance desert warfare is 'Abrehā (c. 535-558 CE). On his military campaigns in the interior of Arabia, see Gajda 2009: 137-46. Strictly speaking, however, these campaigns cannot be classified as Aksumite in that 'Abrehā rebelled against his lord, Kālēb of Aksum, and reigned as a king of Ḥimyar rather than Aksum. At most 'Abrehā's campaigns in Arabia represent an attempt by an Ethiopian expatriate to restore Ḥimyarite control of the Arabian interior and the tribes living there.

innovative step taken by Aksum was the invasion of Nubia. It is to this development and its long-term effects that we now turn.

4. The Fourth Century CE: Aksum in Nubia

The story of Aksum's military operations in Upper Nubia is a familiar one, retold countless times—with varying degrees of accuracy—in secondary literature on Ethiopia and Nubia, as well as in general histories of pre-colonial Africa.[270] Traditionally, the dynamic Aksumite king ʿĒzānā, also famous as the first Christian king of Ethiopia, has been credited with singlehandedly dealing the death-blow to Meroë on the basis of several inscriptions in Greek and Geʿez which he erected at Aksum. In fact, the history of Aksumite military intervention in Upper Nubia during the fourth century is a good deal more complicated than this standard narrative implies, for there is good evidence that the Aksumites invaded Nubia twice during the fourth century, that ʿĒzānā was by no means the initiator of this more aggressive Aksumite policy towards Nubia, and that the *casus belli* cannot be explained away as a straightforward political or economic rivalry between Aksum and Kush. In this chapter it will be argued that during the reign of Ousanas (c. 310-330) a direct military confrontation took place between the two kingdoms in which the Kushite capital of Meroë was involved in some way. But in the reign of Ousanas' son and successor ʿĒzānā (c. 330-370) the Aksumites undertook a much larger-scale invasion of Nubia (See Map 2). Although the Kushites were also affected by this second invasion, the main *casus belli* by that time was the Noba, a people who threatened Aksum's western frontier from their base in the Nile Valley.

4.1. Ousanas and Kush: RIE 186

As we have seen, the third-century *Monumentum Adulitanum II* says nothing of an invasion of Nubia, but states only that the Aksumite army reached the borders of the realm of the "Ethiopians." The earliest evidence for Aksumite involvement with Nubia proper is preserved in

[270] The popular literature on this history is fairly substantial and need not be treated here. Not counting the specialized studies cited in the present work, one may note the descriptions of the Aksumite invasion of Nubia in the more general monographs of Adams 1977: 386-8; Kobishchanov 1979: 82-5 (in which the untenable theory of two Aksumite kings named ʿĒzānā is adopted); Marcus 1994: 7-8; Shinnie 1996: 116-17; Welsby 1996: 197-9; Ehret 2002: 215.

a royal title borne by a fourth-century ruler who erected an inscription, RIE 186, at Aksum to commemorate his military campaigns in northeast Africa.[271] Of particular interest in this inscription is the title borne by the king, which lists the vassals of Aksum. Such royal titles provide a unique insight into how the Aksumites envisioned the geographical extent of their empire. It is only from the fourth century on, however, that such titles are attested in the epigraphic record. The titles borne by third-century Aksumite kings are much terser. Thus one such king, Gadarā, is referred to only as "King of Aksum" (*ngśy 'ksm=*nagāśī 'Aksūm*) on a ritual object[272] from 'Ādī Galamō (RIE 180),[273] while Sembrouthes is only slightly more creative with his title of "King of Kings (βασιλεὺς ἐκ βασιλεῶν) of Aksum"[274] in his Greek inscription from Daqqī Maḥārī (RIE 275).[275] Since the opening lines of *Monumentum Adulitanum II* had either gone missing by the time Cosmas Indicopleustes copied the inscription in 518, or were for whatever reason not included by Cosmas in his copy of the text in the *Christian Topography*, the title borne by the anonymous king who erected *Monumentum Adulitanum II* remains unknown. With RIE 186 we find for the first time a much longer royal title, one which lists a series of lands and peoples on both sides of the Red Sea over which the king of Aksum claims to have held sway.[276] The inscription itself is written in Ge'ez

[271] Bernard et al. 1991: 250-4.

[272] For an illustration of this object, see Bernard et al. 1991: 220. The object itself is shaped like a curved stick, not unlike the throw-sticks used down to the present in the Sudan, and which were among the commodities imported by the ancient Egyptians from Nubia and Punt (Kendall 1989: 703-7, pl. VI). That implements such as these are associated with burials in Predynastic and Early Dynastic Egypt (ibid.: 704) suggests that they had ritual importance, a hypothesis supported by the reference to the offering of throw-sticks to deities in the *Epic of Gilgamesh* (George n.d.: 7).

[273] Bernard et al. 1991: 219-20.

[274] The particle ἐκ in Sembrouthes' title is in fact unnecessary, though this is more likely the result of a careless scribal error than an intentional rendition of the phrase "king from [a line of] kings"—i.e., legitimately descended (Munro-Hay 1981-2: 5).

[275] Bernard 2000: 23-5.

[276] It cannot be deduced from the development of longer royal titles that the territory of Aksum itself increased, for Aksum was already in possession of parts of Yemen in the third century, when only short titles are attested. The longer royal titles from the fourth century, by contrast, date from a time at which Aksum had already lost control of South Arabia (see §3.2). The

using the unvocalized *musnad* script of South Arabia, written from right to left, rather than the more cursive *fidal* script which, though derived from *musnad*, developed in Ethiopia during the early Aksumite period and was written from the opposite direction. RIE 186 employs not only *musnad* but also, in a further attempt to emulate South Arabian monumental culture, mimation, a form of suffixation with *-m* common in Ancient South Arabian but not attested in Ethiosemitic.[277]

The title borne by the king in RIE 186 reads "King of Aksum and Ḥimyar and Raydān and Saba' and Salḥīn and Ṣeyāmō and the Beja and Kush" (*ngś*^{m} *'ksm*^{m} *w-z*^{m} *Ḥmr*^{m} *w-z*^{m} *Rydn*^{m} *w-z*^{m} *Sb*$^{\prime m}$ *w-z*^{m} *Slḥn*^{m} *w-z*^{m} *Ṣym*^{m} *w-z*^{m} *Bg*^{m} *w-z*^{m} *Kš*^{m}=**Nəgūśa 'Aksūm wa-za-Ḥəmēr wa-za-Raydān wa-za-Saba' wa-za-Salḥīn wa-za-Ṣeyāmō wa-za-Begā wa-za-Kāshū*).[278] Priority is given to Arabia, for Arabian places and peoples are listed immediately after the phrase "King of Aksum," while the list of African vassals comes second. There is also a structural difference between the Arabian and African lists, for the former begins with the names of two kingdoms, Ḥimyar with its royal stronghold of Raydān, located at the Ḥimyarite capital of Ẓafār, and Saba' with its corresponding stronghold of Salḥīn at the Sabaean capital of Mārib. In the list of African vassals, the only kingdom mentioned is Kush, the Beja being the inhabitants of the desert regions to the north of the Ethiopian Highlands rather than a state as such, while Ṣeyāmō seems to correspond to the Τιάμαα of *Monumentum Adulitanum II*.[279] The latter were one of the ethnic groups which according to *Monumentum Adulitanum II* dwelled in the mountains "beyond the Nile" (i.e., the Takkazē),[280] by which is probably meant the Samēn Highlands. The main importance of RIE 186 in the present context is that it is the earliest Aksumite inscription that mentions Kush by name.[281] The question as to how early the Aksumites

development of royal titles in Aksum, then, was to a large extent driven by ideological concerns.

[277] Mimation does occur in Sabaic inscriptions from the Diʿmat period, though only in personal names (Robin and Maigret 1998: 784).

[278] RIE 186: 1-4 (Bernard et al. 1991: 251).

[279] That Τιάμαα is to be identified with Ṣeyāmō is supported by 'Ēzānā's Greek inscriptions, which give Τιαμῶ as the equivalent of Ṣeyāmō.

[280] *Top. Chr.* 2.60.5-11.

[281] While the "Ethiopia" of *Monumentum Adulitanum II* is in all likelihood to be identified with Kush, as argued above (§3.3.2), RIE 186 contains the oldest known reference to Nubia as Kush in Aksumite records.

laid claim to Kush can only be settled by identifying the Aksumite king who erected this inscription. Though the identity of this king has been a point of contention for many years, Munro-Hay[282] has argued that the opening of the text should read *W[zn]*^{m} *'l*^{m} *'md*^{m} *b's[y*^{m} *.]šn*^{m}, in which we can recognize a king's name, *Wāzānā, followed by his alternative (birth?) name 'Ella 'Amīdā, and finally his clan affiliation "Man of [...]ś.n."[283] The only king whose name fits this reconstruction is Ousanas, who on his coins is called βισι Γισενε, a Greek transliteration of the Ge'ez **bə'səya Gīśēnē*, "man of [the clan of] Gīśēnē."[284] On the basis of numismatic evidence, then, the fragmentary clan-name of the king, [.]*šn*^{m} given in RIE 186 can be reconstructed as *Gšn*^{m} (=**Gśn*)[285] and the king's name and that of his clan can thus be read as **Wāzānā 'Əlla-'Amīdā bə'səya Gīśēnē*, i.e. "Ousanas 'Ella 'Amīdā, Man of Gīśēnē." Apart from enabling us to identify the ruler who erected RIE 186, the coins of Ousanas also provide valuable chronological evidence, for the gold content of these coins matches the Roman standard of 72 *solidi* to

[282] Munro-Hay 1989b: 27-8.

[283] That RIE 186 has long been attributed to 'Ēzānā is the result of Littmann's reading of the first three words of the royal title as *wld*^{m} *'l*^{m} *'md*^{m}, "the son of 'Ella 'Amīdā" (Littmann 1913: 20-1), a reading accepted by Bernard et al. 1991: 251, 253). Since 'Ēzānā is designated as a son of a king named 'Ella 'Amīdā in his own inscriptions, Littmann (1913: 20-1) was quick to read the element ...*šn*^{m} in the clan-name mentioned RIE 186 as ...*ln*^{m}, which he believed was the final portion of *Ḥālēn, the name of 'Ēzānā's clan, with mimation. Recent re-examinations of the text, however, support the reading of the fragmentary clan-name as ...*šn*^{m} (Bernard et al. 1991: 251, 253; Drewes 2002-2007: 132). As for the *wld*^{m} read by Littmann, Munro-Hay (1989b: 27-8) points out that the only letters apparent from the photograph are the initial *w* and the *m* of mimation. This leaves us with *w..*^{m} *'l*^{m} *'md*^{m} *b's[y*^{m} *.]šn*^{m} for the name of the king and that of his clan. It is unlikely that the initial *w..*^{m} can be reconstructed as *wld*^{m} ("son of"), as this would mean that the king who erected RIE 186 began the text by designating himself not by his name but only by his filiation ("the son of 'Ella-'Amīdā")!

[284] Munro-Hay and Juel-Jensen 1995: 104.

[285] In the *musnad* script used in RIE 186, the Sabaic /š/, more properly s^2, corresponds to the Ge'ez /ś/. The use of the *sigma* to represent this phoneme in the Greek mottoes on Ousanas' coins poses no problems. Firstly, Greek has no equivalent of either /š/ or /ś/, in which case the *sigma* would have been the best approximation. Secondly, the Ge'ez phoneme /ś/ seems to have undergone a shift to /s/ at some point in the language's history. If this process was already underway in the fourth century CE, the /ś/ in Ousanas' clan-name Gīśēnē may well have been pronounced /s/. On the phoneme /ś/ in Ge'ez, see Gragg 1997: 244-5.

the pound which was introduced by the emperor Constantine in the Roman East following his removal of his co-emperor Licinius in 324.[286] In light of this, Ousanas' reign would have extended at least as late as the mid-320s. As for his place in the sequence of Aksumite rulers, we have a vital clue from the reign of the famous 'Ēzānā. In his own inscriptions from Aksum 'Ēzānā calls himself the son of 'Ella 'Amīdā,[287] which RIE 186 gives as another name of Ousanas, thus making Ousanas the father and predecessor of 'Ēzānā. Since his inscription from Aksum (RIE 186) records several fairly extensive campaigns, Ousanas would likely have ruled for more than a decade, in which case a reign of c. 310-330 is plausible. Having made the case for an approximate timeframe for Ousanas' reign, we can deduce that Aksumite claims to Kush date back to the first quarter of the fourth century. But to what extent do such claims reflect the political reality of the time? As we have seen, the implication of the royal title attested in RIE 186 that Aksum held sway over South Arabia during this period is without foundation, for the fourth century witnessed Ḥimyar's establishment of political supremacy throughout South Arabia, as well as the beginning of its military expansion into regions beyond.[288] In the case of Aksum's claims to Kush, however, we are fortunate in possessing epigraphic evidence from Nubia itself that testifies clearly to Aksumite military campaigns in that region, indicating that the inclusion of Kush Ousanas' list of vassals does indeed reflect a political reality.

4.2. Aksum Invades Kush: Two Greek Inscriptions from Meroë

Among the epigraphic evidence for Aksumite warfare in Nubia is RIE 286, an inscription in Greek now kept at the Sudan National Museum (inv. no. SNM 508). The inscription survives in a single fragment whose sides are quite damaged, leaving us with little more than disjointed portions of fourteen lines of text. The original length and width of the inscription are unknown. The name of the king who erected the inscription is missing on the fragment, but his title "King of the Aksumites and Ḥimyarites" ([βασιλεὺς Ἀξω]μειτῶν καὶ Ὁμηρειτῶ[ν]) proves that he can only have been an Aksumite ruler.

[286] Munro-Hay 1999: 15; Hahn 2000: 290.
[287] RIE 187:1, RIE 188:1, RIE 189:1 (Bernard et al. 1991: 255, 259, 263).
[288] See §3.2.

Found in rather obscure circumstances by villagers at Meroë, it was initially published in 1909 by Sayce,[289] to whom the villagers presented the inscription.[290] Reexamination of the inscription by subsequent scholars[291] has helped correct Sayce's drawing of the inscription and his edition of the text, both of which contain many inaccuracies. The following text and translation, based on the edition published in *Fontes Historiae Nubiorum*, read as follows:

1 [I,..............., King of the Aksu]mites and Ḥimyarite[s....]
2 [...son of the invincible god] Ares, when [the people of...]
3 [...], I conv[ey]ed from [...]
4 [...] ...and I pillaged the [...]
5 [...] ...having arrived here [...]
6 [...] (women) of noble birth, and another [...]
7 [...] with the king as far as th[e...]
8 [...] most (things) in the ... [...]
9 [...gen]erals and [their] children [...]
10 [...] I went against [...] at once [...]
11 [...] I will [...] to you [...]
12 [...] subject to pay tribute [...]
13 [...] a bronze (statue?) [...]
14 [...] ...21(?) [...][292]

1 [------------------βασιλεὺς Ἀξω]μειτῶν καὶ Ὁμηρειτῶ[ν----------]
2 [--------υἱὸς θεοῦ ἀνικήτου] Ἄρεως ἀντιδικησάντ[ων-------------]
3 [--------------------------------].ΟΝ παρακο[μί]σας ἀπὸ τῆς [-----]
4 [-----------------------------]ΕΙΑΙΟΙΣ καὶ ἐξεπόρθησα τὰς [-------]
5 [-----------------------------]Α κλειθὲν παρελθὼν ἐνθ[άδε----------]
6 [----------------------------]. γεναῖαι ἕτερον δὲ ΚΑ[-----------------]
7 [----------------------------] σὺν τῷ βασιλεῖ μέχρι τῶ[ν-------------]
8 [---------------------------] τὰ πλεῖστα ἐν τῇ ΣΕΜ[-----------------]

[289] Sayce 1909.
[290] Sayce's account of RIE 286's discovery is very vague. Although he was present at Meroë during Garstang's excavations there, it appears that locals showed him the inscription at a slightly earlier point in time (Shinnie et al. 1982: 55).
[291] For a complete bibliography see Bernard 2000: 47.
[292] English translation *Fontes Historiae Nubiorum III* 1998: 1068-9.

[------------------------στρ]ατηγοὺς καὶ τέκνα [αὐτῶν-------------]
[--------------------------] ἐπῆλθον αὐτί[κα------------------------]
[--------------------------]σομαί σοι ΚΙ[---------------------------]
[-------------------------] ἐπὶ φόροι[ς------------------------------]
[-------------------------] χάλκεον [---------------------------------]
[---------------------------]ΩΝ κα [----------------------------------] [293]

It would be futile to attempt to reconstruct a coherent narrative based on these few lines of badly damaged text, of which not a single complete sentence, clause, or even phrase is preserved.[294] What we can make out from the inscription is a description of a military operation characterized by the pillaging of a number of settlements and involving in some way a king, noble women, generals, and children, after which reference is made to the victorious Aksumites imposing the payment of tribute on the locals.[295] The suggestion that a bronze statue was erected at the conclusion of the campaign is based on similar references in the Greek and Ge'ez inscriptions of 'Ēzānā to the dedication of statues of bronze, gold, and silver to Maḥrem/Ares in gratitude for the god's granting of victory in battle.[296] A possible relic of one such statue may survive at Aksum in the form of a stone slab with depressions for the feet of a statue.[297] The fact that these depressions are 92 cm long implies a total height of 5 m for the statue;[298] roughing it in the field at distant Meroë, the Aksumites may have been forced to make do with a much smaller statue.

Probably related to RIE 286 is a fragment of a second Aksumite inscription in Greek (SNM 24841) which came to light near Temple KC102 (M282) at Meroë during the 1975-76 season of excavations under the direction of Peter Shinnie. That the inscription was situated on the processional way leading to the temple[299] probably reflects an intentional act on the part of the Aksumites of erecting a monument to

[293] Greek text ibid.: 1068.
[294] Burstein 1981: 48.
[295] Ibid.
[296] RIE 185: 17-19 (Bernard et al. 1991: 242-3); RIE 270: 30-1 (Bernard 2000: 6, 11).
[297] Phillipson 1997: 155-6.
[298] Ibid.: 155.
[299] Török 1988: 42.

their victory in a conspicuous place in the city. Currently kept in the Sudan National Museum in Khartoum, the fragment (labeled 6164 in the excavation report) measures c. 26 x 33 cm and bears the last seven lines of an inscription which seems to record the aftermath of a military campaign. In his publication of the inscription, Hägg transcribes the Greek of SNM 24841 as follows:

1]ΡΕΩΣ...[[----------Ἄ]ρεως...[----------]
2].ΜΗΔΕ[..]Σ..[[------------]. μηδὲ [..]Σ..[-----]
3]ΤΟΥ[.]ΣΜΗ̣.Ε̣ΠΑΡ [------------]ΤΟΥ[.]Σ μη[δ]ὲ παρ-
4]ΤΟΥΜΗΔΕΑΙ̣ΓΥΝΑΙ [θένοι ------]του μηδὲ αἱ γυναῖ-
5]ΩΝΑΥΤΟΥΕΚΑΘΙΣΑ [κες --- (παρ)ελθ]ὼν αὐτοῦ ἐκάθισα
6]ΟΝ̣ΑΠΒ̣ΙΔΟΥΣ [------ ἀντίδωρ]ον ἀποδιδοὺς
7]ΔΙΦΡΟΝΤΟΥΤΟΝ [-----τῷ Ἄρει] δίφρον τοῦτον.[300]

These lines Hägg translates as: "(1) ...of [A]res... (2) ...neither... (3) nor young g[irls] (4) ...nor the wom- (5) [en... Having arriv]ed I took my seat here (6) ...giving [as a recompense?] (7) [to Ares?] this throne."[301] The fragmentary reference to the erection of a throne (δίφρος) in the last line of the inscription invites comparison with the allusions in other Aksumite texts to the erection of symbolic thrones following a military victory. As we have seen, *Monumentum Adulitanum II* refers to the Aksumite king's erection of a throne to Ares (=Maḥrem). At the site of Aksum itself numerous stone thrones have been found, several bearing grooves into which the sides and backs were fitted.[302] It is likely that the stelae inscribed with records of military victories which have also been found at Aksum originally formed the sides and/or backs of these thrones.[303] In light of Line 7 of SNM 24841 it would seem that the Aksumite victory over the Kushites at Meroë was commemorated by the erection of a similar throne at the Kushite capital, and that SNM 24841 originally formed part of this throne.[304] If so, RIE 286 probably

[300] Hägg 2004: 106-7.
[301] Ibid.: 107.
[302] Phillipson 1997: 123.
[303] Ibid.
[304] Of interest is the choice of δίφρος as the word for throne in SNM 24841, as well as in *Monumentum Adulitanum II* and the narrative of Cosmas Indicopleustes' *Christian Topography*, when θρόνος is the more common word

also formed part of a throne. That the Aksumites chose to erect inscriptions in Greek at Meroë, as opposed to Ge'ez, reflects the status of Greek as a *lingua franca* in the Hellenistic and post-Hellenistic East, northeast Africa included. Just as we read in the *Periplus* that Zoskales, an Aksumite king of the first century CE, was literate in Greek so too we learn from Diodorus Siculus that the Kushite king Ergamenes, a Kushite king of the early third century BCE referred to in inscriptions as Arkamaniqo,[305] received a Greek education.[306] What may be evidence of instruction in Greek at Meroë is preserved on a column drum at the site inscribed with the Greek alphabet.[307] RIE 286 and SNM 24841 were therefore not simply monuments to a foreign power but were intended to be read by those members of the Kushite elite and diplomatic corps —not to mention visitors from the Roman world—who were proficient in Greek.

4.2.1. Dating RIE 286 and SNM 24841

If RIE 286 and SNM 24841 document the same Aksumite campaign against Meroë, dating the two inscriptions remains difficult given that neither fragment bears a date or a name of an Aksumite ruler. Hägg points out as well that the rough, unsophisticated execution of the latter inscription provides no palaeographic clues for dating.[308] The form of the royal title partially preserved in RIE 286, in which the ruler is described as the king of the Aksumites and Ḥimyarites ([βασιλεὺς Ἀξω]μειτῶν καὶ Ὁμηρειτῶ[ν]), recalls the royal titles given in full in the two Greek inscriptions of ʿĒzānā from Aksum (RIE 270*bis*, recording his campaign against the Beja; and RIE 271, recording his Nubian campaign), which read as follows: Βασιλεὺς Ἀξωμιτῶν καὶ Ὁμηριτῶν

for throne. In Greek, δίφρος can refer not only to a throne, a seat, or a couch, but also a litter, a chariot-board on which two people can stand, and even the chariot itself (Glen W. Bowersock, pers. comm.). It could be that the "throne" on which SNM 24841 and similar Aksumite inscriptions were erected were representations in stone of transportable thrones which, as emblems of the Aksumite king's power, were carried by the Aksumite army on military campaigns.

305 *Fontes Historiae Nubiorum II* 1996: 566-7.

306 Diodorus 3.6.3 (*Fontes Historiae Nubiorum II* 1996: 647).

307 Welsby 1996: 194-5.

308 Hägg 2004: 108.

καὶ τοῦ ʻΡαειδᾶν[309] καὶ Σαβαειτῶν καὶ τοῦ Σιλεῆ[310] καὶ τοῦ Κάσου[311] καὶ Βουγαειτῶν καὶ τοῦ Τιαμῶ.[312] Since titles of this sort are not known to have been borne by Aksumite kings before the fourth century, it is quite plausible that RIE 286 and SNM 24841 can be assigned the reign of an Aksumite ruler in that century, the two great warrior-kings Ousanas and ʻĒzānā being the likeliest candidates. The only possible contender in this regard is an obscure Aksumite ruler of the early fourth century named Wāzēbā, who would seem to have been at one point a co-regent with Ousanas on the grounds of his silver bi-regnal issue with the latter.[313] If Hahn is correct that the coins of Wāzēbā are to be assigned to a brief period between the reigns of Ousanas and ʻĒzānā,[314] this king, perhaps an elder brother of ʻĒzānā, would have been Ousanas' immediate successor. On the other hand, it is not impossible that Wāzēbā ruled briefly (perhaps c. 324-5)[315] only as co-regent with Ousanas and not as a king in his own right. At any rate Wāzēbā is not known to have left any inscriptions, in which case he is far less likely to have undertaken an invasion on the scale of the Nubian campaign described in RIE 286 and SNM 24841. If we are thus left with a choice of either Ousanas or ʻĒzānā, how can we decide which of these two rulers invaded Kush?

A comparison of the royal title in RIE 286 with those borne by both kings is of no help, since all that RIE 286 preserves of this title is "King of the Aksumites and Ḥimyarites," a phrase which appears verbatim in the titles of both Ousanas and ʻĒzānā. Despite this drawback, there are grounds for tentatively dating RIE 286 and SNM 24841 to the reign of Ousanas. It is quite clear that the two inscriptions cannot refer to the Nubian campaign of ʻĒzānā recorded in RIE 189, RIE 190, and RIE 271. The invocation of Ares in RIE 286 and SNM 24841 indicates that the Aksumite king who erected these inscriptions was a pagan, while the records of ʻĒzānā's Nubian campaign, as we will see,

[309] ʻΡεειδᾶν in RIE 271.
[310] Σ[ιλ]εῆλ in RIE 271.
[311] Χάσω in RIE 271.
[312] *Fontes Historiae Nubiorum III* 1998: 1095, 1101.
[313] Munro-Hay 1999: 16.
[314] Hahn 2000: 288.
[315] Munro-Hay and Juel-Jensen 1995: 46. Unlike Hahn (2000), Munro-Hay and Juel-Jensen regard Wāzēbā as the predecessor of Ousanas.

date from the period following that king's conversion to Christianity.[316] One could conceivably attribute RIE 286 and SNM 24841 to an earlier expedition against Nubia which 'Ēzānā undertook before his conversion. His statement in RIE 271 and RIE 189 that he attacked the Noba after they repeatedly broken their oaths with him might in that case suggest that Aksum had already entered into some direct political relationship with the Noba in the early part of 'Ēzānā's reign. However, there is no reason to assume that 'Ēzānā had established this relationship as the result of an invasion of Nubia during his pre-Christian years, particularly given that RIE 189, RIE 190, and RIE 271 record only a single Nubian campaign and give no indication that 'Ēzānā had led his armies against Nubia at an earlier time. Furthermore, RIE 286 and SNM 24841 from Meroë suggest that the Aksumite army reached the Kushite capital, as both inscriptions refer to the Aksumite king's having "arrived here" or having taken his seat "here"—the "here" being by implication Meroë. By contrast there is no incontrovertible reference to Meroë in any of the inscriptions recording 'Ēzānā's Nubian campaign. Indeed, the main target of that campaign was not the Kushites at all but rather the Noba, a people not mentioned in either RIE 286 or SNM 24841, at least insofar as these two inscriptions are preserved. Since Ousanas' proclamation of rule over Kush in RIE 186 pre-dates 'Ēzānā's Nubian campaign by several years—if not decades—RIE 286 and SNM 24841 provide a plausible context for Ousanas' assertion of Kush's vassal status vis-à-vis Aksum. Though we can reject as political fiction Ousanas' claim to be king of South Arabia in light of Ḥimyar's continued independence as well as its military expansion into the very regions of Yemen which Aksum had occupied c. 200-270, RIE 286 and SNM 24841 indicate that the Aksumites invaded Nubia and even erected two stelae commemorating the event at the Kushite capital of Meroë itself. This contrasts dramatically with the situation in South Arabia, for it was not until the reign of Kālēb (c. 510-540) that the Aksumites erected similar victory stelae at the Ḥimyarite capital of Ẓafār.[317]

[316] §4.5.1.

[317] On these inscriptions, see Hatke 2011: 357-61.

4.2.2. The Political Implications of the First Aksumite Invasion of Kush

While Ousanas' claim to be king of Kush, expressed in RIE 186, reflects a genuine instance of Aksumite intervention in Kush, the nature and duration of this intervention are unknown. In his study of RIE 286, Burstein concludes that the inscription does not refer to an attack on Meroë itself on the grounds that the pillaging by the Aksumite army is mentioned before the Aksumite ruler's apparent arrival at Meroë and his erection of a statue there, the Kushite capital being implied by the adverb ἐνθάδε, "here."[318] Seen from this perspective, one might argue that the king's claim in Line 5 of SNM 24841 to have "taken his seat" implies an extended sojourn at Meroë. With so much of both inscriptions missing, however, there is no reason to assume that the texts in their original state did not contain a reference to an actual attack on the city. Nevertheless, Burstein's observations on the sequence of events still deserve consideration. An incident involving noble women, a king, generals, and children, seems to have taken place at Meroë, given that the relevant passage in Lines 6-9 of RIE 286 follows the passage alluding to arrival of the Aksumite army at Meroë in Line 5. The reference to women and children has been compared[319] with a passage in *Monumentum Adulitanum* II (RIE 277) in which the Aksumite king boasts of his having seized men, women, and children in an attack on the nation of Sesea (Σεσέα),[320] located somewhere in the Horn of Africa.[321] On these grounds it is probable that the noble women and the children mentioned in RIE 286 were also prisoners of war captured by the Aksumites in the course of their invasion of Kush. The women and young girls mentioned in Lines 3 and 4 of SNM 24841 were probably also prisoners.[322]

Exactly how long the Aksumite king's sojourn at Meroë lasted and how significant the long-term effects of his campaign are matters of debate. Burstein notes that the narrative throughout RIE 286 is in the

[318] Burstein 1981: 49.
[319] *Fontes Historiae Nubiorum III* 1998: 1067-8.
[320] *Top. Chr.* 2.61.1-5.
[321] Huntingford (1989: 46) very tentatively suggests a location in the Ḥarar highlands. Other scholars favor a location to the west of Aksum, while still others identify Sesea with the Issa, an important Somali tribe. For a discussion of these and other theories, see Bernard 2000: 39.
[322] Hägg 2004: 108.

first person, as are all Aksumite royal inscriptions in Greek, in which case the king mentioned in Line 7 cannot be the Aksumite king.[323] In addition, it is significant that the king is called βασιλεὺς and not βασιλίσκος, as the latter title is reserved in Aksumite inscriptions for minor potentates like Beja tribal chieftains.[324] The only alternative, then, is that the king in question is the Kushite ruler.[325] Burstein's theory thus has significant implications for our understanding of the inscription which, far from indicating a total destruction of Kush, suggests merely the pacification of the kingdom by the Aksumites. In this way, Line 12, which speaks of the payment of tribute, takes on a new meaning as a reference to the reduction of Kush to tributary status.[326] Taking this idea a step further, Burstein argues that the subsequent invasion of Nubia by 'Ēzānā can be explained as a response to a Kushite rebellion against Aksumite suzerainty.[327] Török, however, cautions that, attractive though Burstein's hypothesis is, we must not give undue importance to the fact that the Aksumites merely erected victory inscriptions at the city of Meroë, for it could very well have been the case that these monuments were smashed to pieces after the departure of Aksumite forces.[328] Military invasions, after all, need not result in the establishment of political control. If so, there is no reason to assume that Aksum managed to hold onto Nubia for very long. In fact it is not impossible that the Aksumites and Kushites perceived "tribute" in different ways, the Aksumites regarding as a tributary relationship what Kushites might have seen as nothing more than a system of gift-giving to curry favor with a powerful neighbor.[329] To

[323] Burstein 1981: 49.
[324] RIE 270*bis*: 25 (*Fontes Historiae Nubiorum III* 1998: 1095).
[325] Burstein 1981: 49.
[326] Ibid.
[327] Ibid.
[328] Török 1985: 18.
[329] Spaulding (1995) has approached the *baqṭ* arrangement between the Christian Nubian kingdom of Makouria and Muslim Egypt from this perspective, arguing that the *baqṭ* provided a basis for diplomatic gift-giving and a state-controlled import-export trade. Not enough survives of RIE 286 to determine whether the relationship of reciprocity which Spaulding envisions for Makouria and Muslim Egypt is applicable to Aksumite-Kushite relations in the fourth century. On the possibility of a system of gift-exchange between Aksum and Kush in the fourth century, see §4.6.2.

these points it should be added that ʿĒzānā's inscriptions describe his campaign against Nubia not as a response to a Kushite revolt against Aksumite rule but as a punitive measure meted out to the Noba, on grounds of their having attacked vassals of Aksum. The Kushites, by contrast, seem to have been only tangentially involved. It could be that, out of concern for Aksum's western frontier, Ousanas sought to establish a sphere of influence in Nubia with the belief that a Kushite regime under Aksumite supervision (in the form of suzerainty) would bring greater stability to the nebulous and poorly patrolled region between Kush and Aksum. Not only was security on Aksum's western frontier essential for unhindered access to the gold resources of Sasu but, as Noba attacks on ʿĒzānā's vassals would soon prove, Aksum's frontier was far from impermeable. In fact it is quite possible that the population of the borderland between Nubia and the Ethiopian Highlands had already started to pose problems for the Aksumite regime in the reign of Ousanas.

4.3. Trouble on the Western Front? A Possible Clue in RIE 186

Let us return now to RIE 186, the inscription in unvocalized Geʿez, written in South Arabian *musnad*, which Ousanas erected at Aksum, and which is the earliest known Aksumite inscription that refers to Kush by name. If Kush was already regarded by Ousanas as part of his domain by the time he erected RIE 186, in which the name of Kush appears in the list of the king's vassals, this inscription can be assigned to the period after the Aksumite invasion described in RIE 286 and SNM 24841 from Meroë. Of military operations against Kush before the reign of ʿĒzānā there are no references in any of the known inscriptions from Aksum, though future excavations at the site might one day bring to light such an inscription. On the other hand, mention of what may have been a mopping-up expedition following the invasion of Kush may survive in RIE 186 in the form of a reference to a campaign against an enigmatic land called *MTT*. Little can be understood of the passage in which this name appears,[330] other than that the Aksumite king "reached *MTT*" (*bṣḥ*^{m} *Mtt*^{m}=**baṣḥa MTT*), whose people (*'ḥḏbh*^{m}=**'aḥzābā*) gave tribute (*whb*^{m} *gdh*^{m}=**wahabū gādāhā*).[331]

[330] RIE 186: 21-4 (Bernard et al. 1991: 252).
[331] Ibid.

Whether the people of *MTT* made oaths with the Aksumites as part of their conditions of tributary vassalage depends on if one reads one particular word in Line 23 as *mḥl*^{m} (=**maḥala*, "to make an oath") following Littmann[332] or *msl*^{m} (=**məsla*, "with") following Bernard et al.[333] The key question of course is the location of *MTT*. Moving back in time to the first half of the fourth century BCE, we find a reference to a land called Metete (*Mddt*) in an inscription of the Kushite king Ḥarsiyotef from Temple B500 at Jabal Barkal (Cairo JE 48864). According to this inscription, Ḥarsiyotef had to put down no fewer than three rebellions in Metete during the third, fifth, and sixth years of his reign.[334] Zibelius associates this name with the Med̲j̲ayū (*Md̲3jw*) of the Eastern Desert,[335] long regarded as the ancestors of the Beja,[336] but gives no explanation as to why *Md̲3jw* should be written in such an idiosyncratic fashion in Ḥarsiyotef's inscription,[337] or indeed how this ethnonym became a toponym like Metete in the first place. Although neither the location of Ḥarsiyotef's Metete nor Ousanas' *MTT* can be established with any certainty, the similarly named Mattitae people mentioned by Pliny the Elder[338] are believed by Crawford to have dwelled in the Gash Delta.[339] If Crawford is correct in identifying all

[332] Littmann 1913: 9.

[333] Bernard et al. 1991: 252.

[334] *Fontes Historiae Nubiorum II* 1996: 448-50.

[335] Zibelius 1972: 133-7.

[336] Adams 1977: 58, 389, 419; Shinnie 1996: 67, 118. Like the Graeco-Roman term "Blemmyes" (Barnard 2005) it is probable that "Med̲j̲ayū" was a somewhat contrived term by which the Egyptians referred to all the peoples of the Eastern Desert, implying that these constituted a single ethnic group when in fact there is likely to have been a fair amount of diversity (Liszka 2011). That *Monumentum Adulitanum II* preserves the names of several ethnic groups in the Eastern Desert (§3.3) suggests as much.

[337] Zibelius 1972: 133-7 (VII D a 90=Cairo JE 48864). Whether any connection exists between Metete and the name Meded, mentioned in earlier Kushite inscriptions, is unlikely given that Metete is described in Ḥarsiyotef's inscription as a land, while an inscription from the reign of the Kushite king Irike-Amannote (*floruit* second half of the fifth century BCE) describes the Meded as a people, to wit "western desert-dwellers" (*h̲3stjw imnt*) (Kawa IX: 45 [*Fontes Historiae Nubiorum II* 1996: 407]). That the Meded are located by Irike-Amannote's inscription in the western desert disqualifies them from any identification with the Med̲j̲ayū, much less with Ousanas' *MTT*.

[338] Pliny, *Naturalis historia* 6.190 (*Fontes Historiae Nubiorum III* 1998: 859).

[339] Crawford 1951: 3, 96. It is true that Pliny locates the Mattitae on the "African" (i.e., western) side of the Nile, though in this passage he is

three names—Mattitae, *MTT*, and Metete—with one and the same region,[340] then the *MTT* of RIE 186 is best located somewhere in the borderlands between Kush and Aksum. Ousanas' campaign against *MTT* might in that case have been part and parcel of the establishment of an Aksumite sphere of influence extending westwards into Nubia and involving in the process the subjugation of many of the pastoral groups of the eastern Sudan.

4.4. The Noba: A New Force to be Reckoned with

With the reign of Ousanas' son and successor[341] 'Ēzānā we encounter much clearer evidence of an enemy to the west of Aksum, one hitherto not attested in Aksumite records. The enemy in question is the Noba, a people who, judging from their name, were a Nubian-speaking community quite distinct from the Meroitic-speaking Kushites.[342] Though Egyptian loanwords in Nubian indicate, on the basis of their phonological structure, that Nubian-speaking peoples from Kordofan and Dārfūr had made contact with—and perhaps had even begun to settle in—the Nile Valley as early as the New Kingdom (1539-1075 BCE),[343] direct evidence for the ethnogenesis of a people called "Noba" is not available until the third century BCE. At that point Eratosthenes, in a fragment preserved by Strabo,[344] mentions a people called the Nubae residing to the west of the Nile between Meroë and the bend in the river between the third and fifth cataracts, an area that

somewhat inconsistent in his designation of the western and eastern banks of the river (*Fontes Historiae Nubiorum III* 1998: 859 [n. 454]). Moreover, since the Takkazē River is also occasionally referred to as the Nile in ancient sources (such as *Monumentum Adulitanum II*), it is not impossible that Pliny has gotten his rivers confused, in which case he might have meant that the Mattitae in his day occupied the west bank of the Takkazē, rather than the west bank of the Nile proper.

340 Crawford 1951: 96-8.

341 Assuming, as suggested above (§4.2.1), that Wāzēbā died prematurely following a brief co-regency with Ousanas c. 324-5.

342 On the relationship between Nubian and Meroitic, both of which are classified as Nilo-Saharan languages belonging to the East Sudanic branch, see Rilly 2009.

343 Bechhaus-Gerst 1984/5: 105-6; idem 1996: 37; Jakobi 1993: 69-71; cf. Rilly 2009: 5-6. For a broader treatment of East Sudanic origins in the western Sudan, see Dimmendaal 2007.

344 *Geography* 17.1.2 (*Fontes Historiae Nubiorum II* 1996: 560).

would have included the Bayūḍa Desert.[345] The establishment of a Kushite outpost at Qal'a^{t} Abū Aḥmad in the lower Wādī Hawār in the mid-first millennium BCE[346] may well represent an attempt on the part of Kush to police the region where the *wādī*, originating in eastern Chad and running across the northwestern Sudan, meets the great bend in the Nile at al-Dabba and thus gives direct access to the middle Nile Valley from the west. Such measures may have been prompted by population movements along the Wādī Hawār in which the ancestors of the Noba were involved.[347] Given the difficulty of navigating the bend in the Nile, the Dongola Reach and the Meroë region had long been linked by an overland route across the Bayūḍa Desert.[348] Kushite remains are scarce in the Abū Ḥamad Reach between the fourth and fifth cataracts, even though medieval Christian material has come to light at numerous sites throughout that region.[349] To be sure, a thorough archaeological investigation of this stretch of the Nile Valley is needed before we can properly assess its significance to the Kushite state. Indeed, as we will see in 'Ēzānā's Ge'ez record of his Nubian campaign (RIE 189), the Noba captured at least two Kushite towns in the Nile Valley between Meroë and Napata,[350] though it is impossible to tell how long such settlements had been in existence in 'Ēzānā's time. If the bend in the Nile was in fact a Kushite backwater—ruled from Meroë but relatively little touched by Kushite settlement—it is easy to see how such a vacuum would have been easily filled by Nubian-

[345] Bechhaus-Gerst 1984/5: 117. For an inventory of archaeological sites in the Bayūḍa, see El Tayeb 2002: 52-4.

[346] On this outpost, see Jesse 2009. The dating of its foundation to the mid-first millennium BCE is based on C^{14} dates between c. 700 and 400 BCE obtained from the site (ibid.: 8). Possibly related to this apparent Kushite interest in the western frontier is the evidence for Kushite occupation of the Bayūḍa's Wādī Muqaddam, though this may date at as early as the eighth century BCE (Kendall 2007), before the foundation of the outpost at Qal'a^{t} Abū Aḥmad.

[347] Rilly (2009: 6) suggests that some Proto-Nubians may have resided in areas of the middle Wādī Hawār until the first millennium BCE, which fits nicely with the date of the Kushite fortress at Qal'a^{t} Abū Aḥmad and might support the hypothesis that the fortress was founded as a defense against the ancestors of the Noba.

[348] Edwards 2004: 155.

[349] Idem 1989: 81-92; cf. El Tayeb 2002: 54-6.

[350] See §4.5.2.3.

speaking groups, whose settlement may be reflected in Graeco-Roman references to the Nubae as dwelling in this very region.[351] Conflicts between Kush and the Noba are indicated by prisoner figures dating from the first century BCE to the first century CE which were inscribed with the ethnonym "Noba" in Meroitic and magically "punished."[352]

From the bend in the Nile these Nubian-speakers would have been able to expand northwards into Lower Nubia, in the course of which they attracted the attention of Graeco-Roman authors, who called them Nobatae or Nobades, while other groups pushed southwards towards Meroë and beyond.[353] Citing Eratosthenes, Strabo alleges that the Nubae were not subject to the "Ethiopians" (i.e., Kushites),[354] though that may well have changed in later centuries. Török suggests that at some point in their history the Noba became federates of the Kushite state,[355] a not inconceivable scenario in that their more northerly cousins the Nobatae/Nobades are known to have entered into a federate status with the Roman Empire by the fifth

[351] A number of sites in the Abū Ḥamad Reach, as well as in the area of the ʻAṭbara-Nile confluence and the region to the south, may represent a later stage in the settlement of Nubian-speakers in the middle Nile Valley. The Tanqasi Culture associated with these sites, so called after the site where it was first identified, is distinct from that of Kush, and as it dates from the fourth and fifth centuries CE it has long been connected with the Noba (Kirwan 1957; Bechhaus-Gerst 1984/5: 95-8; Shinnie 1996: 117). Further excavations, however, are needed to clarify the relationship between the Noba and the pottery types regarded as diagnostic of late and post-Kushite times in Upper Nubia, for as El Tayeb (2002: 72-6) cautions, the identification of a distinct pottery type with the Noba remains controversial, as is the issue of cultural continuities between the Kushite and post-Kushite periods. In a similar vein Edwards (2004: 210) notes that "if there were any significant population movements in the late Meroitic period they have left little obvious trace archaeologically." We should probably in that case view Noba settlement in Nubia as a gradual trickle of migrants from the west over a long period, their push towards the Aksumite frontier during the fourth century CE representing a later stage in the history of the Noba.

[352] Török 2011: 517.

[353] Nubian toponyms occur as far south as Kosti on the White Nile, though on the basis of this evidence alone it is impossible to tell how far back Nubian presence goes, except that it probably predates the Arabizing trend which began in the northern Sudan around the sixteenth century (Thelwall and Schadeberg 1983: 222).

[354] *Geography* 17.1.2 (*Fontes Historiae Nubiorum II* 1996: 560).

[355] Török 1985: 19.

century.[356] As we know from the history of the Arab clients of the Romans and Sāsānids, a state's inability to prevent federate polities from raiding foreign territory could at times become an international incident.[357] In light of the tantalizing reference in Line 12 of RIE 286 to the Kushite payment of tribute to Aksum, an increasing aggressiveness on the part of the Noba is likely to have led to its disruption—assuming, of course, that the Kushites were regularly paying their tribute all along. Whether Noba raids were the *casus belli* in Ousanas' invasion of Kush cannot be determined on the basis of what little remains of the Aksumite inscriptions from Meroë, though there is little doubt that it was hostile actions by the Noba which prompted the Aksumite army to return to Nubia in the reign of Ousanas' son ʻĒzānā. It is to that story that we now turn.

4.5. ʻĒzānā's Nubian War

For the reign of ʻĒzānā we have the good fortune to possess three inscriptions from the city of Aksum recording what appears to be the same invasion of Nubia:[358] the first in Greek (RIE 271),[359] the second in vocalized Geʻez (RIE 189),[360] and the third in pseudo-Sabaic Geʻez written in the South Arabian *musnad* script (RIE 190).[361] Apart from the variety of languages and scripts employed, the inscriptions differ only in terms of which details of the invasion are selected for mention. Since the account of the war preserved in RIE 189 has been known to the scholarly world since the first half of the nineteenth century[362] this version has, for far longer than the other two, served as the primary source of information on Aksumite military activities in Nubia. But if Aksum had reduced Kush to temporary vassalage at some point prior to ʻĒzānā's invasion of Nubia, as argued above,[363] this latter invasion

[356] See §5.2.
[357] See in particular the conflict between the Roman's Ghassānid clients and the Sāsānids' Lakhmid clients (Procopius, *De Bell. Pers.* 2.1).
[358] Brakmann 1994: 68.
[359] Bernard 2000: 15-21; *Fontes Historiae Nubiorum III* 1998: 1094-1100.
[360] Bernard et al. 1991: 262-7.
[361] Ibid.: 268-71.
[362] For a bibliography of early literature on RIE 189, see Bernard et al. 1991: 262.
[363] §4.2.2.

would then be not the beginning but rather the culmination of a longer period of Aksumite interaction with—and intervention in—the middle Nile valley. When compared with what (admittedly little) can be made out of RIE 286 and SNM 24841, the records of ʿĒzānā's Nubian war, particularly the longest version, preserved in RIE 189, suggest that ʿĒzānā's was a military campaign which affected a much larger area of Nubia than Ousanas' did.[364] For all that, its long-term effects on Kush are somewhat obscure, particularly since ʿĒzānā's inscriptions indicate that the main source of trouble in Nubia was not the Kushites at all but rather the Noba. A synthesis of the information provided by all three of inscriptions recording ʿĒzānā's Nubian campaign is in order, particularly as no such synthesis has yet been attempted. We will begin with ʿĒzānā's Greek inscription (RIE 271), as it is this text that provides a date for the campaign. After this we will examine his two Geʿez inscriptions (RIE 189 and RIE 190), both of them important for the information they provide on the course of the campaign. Whether this was the order in which these inscriptions were carved is impossible to determine but is ultimately irrelevant, given that all three appear to present different versions of the same narrative.

4.5.1. The Greek Account: RIE 271

RIE 271 consists of thirty-three lines of Greek text on a stele recording ʿĒzānā's campaign against Nubia and was discovered at Aksum in 1969. Since the text ends abruptly in the initial part of the narrative, right as ʿĒzānā departs for Nubia, the remaining portion must have been continued on another as yet undiscovered stone.[365] On the other side of the stele, the badly damaged Geʿez version in *musnad* was carved (RIE 190). The opening portion of RIE 271 (Lines 1-22) consists of a religious invocation and a statement of ʿĒzānā's royal title:

[364] An alternative theory holds that ʿĒzānā never set foot in Nubia but instead merely conducted a campaign against tribes in the Ethiopian Highlands to the west of Aksum (Welsby 1996: 198). Such a theory is, however, quite untenable, for the erection of RIE 286 and SNM 24841 at Meroë clearly demonstrates Aksumite military intervention in Nubia (ibid.), in addition to which RIE 189 mentions several Nubian toponyms and describes ʿĒzānā's attack on the Kushites, who maintained no presence as far east as the Ethiopian Highlands, least of all in the fourth century CE.

[365] *Fontes Historiae Nubiorum III* 1998: 1100.

By faith in God and by the power of the Father and the Son and the Holy Ghost, to Him who has saved my kingdom through faith in His Son Jesus Christ, to Him who helped me and who always helps me: I, ʻĒzānā, King of the Aksumites and Ḥimyarites and of Raydān and the Sabaeans and of Salḥīn and of Kush and the Beja and of Ṣeyāmō, man of Ḥalen, son of ʼElla-ʻAmīdā and servant of Christ, thank the Lord my God, and I cannot fully express my thankfulness to Him, because my mouth and my mind cannot [express] my thankfulness [for what] He made with me, because He gave me strength and power and bestowed on me a great name through His Son in whom I have placed my faith, and made me the guide of my whole kingdom through faith in Christ, by His will and by the power of Christ, because He guided me and I have faith in Him and He Himself became my guide.[366]

(Ἐν τῇ πίστει τοῦ Θ[εοῦ καὶ τ]ῇ δυνάμι τοῦ [Πα]τρὸς καὶ Υἱοῦ καὶ [Ἁ]γί[ο]υ [Π]νεύματος τ[ῷ] [σ]ώσαντί μοι τὸ Βασ[ίλ]ιον τῇ πίστι τοῦ Υἱ[οῦ] αὐτοῦ Ἰησοῦ Χριστοῦ τῷ βοηθήσαντί μο[ι] τῷ καὶ πάντοταί μοι βοηθοῦντι ἐγὼ Ἀζανᾶς Βασιλεὺς Ἀξωμιτῶν καὶ Ὁμηρι[τῶν κ]αὶ τοῦ Ῥεειδᾶν καὶ Σαβαειτῶν καὶ τοῦ Σ[ιλ]εῆλ καὶ τοῦ Χάσω καὶ Βουγαειτῶν [κ]αὶ τοῦ Τιαμῶ Βισι Ἀληνε υἱὸς τοῦ Ἐλλε-αμίδα δοῦλος Χριστοῦ εὐχαριστῶ Κυρίῳ τῷ [Θεῷ] μου καὶ οὐ δυνάμαι εἰπῖν πλίρης τὰς εὐ[χ]αριστίας αὐτοῦ ὅτι οὐ δύναται τὸ στό[μ]α μου καὶ ἡ διάνοια μου πάσας τὰς εὐχαριστίας ἅσπερ ἐποίησεν μετ' ἐμοῦ ὅτι ἐπ[οί]ησεν ἐμοὶ ἠσχὺν καὶ δυνάμιν καὶ ἐχαρίσ[α]τό μοι ὄ[ν]ομα μέγα διὰ τοῦ Υἱοῦ [α]ὐτοῦ εἰς ὃν ἐπ[ί]στευσα [κα]ὶ ἐποίησέν μαι ὁ[δ]ηγὸν πάσης τῆς Βασιλίας μου δια τὴν πίστ[ι]ν τοῦ Χριστοῦ τ[ῷ] θελήματι [αὐ]τοῦ καὶ δυνάμι τοῦ Χριστοῦ ὅτι αὐτὸς ὁδήγησέν μαι καὶ εἰς α[ὐ]τὸν πιστεύω καὶ αὐτὸς ἐγένετό μοι ὁδηγός.)[367]

[366] Translation based on ibid.: 1102.
[367] Greek text ibid.: 1101.

'Ēzānā's Greek title is clearly patterned after that of his father Ousanas in the unvocalized Ge'ez of RIE 186, the only difference here in RIE 271 being that Kush (Χάσω) stands at the beginning of the list of Aksum's African vassals. In Ousanas' RIE 186, by contrast, Kush (*Kś^{m}*) comes at the very end of the list.[368] There is no reason to give any weight to the novel position of Kush at the heading of the African list in RIE 271, however, for the name Kush (*Kāsū*) occurs again at the very end of the list of vassals in the version of the royal title given in RIE 189, the account of 'Ēzānā's Nubian campaign in vocalized Ge'ez.[369] This indicates that the order in which 'Ēzānā's vassals are listed in his royal titles does not reflect the relative importance of these vassals to Aksum, nor their relevance to the subject-matter of the inscriptions in which they occur. Certainly the claim to Kush had importance to 'Ēzānā, as Kush is listed among the king's vassals in his title in several of his Ge'ez inscriptions from Aksum (unvocalized RIE 185 I+II and RIE 185*bis* I+II; vocalized RIE 187 and RIE 188)[370] together with two of his Greek inscriptions (RIE 270 and RIE 270*bis*) from the same site.[371] On the basis of the reference to 'Ēzānā as the "son of Maḥrem unconquered by the enemy" (*walda Maḥrəm za-'əy-yətmawā' la-ḍar*) in the Ge'ez inscriptions[372] and "son of the invincible god Ares" (υἱὸς θεοῦ ἀνικήτου Ἄρεως) in the Greek,[373] all four inscriptions must be dated to the period before 'Ēzānā's conversion to Christianity, and thus before his Nubian campaign. Such claims to Kush by 'Ēzānā in his pre-Christian days undoubtedly reflect political rhetoric, rather than political reality, as there is no evidence that Ousanas' Nubian campaign

[368] RIE 186:3-4 (Bernard et al. 1991: 251); cf. RIE 187:3 (ibid.: 255); RIE 188:4 (ibid.: 260); RIE 270:5 (Bernard 2000: 6); RIE 270*bis*:4 (Bernard 2000: 12; *Fontes Historiae Nubiorum III* 1998: 1095, 1096).

[369] RIE 189:4 (Bernard et al. 1991: 263).

[370] RIE 185 I:2 (Bernard et al. 1991 : 242); RIE 185 II:1 (ibid.: 243); RIE 185*bis* I:3 (ibid.: 246); RIE 185*bis* II:2 (ibid.: 247); RIE 187:3 (ibid.: 255); RIE 188:4 (ibid.: 260).

[371] RIE 270:5 (Bernard 2000: 6); RIE 270*bis*:4 (*Fontes Historiae Nubiorum III* 1998: 1095, 1096; Bernard 2000: 12).

[372] RIE 185 I:2-3 (Bernard et al. 1991: 242); RIE 185 II:3-4 (ibid.: 243); RIE 185*bis* I:3-4 (ibid.: 246); RIE 185*bis* II:3-4 (ibid.: 247); RIE 187:4 (ibid.: 255); RIE 188:5-6 (ibid.: 260).

[373] RIE 270:5-6 (Bernard 2000: 6); RIE 270*bis*:4-5 (Bernard 2000: 12; *Fontes Historiae Nubiorum III* 1998: 1095, 1096).

led to any long-term Aksumite rule over Kush, let alone of the sort that continued unbroken into the reign of his son. This did not, however, prevent ʻĒzānā from believing that Kush was still his by right.

Of far greater historical significance than royal titulary are the explicitly Christian references in RIE 271, the first of their sort to occur in any Aksumite inscription. These references—to wit the mention of Jesus Christ and the Trinity—give us an idea of the timeframe in which the inscription was erected, and hence the timeframe of ʻĒzānā's Nubian campaign itself. This epigraphic evidence of ʻĒzānā's conversion to Christianity is supported by numismatics, for it is during the reign of ʻĒzānā that the pagan symbols of the moon-disc and crescent are replaced by the Cross.[374] The story of the Christianization of the Aksumite royal house at the hands of Frumentius, a Roman missionary of Syrian origin, is well known thanks to the *Historia ecclesiastica* of Rufinus of Aquileia (345-410)[375] and need not be repeated here except insofar as it bears directly on the chronology of ʻĒzānā's reign. Rufinus writes that as a boy Frumentius and another youngster named Aedesius sailed to India with their teacher, a philosopher from Tyre named Meropius.[376] On their return journey they made a stop on the Ethiopian coast, whereupon the locals put Meropius to death but spared the two boys, whom the Aksumite king took under his protection.[377] While Aedesius served as the king's cup-bearer Frumentius rose through the ranks to become the official in charge of the king's accounts and correspondence.[378] Following the death of the Aksumite king, Frumentius acted as advisor to the king's successor, still a minor at the time.[379] When at length Frumentius and Aedesius were allowed to leave Ethiopia, Frumentius went straight to the Alexandrian patriarch Athanasius (d. 373), who appointed him bishop of the Aksumite realm.[380] This meeting likely took place between Athanasius' appointment as patriarch on 8 June 328 and the beginning

[374] Munro-Hay and Juel-Jensen 1995: 41.
[375] Rufinus, *Historia ecclesiatica* 10.9-10.11 (transl. Amidon 1997: 18-23).
[376] Ibid.: 10.9 (Amidon, loc. cit.: 19-20).
[377] Ibid.
[378] Ibid.
[379] Ibid.
[380] Ibid.: 10.10 (Amidon, loc. cit.: 20).

of his first exile on 7 November 335.[381] Assuming, then, that Frumentius left Ethiopia at some point between June 328 and July 335, or possibly even c. 337-339 in the interim between Athanasius' first and second exiles, he would likely have first arrived in Ethiopia as a boy during the second decade of the fourth century, a timeframe that suits the period of the reign of 'Ēzānā's father Ousanas (c. 310-330) adopted in this study.[382] This would make Ousanas the king in whose reign Frumentius and his traveling companions first landed in Ethiopia and 'Ēzānā the successor who came to the throne as a minor, Wāzēbā (his brother?) having died some years earlier. That Frumentius' patron Athanasius was exiled no fewer than five times during his career was the result of a fierce theological debate that raged in the eastern half of the Roman Empire during this period. The point of contention concerned the relationship of the Son to the Father in the Christian Trinity. One influential presbyter in Alexandria named Arius (d. 336) contended that the Son was not co-eternal with, and therefore not equal to, the Father.[383] Athanasius could not countenance such a position and argued instead that the Son not only existed from all eternity but was also one with the Father in divinity.[384] The consequent bickering over the question as to whether or not the Godhead could be shared with any created being was soon to exert an influence on ecclesiastical affairs at Aksum for, on account of Athanasius' opposition to Arianism, the legitimacy of his appointment of Frumentius as bishop of Aksum

[381] Not until after Constantine died on 22 May 337 was Athanasius able to return to Alexandria, only to be exiled again, this time by Consantius II, on 16 April 339, his second exile lasting until 21 October 346. It cannot be excluded, of course, that Frumentius was ordained bishop of Aksum during the two-year period between Athanasius' first and second exiles, though the longer period between 8 June 328 and 11 July 335 is a more probable timeframe for his ordination. It is far less likely that Frumentius was ordained bishop after the end of Athanasius' much longer second exile in October 346. On the life and career of Athanasius, see Barnes 1993; Brakke 2000.

[382] Since Frumentius was still a boy when he arrived in Ethiopia, his trip to India with Meropius could not have lasted much more than a year, as Meropius would hardly have undertaken such a journey with a very young child.

[383] Kelly 1958: 226-31. On the life and career of Arius, see Williams 1987. On Arian doctrine in the fourth century, see Rankin 2000.

[384] Kelly 1958: 243-7; Weinandy 2007: 49-79.

was called into question. In his *Apologia ad Constantium* Athanasius quotes in full a letter sent by the emperor Consantius II (337-361) to 'Ēzānā and his brother Śe'āzānā,[385] in which the Roman emperor sought to persuade the two royal Aksumites that Frumentius' ordination was invalid and that they should send him back to Egypt to be re-instructed and consecrated by George of Cappadocia.[386] This Arian churchman is known to have held office as bishop of Alexandria from 356 to 362, during Athanasius' third exile, thus providing a timeframe for Constantius' letter. Constantius warned that failure to comply with this request would result in the sacrilegious and impious discourse (λόγος) of Athanasius corrupting the subjects of Aksum, overturning the churches established there, and in the end bringing destruction upon the nation itself.[387]

For all the lack of ambiguity in Consantius' letter regarding the emperor's distrust of Frumentius, questions have been raised as to whether the text really establishes that the royal house of Aksum had adopted Christianity by this time. Dihle believes that, although there was a Christian community in Ethiopia when Constantius wrote his letter, 'Ēzānā and Śe'āzānā had not yet embraced Christianity.[388] If they had, Dihle argues, Constantius would undoubtedly have addressed them as fellow Christians and would have also presented the dogmatic and political grounds for the banishment of Athanasius and the appointment of another patriarch in his place, namely George of Cappadocia.[389] In this connection Dihle makes much of Constantius' warning to the Aksumite brothers that the influence of a bishop not ordained by the Arian George would have dire effects on the Christian community as well as the "nation" (ἔθνος), which he takes to mean

[385] This Śe'āzānā, together with another brother of 'Ēzānā named Ḥadefā (*Ḥdfh*='Αδιφᾶν), led a campaign against the Beja prior to 'Ēzānā's conversion to Christianity, as recorded in Ge'ez in RIE 185 I and II, and in Greek in RIE 270. Σαζανᾷ, the Greek form of Śe'āzānā's name given in Athanasius' *Apologia* as well as in RIE 270, appears in the unvocalized Ge'ez of RIE 185 I and II as *Š'd̲n^{m}* and *Ś'zn* respectively (Bernard et al. 1991: 242, 243; *Fontes Historiae Nubiorum III* 1998: 1095).
[386] *Apologia* 31.13-17 (transl. Szymusiak 1987: 161).
[387] Ibid. 31.36-41 (transl. Szymusiak 1987: 163).
[388] Dihle 1965: 53; idem 1989: 464.
[389] Dihle 1965: 53.

that the Aksumite royal house was not yet Christianized.[390] The implications of Dihle's interpretation of Constantius' letter are significant for the dating of 'Ēzānā's Nubian campaign, for if 'Ēzānā was still a pagan for at least part of George's term as bishop of Alexandria between 356 and 362, the Christian references in RIE 271 could be taken to imply that the inscription, and therefore the Nubian campaign it describes, must postdate this six-year period. Furthermore, if one allows several years for the sending of Constantius' letter to Aksum, the conversion of 'Ēzānā, and his mounting of a campaign against Nubia, this would bring us well into the 360s, "perhaps closer to 370 than to 360" in the opinion of Török, who accepts Dihle's hypothesis.[391] This conclusion might then have significant implications for dating the end of Kush. Since RIE 271 and RIE 189 mention the Kushites not only as a name in the list of 'Ēzānā's vassals but also as a people directly affected by the king's military ventures, Török's dating of the campaign to the late 360s implies that Kush still existed as a polity at this time. As confirmation of this late date for Kush's demise, Török notes a pair of bracelets found in one of the latest pyramid graves in Meroë's West Cemetery (Bagrawiyya W 130), which he claims is an imitation of a particular style of Roman jewelry manufactured in the mid-fourth century.[392] He bases this date on the depiction of a similar bracelet in the hypogeum of Trebius Justus on the Via Appia, dating from the mid-fourth century. Since the Kushites marked only royal graves with pyramids, following Egyptian practice, assigning Bagrawiyya W 130 to the decade 360-370 would imply that the royal house of Kush was still in existence at that time.

As we will see, however, none of 'Ēzānā's inscriptions state that his Nubian campaign dealt the final death-blow to Kush, only that he fought the Kushites in the course of his war with the Noba. This being the case, the evidence from tomb Bagrawiyya W 130 at Meroë, suggesting that Kush survived as late as 360-370, is not relevant for dating 'Ēzānā's Nubian campaign. Nor does Consantius' letter help either, for the case that the letter was addressed to two still-pagan kings of Aksum is difficult to sustain. While Constantius does not

390 Ibid.
391 Török 1988: 37.
392 Ibid.

explicitly refer to the Christian faith of ʻĒzānā and Śeʻāzānā in his letter, he does not state that they were pagan either, and if the Aksumite brothers had already embraced Christianity, Constantius may have seen no need to belabor the obvious by reminding them of their new religion. Indeed the fact that Constantius stresses "pure" doctrine in his letter is quite likely *because* the Aksumite royalty were Christian and could thus appreciate the importance of correct doctrine.[393] For this reason, the fact that the letter never mentions the Trinity around which so many of the Christological debates engendered by Arianism revolved need not be taken as evidence that the Aksumite addressees were still pagan and would thus not be interested in such matters. As Brakmann points out, Trinitarian references are similarly lacking in a letter sent by Constantius to the Christians of Alexandria.[394] Regarding the term ἔθνος, it is true that this does in some contexts have the sense of "pagan" by virtue of its association not only with nations in general but specifically with foreign or barbarian nations.[395] Whether it carries such religious overtones in Constantius' letter is not clear, however. We have seen that in his letter, Constantius warns the Aksumites about what would befall their people, the churches in their land, and the nation if Frumentius were allowed to continue his work and thus spread the doctrines propounded by Athanasius, though it is by no means clear that "nation" means anything other than the Aksumite realm. That the majority of Aksum's subjects were still pagan in the mid-fourth century can hardly be doubted, but if, for the sake of argument, these elements are what Constantius really meant by the "nation" it need not follow that ʻĒzānā and Śeʻāzānā were also pagan. In addition, arguments for dating RIE 271—and thus ʻĒzānā's Nubian campaign—to the late 360s overlook the Aksumite numismatic evidence. Bearing in mind Ousanas' adoption of the weight standard employed by Constantine in 324,[396] it is clear that ʻĒzānā's father was still on the throne in the 320s. Even if one were to insert Wāzēbā's reign between those of Ousanas and ʻĒzānā, as proposed by Hahn, there is no evidence

[393] Brakmann 1994: 76-7 (n. 376).
[394] Ibid.: 77.
[395] De Blois 2002: 22 (n. 110, 111).
[396] See §4.1.

that Wāzēbā reigned for more than a few years. In either case a date of c. 330 is probable for the beginning of 'Ēzānā's reign,[397] which fits well with the hypothesis put forward in this study that Frumentius, having spent already spent a few years in Ethiopia before 'Ēzānā came to the throne, left the Aksumite kingdom sometime between 328 and 335, at which point he was ordained Ethiopia's first bishop by Athanasius. To be sure, Rufinus says nothing of the conversion of 'Ēzānā, though the omission of this important detail can likely be attributed to his informant, who was none other than Aedesius, with whom Frumentius had shared so many of his adventures in Ethiopia. Rufinus tells us that, while Frumentius returned to Ethiopia after his investiture by Athanasius, Aedesius became a presbyter at Tyre,[398] and appears to have lost all contact with his erstwhile companion. If 'Ēzānā and other members of the royal house of Aksum like Śe'āzānā embraced Christianity following Frumentius' return to Ethiopia as that country's first bishop, the fact that Aedesius was no longer present in Ethiopia may explain why he made no mention of these events when speaking with Rufinus. If Frumentius was appointed bishop of Aksum between 328 and 335, or even c. 337-339 during Athanasius' second episcopate, his return to Ethiopia probably took place during the second half of the 330s, in which case this the traditional Ethiopian date of 333 EC (340-1 CE)[399] for the conversion of Aksum's royal house[400] is quite plausible. Since RIE 271 contains explicit Christian references, it cannot predate 340-1, with the result that the invasion of Nubia documented by that inscription must be dated to sometime after 340-1.

For a more precise date for the invasion, we turn now to the narrative portion of RIE 271, which mentions the month and day on which 'Ēzānā set out for Nubia.

[397] Munro-Hay 1999: 15-16.
[398] Rufinus, *Historia ecclesiastica* 10.10 (transl. Amidon 1997: 20).
[399] Ethiopia has historically followed the Julian calendar, resulting in a seven- to eight-year gap between the Ethiopian year (EC) and the year in the Gregorian calendar.
[400] Munro-Hay 1999: 16. Hahn (2000: 295) prefers to see c. 340 as the date of Frumentius' appointment as Ethiopia's first bishop by Athanasius, believing that 'Ēzānā did not convert until the later 340s.

²²·I went forth to war on the Noba, because the Mangurto and Khasa and Atiadites ²⁵·and Barya cried out against them saying: "The Noba have subdued us, come and help us, because they have oppressed and killed us." I stood up with the power of the God Christ, in whom I have placed my faith, and he guided me. I stood up ³⁰·from Aksum the eighth day in the Aksumite month of Maggābīt, a Saturday, with faith in God, and I arrived in Mambaria and from that place I procured supplies...⁴⁰¹

(²²·Ἐξῆλθα πολεμῆσαι τοὺς Νωβα ὅτι κατέκραξαν κατ' αὐτῶν οἱ Μανγαρθω καὶ Χασα καὶ Ἀτιαδιται ²⁵·καὶ Βαρεωται λέγοντες ὅτι κατεπόνησαν ἡμᾶς οἱ Νωβα βοηθήσατε ἡμῖν ὅτι ἔθληψαν ἡμᾶς ἀποκτένοντες. Καὶ ἀνέστη[ν] ἐν τῇ δυνάμι τοῦ Θεοῦ Χριστοῦ εἰς ὃν ἐπίστευσα καὶ ὁδήγησέν με. Καὶ ἀνέστην ἀ³⁰·πὸ Ἀξώμεος ἐν μινὶ κατὰ Ἀξωμιτὰς Μαγαβιθε η ἡμέρα σαμβάτω πίστι τοῦ Θεοῦ καὶ ἔφθασα εἰς Μαμβαριαν καὶ ἐκῖθεν ἐσιταρχησά[μην...])⁴⁰²

Though this opening portion, describing the background of, and preparations for, the campaign, is all that survives of the narrative section of RIE 271, it is of vital importance for dating the invasion of Nubia, as it informs us that ʿĒzānā's army departed from Aksum on the eighth day of the Ethiopian month of Maggābīt (Μαγαβιθε<መጋቢት), which is here specifically stated to have fallen on a Saturday. In the Julian calendar Maggābīt 8 corresponds with March 4, which fell on a Saturday in the years 349, 355, and 360.⁴⁰³ Since the Christian references in RIE 271 leave us in little doubt that the inscription post-dates ʿĒzānā's conversion to Christianity, and since the king's conversion may be confidently dated to c. 340-1—or at least no earlier than that—any of these years is a potential date for the Nubian campaign.⁴⁰⁴ Once again the religious language used in the inscription

---

⁴⁰¹ Translation *Fontes Historiae Nubiorum III* 1998: 1102.
⁴⁰² Greek text ibid.: 1101.
⁴⁰³ Török 1988: 37-8.
⁴⁰⁴ There is no evidence to support Török's contention (loc. cit.) that RIE 271 should be assigned to an otherwise unattested Aksumite ruler whose name

sheds light on the matter. In a recent study of the Christology of RIE 271, Black draws attention to the use of the article τοῦ in both the Trinitarian phrase τοῦ [Πα]τρὸς καὶ Υἱοῦ καὶ [Ἁ]γί[ο]υ [Π]νεύματος ("the Father and the Son and the Holy Ghost")[405] in the opening of the inscription and in the phrase τοῦ Θεοῦ Χριστοῦ ("the God Christ") in Line 28.[406] In the Trinitarian invocation, a string of nouns is joined by the conjunction καὶ, yet the article τοῦ precedes the first noun alone, indicating the unity, equality, or identity of all nouns following the article.[407] Thus the three persons of the Trinity are here described as one. In the phrase "the God Christ" the identification of Christ the Son with God the Father is even more explicit.[408] This is the very doctrinal position to which Arian Christians were opposed, and which Consantius sought to correct by having Frumentius re-indoctrinated by the Arian George of Cappadocia. It is probable, then, that RIE 271 reflects an anti-Arian stance adopted by Aksum in the face of the pro-Arian pressure exerted by Constantius on the recently Christianized kingdom.[409] The earliest hint of this pressure is indicated in Constantius' letter which, since it most likely dates from the first part

is partially preserved as ΑΓ..ΑC, particularly when the king who erected this inscription names 'Ella-'Amīdā as his father and Ḥalēn as his clan. Since 'Ēzānā is the only Aksumite who is known to have claimed kinship with both, RIE 271 must be assigned to his reign.

[405] Black 2008: 104-5.

[406] Ibid.: 107-8.

[407] Ibid.: 104-5.

[408] Ibid.: 107-8.

[409] In the years before George's episcopate these doctrinal issues would have been less pressing, such that the Aksumites would have felt less of a need to emphasize such doctrines as the identity of Christ with God which were the distinguishing beliefs of the non-Arian camp. Perhaps 'Ēzānā felt the need to take a firmer doctrinal stand against Arianism, as he seems to in RIE 271, following the mission of Theophilus Indus. This Arian Christian of South Asian origin is reported by Philostorgius to have evangelized the Ḥimyarites of South Arabia sometime in the 350s, perhaps 356, after which he traveled to Ethiopia (Philostorgius 3.4, 3.6). It may be significant that, while Philostorgius recounts Theophilus' work in Ḥimyar in some detail, and even claims that the local king built three churches under Theophilus' influence, he has very little to say about Aksumite Ethiopia, a striking omission which might suggest that his attempt to promote Arianism there failed (Fernandez 1989: 362). All the same, the experience of his mission may have been enough to prompt 'Ēzānā to publicly assert his anti-Arian stance. For an in-depth study of Theophilus Indus, see Fiaccadori 1992.

of George's episcopate, thus c. 356-7, would mean that RIE 271 dates from sometime thereafter. This disqualifies 349 and 355 as years in which RIE 271 could have been erected, thus leaving us with 360. We will therefore proceed with March 4, 360 as the likeliest date for the beginning of 'Ēzānā's Nubian campaign. Nowhere in the extant text of any of 'Ēzānā's inscriptions is it stated how long the campaign lasted, though such an undertaking must have lasted several months. If the Aksumite army wished to return home before the height of the rainy season hit Ethiopia in July-August, four months is a likely timeframe.

Having made the case for dating the Nubian campaign to 360, let us now take a closer look at the narrative preserved in RIE 271. While the Aksumite inscriptions in Greek found at Meroë (RIE 286 and SNM 24841) attest to an Aksumite conflict with the Kushites, followed by the imposition of the payment of tribute, the passage in RIE 271 quoted above indicates quite clearly that 'Ēzānā's campaign in Nubia was concerned not with the overthrow of Kush at all but rather with aiding the Mangurto, Khasa, Atiadites, and Barya against the Noba. This is the first time in which the Noba appear in Aksumite records. The Noba have been introduced above as the Nubian-speaking people who first made contact with the middle Nile Valley during the Late Bronze Age and who had attained a degree of political power there by the fourth century CE if not earlier.[410] Of the other peoples mentioned by name, only the Khasa and the Barya are known from non-Aksumite sources and, indeed, are still known by these names today. The present-day Khasa are nomadic pastoralists who live along the Sudanese-Eritrean border and speak Tigrē, but are of Beja origin and belong to the Banī 'Āmir ethnic group.[411] Ibn Sa'īd (d. 1286) says of the Khasa, "they are the [most] reprehensible among the Ethiopian races, and it is well known about them that they castrate those who fall into their hands and offer human penises as nuptial gifts, taking pride in this!" (*hum madhmūmūna bayna ajnās il-Ḥabasha wa-qad ishtahara 'anhum annahum yakhṣūna man yaqa'u ilā aydīhim wa-yadfa'ūna dhukūr al-ādamiyyīna fī*

[410] See §4.4.

[411] Kirwan 1972: 462. Today a distinction is made between the name Khāsa, by which Arabs refer to all Tigrē-speakers, and the name Hāsā, which refers to the Tigrē-speakers from the region of Tokar and Port Sudan and thus distinguishes them from Eritrean Tigrē-speakers (Morin 1996: 252-3).

ṣadaqātihim wa-yaftakhirūna bi-dhālika).[412] As for the Barya, who still live north of Bārantū in western Eritrea[413] and are more properly known as the Nara,[414] their identification with the Βαρεωται of RIE 271 is evident from the vocalized Geʻez account of the Nubian campaign (RIE 189), in which their name is given as *Bāryā* (ባርያ). Barya also survives in Amharic as a word for "slave,"[415] reflecting this ethnic group's historically subservient status vis-à-vis the Ethiosemitic communities of the Horn of Africa.[416] While the territory of the Barya may once have extended further over a much wider area than it now does, Ibn Ḥawqal locates the Barya in the area of the Barka River,[417] where they continue to dwell today. Together with the Bazayn, a people of Beja origin, the Barya are reported by Ibn Ḥawqal to have constituted "many tribes" (*qabā'il kathīra*),[418] suggesting that 'Ēzānā's Barya subjects were an ethnic group rather than a single clan. Of the Barya's lifestyle Ibn Ḥawqal says that "they live in mountains and valleys, possess cattle and sheep, and farm" (*yaskunūna fī jibāl wa-awdiya wa-yaqtinūna l-baqar wal-shāᵗ wa-yazraʻūna*).[419]

In contrast to the Khasa and Barya, nothing at all is known of such groups as the Mangurto and the Atiadites.[420] The Μανγαρθω of RIE 271 correspond with the Mangurto (መንጉርቶ) of RIE 189, while the name Ἀτιαδιται appears only in RIE 271. In view of the location of the Khasa and Barya, who both complained to 'Ēzānā of attacks by the Noba, it is likely that the Mangurto and Atiadites lived somewhere between the eastern Sudan and the Ethiopian Highlands. The fact that the Mangurto, Khasa, Atiadites, and Barya sought 'Ēzānā's help against the Noba indicates that, having already settled in certain areas of the

412 Ibn Saʻīd 1970: 98. This grisly custom was still practiced as late as the twentieth century by the Afar nomads of the Danakil Desert.
413 Kirwan 1972: 462; Bender 1968: 1; Huntingford 1989: 58.
414 Rilly 2009: 1.
415 Bender 1968: 1; Huntingford 1989: 58; Levine 2000: 56.
416 The name "Noba" may also be derived from a Northeast Sudanic word meaning "slave" in both Meroitic (*nob*) and Proto-Nubian (**nogu*) (Rilly 2009: 3).
417 Ibn Ḥawqal 1938-9: I: 55.
418 Ibid. In the same passage he states that the Barya and Bazayn were made up of "many nations" (*umam kathīra*).
419 Ibn Ḥawqal, loc. cit.
420 Kirwan 1972: 462.

middle Nile Valley, the Noba were now pushing eastwards, towards the frontier of the Aksumite kingdom. Clearly whatever order the Aksumites might have hoped to establish in Nubia in, as argued in this study, Ousanas' reign had been eroded by Noba raids on Aksum's western frontier, thus prompting 'Ēzānā to take action. The course of the route which 'Ēzānā took from Aksum to Nubia is not clear from RIE 271, for the location of Mambaria is unknown and this toponym is not attested in RIE 189 nor—as far as we can tell—RIE 190. Bernard's suggestion that Mambaria is not a toponym at all but rather a Greek transliteration of the Ge'ez **manbarəya>mambarəya* ("my throne")[421] is unlikely, for the use of the term δίφρος in *Monumentum Adulitanum II* and SNM 24841 proves that the Aksumites knew of a Greek approximation of the Ge'ez *manbar*, and thus would hardly have needed to transcribe the Ge'ez term in Greek. Even this assumes that RIE 271 was carved by an Aksumite trained in Greek; if it was the work of an itinerant Greek-speaking foreigner employed by 'Ēzānā the scenario of Ge'ez influence would be even less probable. Moreover, while the erection of symbolic stone thrones was common in ancient Aksum, it is highly unlikely that the place at which the Aksumite army stopped to procure supplies for a military campaign was named after one of 'Ēzānā's "thrones." Morphologically Mambaria suggests a possible connection with the Barya, a not implausible hypothesis given that the Barya were a frontier people whose territory lay on the route leading northwest from Aksum to Nubia. It is possible, then, that the Aksumite army took such a route, by way of the Barya country, when invading Nubia. RIE 271 breaks off abruptly at this point, so for details as to what happened after 'Ēzānā procured supplies at Mambaria we must turn to RIE 189.

4.5.2. The Vocalized Ge'ez Account: RIE 189

A 52-line inscription in fully vocalized Ge'ez, RIE 189 from Aksum survives in full and provides the longest and most detailed account of 'Ēzānā's Nubian campaign. In terms of its relationship to RIE 271 much has been made of the fact that, though RIE 189 begins with a religious invocation like its Greek counterpart, this Ge'ez version is much less explicitly Christian. Thus, while RIE 271 invokes the Christian Trinity,

[421] Bernard 2000: 17.

RIE 189 commences with the doctrinally neutral but still recognizably monotheistic formula "By the power of the Lord of Heaven who is in heaven and [on] earth, the Victorious" (*ba-ḫayla ʾəgzīʾa samāy za-ba samāy wa-mədr mawāʿī*).[422] Some scholars have taken the doctrinally neutral wording of RIE 189's religious references as evidence of a transitional stage between Aksumite pantheism and normative Christianity,[423] in which case one might assign RIE 189 to a period in ʿĒzānā's reign immediately prior to the king's formal conversion to Christianity, and thus before RIE 271 with its explicit invocation of the Christian Trinity. Yet the content of the two inscriptions is similar enough for them to be close in date. To be sure, RIE 271 can hardly be described as a translation of RIE 189, particularly given that neither the Atiadites nor the toponym Mambaria appear in RIE 189. However, the mere fact that the two inscriptions select different details of ʿĒzānā's campaign proves only that the scribes who produced them were not working from the same *Vorlage*. In both RIE 189 and RIE 271, the war with Nubia is said to have begun after ʿĒzānā received reports that his vassals were being attacked by the Noba, and it seems unlikely that the Aksumite king should have launched two separate invasions of Nubia in response to Noba attacks on more or less the same peoples. In all likelihood, then, RIE 189 and RIE 271 refer to one and the same invasion of Nubia, the difference between them in terms of religious terminology reflecting not a gradual development of ʿĒzānā's faith from vague monotheistic inclinations to Christianity, but rather an attempt to express the same Christian faith in different ways. If so, the Geʿez version could have been produced by an Ethiopian still accustomed to indigenous habits of describing the divine[424] while the Greek version was produced by an individual better trained in Christian theology, perhaps a Greek or Greek-speaking Near

[422] RIE 189:1 (Bernard et al. 1991: 263).

[423] For a survey of the relevant literature, see Kaplan 1982: 103.

[424] Levine (2000: 66) notes that nearly all the peoples of Greater Ethiopia believe in a supreme deity, without exception associated with the sky and conceived as masculine, and cites examples of this phenomenon among Cushitic, Omotic, and East Sudanic communities. This recalls the manner in which the Christian deity is designated in RIE 189, though in the latter case the deity is called the Lord of Heaven residing both in heaven *and* on earth.

Easterner.[425] In this way, Christian ideas about the divine were expressed in Ge'ez in terms of what Kaplan calls Aksum's "traditional cosmological structure."[426] If, then, RIE 189 and RIE 271 are different versions of the same narrative we can date the events described in RIE 189 to the late winter to early summer of 360, following RIE 271's date of Saturday, 8 Maggābīt (=March 4) for 'Ēzānā's departure from Aksum.

4.5.2.1. The Haughty Noba

After the invocation of the Lord of Heaven, RIE 189 gives the king's name as 'Ēzānā Son of 'Ella 'Amīdā, the Man of the Ḥalen [Clan] (*'Ēzānā walda 'Ǝllē 'Amīdā bə'səya Ḥalən*),[427] followed by the list of Aksum's (putative) Arabian and African subjects: "King of Aksum and Ḥimyar and D͟hū-Raydān and Saba' and Salḥēn and Ṣeyāmō and the Beja and Kush" (*Nəgūśa 'Aksūm wa-za-Ḥəmēr wa-za-Raydān wa-za-Saba' wa-za-Salḥēn wa-za-Ṣəyāmō wa-za-Bəgā wa-za-Kāsū*).[428] This list contains nothing of interest, as it repeats the same names that occur in the lists in 'Ēzānā's earlier inscriptions, as well as in Ousanas' RIE 186.[429] Completing the introductory portion of RIE 189 is another formula containing religious references: "King of Kings, Son of 'Ella 'Amīdā, unconquered by the enemy! By the power of the Lord of Heaven Who has given to me, the Lord of All in Whom I believe, the king unconquered by the enemy. No enemy stands before me nor follows after me!" (*nəgūśa nagaśt walda 'Ǝllē 'Amīdā za-'ay-yətmawā' la-ḍar ba-h̲ayla 'əgzī'a samāy za-wahabanī 'əgzī'a kʷəllū za-bōtū 'amankū nəgūś za-'ay-yətmawā['] la-ḍar qədmēya 'ay-yəqūm ḍar wa-dəh̲rēya 'ay-yətlū ḍar*).[430] After

[425] Brakmann 1994: 73.

[426] Kaplan 1982: 108. Kaplan's main argument, though valid in the opinion of the present author, is undermined by his theory (ibid.: 107) that, as part of the long-term process of conversion to Christianity, 'Ēzānā must necessarily have passed through an intermediate stage of cosmological speculation, marked by a monotheizing paganism centered on the cult of 'Astar. No evidence for such an intermediate period survives in the epigraphic record.

[427] RIE 189: 1-2 (Bernard et al. 1991: 263).

[428] RIE 189: 2-4 (ibid.).

[429] See §4.1.

[430] RIE 189: 4-7 (Bernard et al. 1991: 263). Note that the particle of negation employed here (*'ay-*) represents an earlier stage in the phonological development **'al->'ī* (Gragg 1997: 257). The fourth century CE would seem to mark a transitional stage in this process during which both *'ay-* and the Classical Ge'ez *'ī-* were still used interchangeably, as the latter form appears several times elsewhere in RIE 189, thus *'ī-yəfalləs* in Line 8 and *'ī-sam'anī* in

this introductory portion of RIE 189 with its religious references we come to the narrative proper, wherein we are told the familiar story of why ʿĒzānā took up arms against Nubia in the first place:[431]

> [7.]By the power of the Lord of All I made war on the Noba once [8.]the confederations of the Noba[432] had made war, having acted haughtily. "They (i.e., the Aksumites) will not cross the Takkazē!"[433] said the confeder[9.]ations of the Noba. At that time they had wrought havoc upon the peoples of the Mangurto and the <u>Kh</u>asa and the Barya, and the blacks [10.]made war on the reds.
>
> ([7.]*Ba-<u>h</u>ayla 'əgzīʾa kʷəllū ḍabaʾkū Nōbā sōbē* [8.]*'aḍrara 'əḥzāba Nōbā sōbē tamakaḥa. Wa-'ī-yəfalləs 'əm-Takkazī yəbē 'əḥzā*[9.]*ba Nōbā. Sōbē gafʿa 'əḥzāba Mangūrtō wa-<u>H</u>asā wa-Bāryā wa-ṣalīm* [10.]*ḍabʾa qayyəḥ ḍabʾ*[*a*]).[434]

Line 13 (Bernard et al. 1991: 263).

[431] It will be noted that the phonology of the Geʿez in this inscription differs slightly from that of Classical Geʿez.

[432] In RIE 189 not only the Mangurto, the <u>Kh</u>asa, and the Barya but also the Noba themselves are described as *'əḥzāb* (Classical Geʿez *'aḥzāb*, sing. *ḥəzb*), a somewhat ambiguous term used to describe groups of people ranging in size from tribes to nations. With the development of a Christian literature in Geʿez, *'aḥzāb* took on the connotation of "gentiles" (cf. Syriac *ʿammē*). A few lines later in RIE 189 ʿĒzānā refers to his troops as his *'aḥzāb*, and it is in this military sense that the sixth-century Aksumite king Kālēb uses the term when referring to the invasion forces which he dispatched to Ḥimyar in 518 (RIE 191: 35 [Bernard et al. 1991: 273]). On the nuances of this term in Kālēb's Geʿez inscription from Mārib, RIE 195 I, see Hatke 2011: 366-8; cf. Merid Wolde Aregay 2005: 159, 180 (n. 3). This Ethiopian habit of calling armed divisions *'aḥzāb* was apparently a long-standing one, for the Aksumite forces which occupied the Tihāma region of western Yemen c. 200-270 CE are also referred to in South Arabian inscriptions as *'ḥzb* (=*'*aḥzāb*) (Hatke 2011: 366-8). When applied to non-Aksumite groups, however, the term is best translated as "confederations" for lack of any more precise information on the social and political structure of Aksum's neighbors to the west. It should be noted that *'aḥzāb* has no equivalent in the Greek account of ʿĒzānā's Nubian campaign (RIE 271), wherein the different ethnic groups are simply mentioned by name, without their designation as ἔθνος, for example.

[433] The verb used here, *yəfalləs*, is grammatically singular, but since collective groups such as the Noba or the Aksumites are typically treated as singular throughout RIE 189, it seems better to take the Aksumites rather than ʿĒzānā as the subject of this sentence.

[434] RIE 189 (Bernard et al. 1991: 263).

Whereas RIE 271 credits the Mangurto, K̲hasa, Atiadites, and Barya for reports of the Noba's aggressions, RIE 189 states only that the Noba had attacked the Mangurto, K̲hasa, and Barya, without specifying how 'Ēzānā came by this information. We have already encountered these peoples in RIE 271, the striking difference in RIE 189 being the omission of the Atiadites. It is, however, easy to explain why the latter are not mentioned by name here. As suggested above,[435] it is likely that the At- element attested in such ethnonyms as the Atalmo of *Monumentum Adulitanum II* and the Atiadites of RIE 271 corresponds with the prefix **Ad* found among several Beja confederations, including the Banī 'Āmir. If so, it could be that the Atiadites of RIE 271 were a clan of the K̲hasa mentioned in RIE 189, given that the K̲hasa are a section of the Banī 'Āmir. Another noteworthy point in the narrative of RIE 189 is the statement that "the blacks made war on the reds" (*ṣalīm ḍab'a qayyəḥa ḍab'[a]*). Elsewhere in RIE 189 we hear of 'Ēzānā's attacks on the Red Noba (*Nōbā qayyəḥ*)[436] but not, however, on a corresponding Black Noba. Indeed there are no references to a "Black Noba" as such anywhere in the inscription.[437] The allusion to color in this passage seems instead to be idiomatic. Drewes notes that black and red are sometimes employed in Arabic as contrastive adjectives which, when used in conjunction, indicate "everyone,"[438] hence the expression *ḥarb al-aḥmar wal-aswad* ("a war between everyone," literally "a war between the red and the black").[439] If the reference in RIE 189 to the blacks making war on the reds is similarly taken as an idiomatic expression—as opposed to a rather dubious allusion to a race war—this would support the hypothesis presented here that RIE 189 uses different and at times vaguer terminology to express the ideas more explicitly stated in RIE 271. Thus Christ and the Trinity are

---

[435] §3.3.
[436] §4.5.2.3.
[437] Hintze 2000: 50.
[438] Cf. English "young and old" and "big and small," both expressions signifying "everyone."
[439] Drewes 1962: 98 (n. 2). In Ethiopian inscriptions from the pre-Aksumite period Drewes (ibid.) identifies a prototype for this idiomatic expression in the form of *'dmhy w-ṣlmhy* ("its reds and blacks"), which also seems to have the sense of "everyone" given the use of a parallel phrase *ms²rqhy w-m'rbhy* ("its east and west").

replaced in RIE 189 by a vague "Lord of Heaven," while the name of a particular Beja clan in RIE 271, the Atiadites, is replaced in RIE 189 by the name of the larger tribe to which these may have belonged, to wit the Khasa. That the Aksumites made a distinction between different groups of Noba illustrates some of the ambiguities inherent in ethnic labels, a problem all the more acute in that we do not know what the Noba called themselves during this period, or even if they saw themselves as a unified group.[440] Given the diversity in lifestyles among the Noba described in RIE 189, it is likely that the term "Noba" encompassed a fairly diverse group.[441] All the same the term "Noba" will be retained here as a broad term for a group which was regarded as separate from Kushites and was so designated by the Aksumites and indeed by the Kushites themselves.

The Noba's boast of impunity mentioned in RIE 189 indicates that by 'Ēzānā's reign the Takkazē River, which flows from the highlands of Lasta in north-central Ethiopia and meets the 'Aṭbara in the eastern Sudan, marked some sort of boundary between the area under direct Aksumite rule and the more nebulous frontier region beyond, now occupied or at least harassed by the Noba. Evidently whatever territory the Aksumites had gained to the west of the Takkazē had been lost by the time 'Ēzānā came to power. Rufinus' statement that 'Ēzānā came to the throne as a minor suggests a possible juncture at which the Aksumites were unable to enforce their rule in the "wild west" of their realm. Suggestive in this regard is archaeological evidence of a break in the occupation of the eastern Sudan at this time. Excavations have revealed that the Ḥājiz Group which dominated the region between the Gash and 'Aṭbara Rivers in the early first millennium CE came to an end in the third to fourth centuries, when it was replaced by the culturally distinct Khatmiyya Group.[442] The origins of the latter group are uncertain, though its funerary traditions and pottery have been compared with those of the central Sudan.[443] On these grounds it is tempting to identify such material with the Noba, whose attacks on the peoples of Aksum's western frontier might

[440] On the problem of the term "Noba" see Edwards 2011: 505-8.
[441] See §4.5.2.2.
[442] Manzo 2004: 75.
[443] Ibid.: 75-7.

conceivably had led to the cultural hiatus noted in the eastern Sudan. On the other hand, similarities between Khatmiyya pottery and Eastern Desert Ware, associated by many with the Blemmyes/Beja, might imply instead that the Khatmiyya Group represents the southernmost extension of the Eastern Desert culture, rather than an offshoot of the Noba. Conceivably, an upheaval in the eastern Sudan of the sort caused by Noba raids may have facilitated the influx of the Blemmyes/Beja, or else raids by the latter on the Aksumite realm, already documented in inscriptions from the earlier part of ʻĒzānā's reign (RIE 185 I+II; RIE 270),[444] weakened Aksum's hold on its western frontier and thereby facilitated the Noba's attacks.[445] The relative scarcity of occupation sites between the Gash and ʻAṭbara during the Khatmiyya Period is certainly suggestive of the nomadic lifestyle that characterizes the pastoralists of the Eastern Desert, and the distribution of seasonal Khatmiyya camps between the Kasalā region and the Eastern Desert are paralleled by the seasonal movements of the modern Hadendowa Beja.[446] That ʻĒzānā had to deal militarily not only with the Noba but also, at an earlier point in his reign, with the Beja illustrates the seriousness of the influx of pastoral groups from the Eastern Desert at about the time that the Ḥājiz Group came to an abrupt end.

Exactly why the Noba initiated their aggressions against the Mangurto, Khasa, and Barya is nowhere stated in RIE 189 or RIE 271. There is little doubt, however, that Noba expansion to the east was part of a broader process of migration by Nubian-speakers into the middle Nile Valley and beyond—the same process, indeed, which had brought groups like the Nobatae/Nobades into conflict with the Roman by the last third of the third century CE. In time, the Romans managed to reach an understanding with these groups, such that they established

[444] For a discussion of this material, see §4.5.2.4.
[445] Significantly, it is nowhere stated in any of ʻĒzānā's inscriptions that the Noba actually settled in those parts of the Aksumite frontier occupied by the Mangurto, Khasa, and Barya. Rather, RIE 189 indicates that their area of permanent settlement was limited to the Nile Valley. If so, then the replacement of the Ḥājiz Group by a foreign culture like the Khatmiyya, suggesting as it does the sustained presence of a new population in the eastern Sudan, is unlikely to be attributed to short-term Noba raids.
[446] Manzo 2004: 80-1.

a federate relationship with them in the fifth century.[447] Török may be correct in hypothesizing a similar federate status of the Noba vis-à-vis Kush, though it is impossible to tell how long such a relationship might have lasted. For his part, ʿĒzānā sought to make peace with the Noba, but to no avail.

> [10.]Twice and thrice did they break their pledges [...], [11.]spending the winter season (?) killing neighboring communities, as well as the envoys and messengers whom I had [12.]sent to them to inquire into their plundering. And they pillaged their possessions and stole [13.]their [.....].
>
> ([10.]*Wa-ʾamāsana kaʿba wa-śels*[*a*] *la-maḥalāhū* [...] [11.]*ʾakrīmō yəqattəl ʾagwārīhū wa-tanbālāna wa-ḥawārəyāna za-fana*[12.]*wkū lōtū yəsməʿəwwō hēdōmū. Wa-barbarōmū nəwāyōmū wa-saraqōmū* [13.][.]*nawōmū.*)[448]

As Hintze notes in his study of RIE 189, ʿĒzānā does not call himself "King of the Noba," but seems nevertheless to have maintained relations of some sort with the Noba in which the latter were bound by pledges.[449] That Kush, by contrast, does merit mention in ʿĒzānā's title as one of Aksum's vassals is likely because the Kushites had greater prestige than the hitherto peripheral Noba. The Noba may also have been regarded by ʿĒzānā—correctly or not—as in some way subject to Kush rather than as a legitimate, autonomous polity.

4.5.2.2. Pillaging the Towns of the Noba

Unable to come to terms with the Noba through diplomatic means, ʿĒzānā embarked on a punitive campaign which brought the Aksumite army to the banks of the Nile for the second time since the reign of his father Ousanas.

> [13.]Then, when I had sent them [further] messages they did not heed me, and they refused to desist and [...]. [14.]But

[447] See §5.2.
[448] RIE 189 (Bernard et al. 1991: 263).
[449] Hintze 2000: 50. Kālēb (c. 510-540) was the first and, as far as we know, the only Aksumite king who styled himself "King of the Noba." On this point, see §5.1.

they retreated once I made war on them and I rose up by the power of God [15.]and killed [them] by the Takkazē at the ford of Kemalke while they took to flight [16.]without making a stand. And I pursued the fugitives for twenty-three days, kil[17.]ling them, taking prisoners, and seizing booty wherever I halted, while [18.]my troops who had gone forth into the surrounding country brought back [further] prisoners [and] booty and I burned their towns [19.]of brick and those of straw. And they (i.e., the Aksumite troops) pillaged their grain and copper and iron and [20.] [.....] and destroyed the idols in their temples and the storehouses of grain and cotton and cast [21.]them into the Nile. And many—I know not their number—died in the water [22.]as their boats sank from being overloaded with people, [23.]women and men. And I took captive two officials who [24.]came as spies riding camels, named [25.]Yesaka and Butale, together with a man of noble birth belonging to the royal house. Of those officials who died were [26.]Danokwe, Dagale, Anakwe, Ḥaware, Karkara, their priest [.....], [27.]and they (i.e., the Aksumite troops) stripped from him a silver ornament and a vessel of gold. The officials who [28.]died were five and the priest one.

([13.]*Sōbē lə'īkəyanī 'ī-sam'anī wa-'abaya h̲adīga wa-sa[...].* [14.]*Wa-tah̲alafa 'əmzə ḍaba'kəwwōmū wa-tanśa'kū ba-h̲ayla 'Əgzī'a-* [15.]*Bəḥēr wa-qatalkū ba-Takkazī ba-ma'dōta Kəmalkē wa-'əmzə g^{w}ayyū wa-*[16.]*'ī-qōmū. Wa-talawkū watga 'əśrā wa-śalūsa mawā'əla 23 'ənza 'ə*[17.]*qattəlō wa-'əḍēwəwō wa-'əmaharəkō ba-wə'əda h̲adarkū 'ənza ḍēwāwa* [18.]*məhrəkā yāgabbə' 'əḥzābəya za-wafara 'ənza 'awə'ī 'əhgūrīhū* [19.]*za-nədq wa-za-ḥaśar. Wa-yəbarabərū 'əklō wa-bərtō wa-h̲aṣīnō wa[...]*[20.]*so wa-yāmāsənū śə'la 'abyātīhū wa-mazāgəbta 'əkl wa-ṭūṭ wa-yā*[21.]*ṣadəfəwwō wəsta falaga Sēdā. Wa-bəzūh̲ za-mōta ba-wəsta māy za-'ī-yā*[22.]*'ammər h̲^{w}əlqō wa-'ənza 'əḥmārīhōmū yāsaṭəmū 'ənza məl'a sab*[23.]*' wəstētū 'anəst wa-'əd. Wa-ḍēwawkū magabta kəl'ēta 2 'əlla* [24.]*maṣ'ū 'a'yənta 'ənza yəṣa'anū 'arkūbāta wa-'asmātīhōmū* [25.]*Yəsakā 1 Būtālē 1 wa-'əngabēnāwē kābra 1.*

Wa-'əlla mōtō magabt [26.]*Danōkwē 1 Dagalē 1 'Anakwē 1 Ḥawārē 1 Karkārā 1 mārīhōmū 1* [..][27.]*salū wa-salabəwwō qədāda bərūr wa-ḥəqata warq. Kōnū magabt 'əlla* [28.]*mōtū 5 wa-mārī 1.*)[450]

Thus we learn that this stage of 'Ēzānā's invasion of Upper Nubia involved a division of the Aksumite army, the king leading the main division for a period of twenty-three days and at the same time sending out smaller detachments to raid the surrounding countryside. In view of its association with the Takkazē, it has been suggested that the ford (*ma'dōt*) of Kemalke was located in the area of present-day Khashm al-Qirba in the Sudan's Kasalā Province,[451] a plausible hypothesis given that town's location on the 'Aṭbara just north of the embouchement of the Takkazē.[452] This ford of Kemalke probably served as 'Ēzānā's headquarters for the duration of the Nubian campaign.[453] While the Aksumite raiding parties plundered the Noba's towns, 'Ēzānā himself captured two spies and a nobleman of the Noba. Of interest as an indication of social conditions in Nubia at this time is the statement in RIE 189 that, although some of their settlements were built of straw (presumably meaning that they consisted of thatched huts), the Noba also lived in towns with temples and storehouses,[454] and possessed grain, copper, iron, and cotton. By this stage, then, the Noba cannot be generalized as a nomadic horde still fresh from the desert but were to a large degree, perhaps predominantly, sedentary folk with a reasonable amount of resources at their disposal.[455] That other Noba had a rather

[450] RIE 189 (Bernard et al. 1991: 263-4).
[451] Kirwan 1972: 463.
[452] Kirwan (1960: 167) compares the name Kemalke with the Galla (i.e., Oromo) word *malka*, meaning "ford," but since there is no evidence of an Oromo presence this far north, let alone as early as the fourth century CE, this etymology is untenable.
[453] Hintze 2000: 52.
[454] It is unknown what the Noba's temples looked like. Worthy of note, however, is Building G at Soba, which has been interpreted by its excavator as a temple (Welsby 1998: 272, 275-8; idem 1999: 667-8), and which appears to belong to a cultural tradition different from that of Meroë. While the date proposed for this structure on the basis of pottery and C^{14} evidence (Welsby 1998: 272-3) is much too late for it to have any connection with the temples of the Noba destroyed by 'Ēzānā's troops, it raises interesting questions regarding the non-Kushite traditions of religious architecture in Upper Nubia in Late Antiquity.

different lifestyle and lived in towns of straw could be another reflection of the diversity that existed within the Noba.[456]

Of the Kushites, who are distinguished by name (*Kāsū*) from the Noba, we hear nothing until later on in RIE 189.[457] It may well have been the case that there were Kushites still living in the towns now occupied by the Noba, it was the latter who held real political power. If so, they would have done so not from Meroë, which is nowhere mentioned in any of 'Ēzānā's inscriptions in connection with his Nubian campaign.[458] The site of El Hobagi, 70 km upstream from Meroë, is one possible candidate for a Noba stronghold, particularly given the C^{14} dates indicating a fourth-century occupation of the site (GiF-7199 1600±50 b.p.),[459] a period overlapping with 'Ēzānā's reign. The culture of the inhabitants of El Hobagi is noticeably different from that of Meroë. A grave tumulus at the site, measuring some 40 m in diameter, may well mark the burial of a member of the local elite,[460] and contains libation vessels decorated in late Kushite style—in one case with Meroitic hieroglyphs.[461] These funerary materials have been taken as evidence that the local population shared much with the Kushites in terms of culture,[462] which is quite possible in that many Noba had been living in the Nile Valley long enough to have established permanent settlements and as a result enjoyed sustained contact with Kushite

[455] This is another reason why the Khatmiyya Group of the eastern Sudan, which may have had a more nomadic economic base (Manzo 2004: 80-1), is more likely connected with the Beja than with the Noba.

[456] Sites of Post-Kushite date consisting of small, impermanent structures have been excavated in the fourth cataract region and are thought to represent a population with a pastoral economy (Edwards 2011: 513-14). The Noba who dwelled in "towns of straw" may have been among such groups.

[457] See §4.5.2.3.

[458] It is unlikely that Meroë can be identified with the town of Alwa mentioned later on in RIE 189, as suggested by Hintze (2000: 52). On this point, see §4.5.2.3.

[459] Lenoble and Sharif 1992: 629.

[460] Török (1999: 135-6) cautions us that, since we do not know enough about the social hierarchy of this period, it cannot be assumed that the occupants of the largest tumuli at El Hobagi were kings as opposed to simply high-ranking officials or noblemen. He compares the elite burials of El Hobagi to those of the uppermost, yet still non-royal, echelon of Nubian society at more northerly sites like Qustul, Firka, and Gemai.

[461] Lenoble and Sharif 1992: 630-4.

[462] Ibid.

culture. An equally valid explanation, though, is that such items were looted from Kushite tombs, if not seized in raids on neighboring Kushite settlements.[463]

That several Noba are mentioned by name in RIE 189 is a clear indication that these were individuals of some social standing. Two of them, Yesaka and Butale, are described as "officials" (*magabt*) while a third is called simply "a nobleman of the royal house" (*'əngabēnāwē kābra*).[464] Still other Noba—who must also have been high-ranking given that they too are named in the inscription—met their end at the hands of the Aksumites, though we are not told how. That a priest was among those killed may reflect a symbolic act of severing the enemy's link with the divine, similar in its implications to the destruction of the idols in the Noba's temples and signifying to the Noba that any appeal for divine help would be in vain. That said, there is no indication in the inscription of any religious zeal on the part of ʻĒzānā, recent convert to Christianity though he was. He acknowledges the power of God and alludes to the role of divine aid in battle, but one

[463] Shinnie and Robertson 1993: 897. Shinnie and Robertson, quite correctly in the opinion of the author, call into question many of interpretations put forward by Lenoble and Sharif (1992).

[464] Leslau (1991: 29) gives *'angəbənāwī* as a variant of the term *'angabēnāy*, which he interprets as "noble" or "offspring of a noble family." *'Angabēnāy* appears in a fragment of Kālēb's Geʻez inscription from Ẓafār in Yemen, RIE 263 (Bernard et al. 1991: 350), apparently in reference to that king's conflict with the royal house of Ḥimyar. For a discussion of this fragment and the term *'angabēnāy*, see Hatke 2011: 358-61. Kirwan, however, takes the *'əngabēnāwē* of RIE 189 as a proper name (Kirwan 1960: 164), but adds in a footnote that this may be "possibly tautological" (ibid.: n. 3). Despite this cautionary note, Angabenawi is accepted without comment as a proper name by Burstein (2009: 118), who incorrectly gives the source for the translation as Kirwan's article "A Survey of Nubian Origins" (Kirwan 1937: 50-1). In fact, Kirwan's translation in the latter article omits the section on the capture of the spies in which the term *'əngabēnāwī* appears. The mistranslated passage in Burstein's work reads as follows: "And I captured two nobles, who had come as spies, riding on camels. Their names were Yesaka, Butale, and the chieftain Angabenawi" (Burstein 2009: 118). Since the inscription refers to only two noblemen (*magabt*) it would appear instead that "their names" (*'asmātīhōmū*) refers only to Yesaka and Butale—the dual does not exist in Geʻez except in a few vestigial forms—and that the *'əngabēnāwī* was simply another member of the Noba elite who had also been captured at the time. It is likely, then, that what Bernard et al. (1991: 264) read as *'əngabēnāwē kābra* in RIE 189 is a construct phrase meaning something like "one of noble birth and/or belonging to the royal house."

does not get the sense in RIE 189 that he was intent on destroying signs of paganism as a religious duty, much less on converting the Noba to Christianity. By contrast, the religious sentiments of the sixth-century Aksumite king Kālēb are much more explicit in a reference to his "zeal for the name of the Son of God" (*qn'y b'nt sm wld 'gz'bḥr=*qanī'əya ba'ənta səma walda 'Əgzī'ābḥēr*), contained in the account of his first invasion of South Arabia in 518.[465]

In addition to the information it provides on Noba society in the fourth century, the passage of RIE 189 describing the attacks on Noba settlements sheds interesting light on the industrial economy of Upper Nubia at that time. The raw materials mentioned are grain, copper, iron, and cotton. That copper (*bərt*) was seized by the Aksumite troops is curious in that, although numerous bronze items were imported by the Kushites, and although there is evidence of copper working at a much earlier date at Kerma, there is little trace of a copper-working industry during the period with which we are presently concerned.[466] RIE 189, however, gives us reason to reconsider the possibility of such an industry. Cotton, referred to in RIE 189 as *ṭūṭ*, also calls for special comment here. Despite attempts to interpret *ṭūṭ* as "yarn," "fiber," "flax," or "linen,"[467] archaeological evidence for the widespread use of

[465] RIE 191:36 (Bernard et al. 1991: 273). On this passage in Kālēb's inscription, see Hatke 2011: 141-3.

[466] Edwards 1989: 155-6. Although copper ores in the far southwest of the Sudan lie well beyond the known range of Kushite trade networks (ibid.: 156), copper ore also exists at Abū Siyāl in the desert of southeastern Egypt (Lucas 1927: 164-5) and at Tokar in the eastern Sudan (Nibbi 1997: 307). The exploitation of this particular source in antiquity is indicated by the traces of ancient slag and furnaces at the site (ibid.), which might explain the copper slag at Qubbān in Egyptian Nubia, as well as the reference to the collection of Nubian copper by the Egyptians during the Twelfth Dynasty, c. 1991-1802 BCE (Ogden 2000: 150-1). If Edwards (1989: 156) is correct that unworked copper was imported by the Kushites, it is possible that its source lay in the Eastern Desert.

[467] Gervers 1992: 15. Gervers' observation that a Ge'ez word for linen, *'agē*, is translated as *ṭəṭ* in Amharic in eighteenth-century texts need not indicate that the Ge'ez *ṭūṭ* had this same connotation in the mid-fourth century. Though *ṭəṭ* is clearly a cognate of *ṭūṭ*, the Amharic term may not have acquired the meaning of "linen" until well after 'Ēzānā's time. Even then, there is no reason to assume that *ṭəṭ* was regularly used as a term for linen. Gervers may well be correct that the derivation of the more common Arabic term for cotton, *quṭn*, from the Old Babylonian *kitinnu* points to the transfer of the word for linen to cotton as one fiber replaced the other in use, but it

cotton fabric in Kush during the Roman period[468] leaves little room for doubt that cotton was an important Nubian commodity well before 'Ēzānā's time. Conspicuous by its absence among the raw materials seized by the Aksumites is gold. A gold vessel stripped from a Noba priest is the sole reference to the metal in RIE 189. This is particularly surprising given Nubia's long-standing fame for its gold,[469] though as Edwards points out value-systems involving precious metals like gold and silver are by no means universal.[470] The reference to iron is interesting in light of the evidence of extensive iron smelting at Meroë, most notably in the form of slag mounds at the site.[471] Judging from slag found at a level which has been C^{14}-dated to the sixth century BCE, it would appear that the origin of Meroë's iron industry

cannot be assumed on this basis that a similar lexical development took place in early Ethiopia. In fact the evidence from Ethiosemitic militates against such a supposition. To begin with, *ṭaṭ* is by no means a common term for linen in Amharic but is most commonly used by speakers of that language to refer to cotton. Similarly, *ṭaṭ* in the Gurage languages and *ṭūṭ* in Tigrinya and Ḥararī both mean "cotton" rather than "linen." On the diffusion of cotton in the ancient Near East, see Álvarez-Mon 2010: 34-42.

468 Based on cotton seeds found in Egyptian Nubia by the Archaeological Survey of India, it is known that the cotton plant grew in Nubia as early as the mid-third millennium BCE, though it was not until the Roman period that the Nubians used cotton to produce textiles (Chowdhury and Buth 1971; cf. Wild et al. 2007). The earliest archaeobotanical evidence for the use of cotton in the Nile Valley comes from Qaṣr Ibrīm (Van der Veen and Morales 2011: 111). Addition archaeological and textual evidence has been found for the cultivation of cotton in the Egyptian oases during the Roman period (Gradel et al. *in press*). Fragments of cotton fragments were discovered by Reisner in the course of his excavations at Meroë's West Cemetery in 1922-3 (Griffith and Crowfoot 1934: 9), and textiles recovered from Kushite-period tombs at Ballaña and Qustul in Egyptian Nubia were largely of cotton (Welsby 1996: 160). Of the 115 Kushite-period textile fragments from Qaṣr Ibrīm, all but three were made of cotton (Adams 1987: 86). Even Gervers, for all his reservations about interpreting RIE 189's *ṭūṭ* as cotton, has no trouble acknowledging that 75% of the textiles from Cemetery III at Jabal 'Adda, also located in Egyptian Nubia, are believed to be of cotton (Gervers 1992: 16). On the Kushite production of cotton in the broader context of long-distance trade during the Roman period, see Gradel et al. *in press*.

469 Klemm et al. 2001.

470 Edwards 2004: 137-8. Writing in the mid-fifth century BCE, Herodotus (3.23) states that bronze was the most precious metal to the Kushites, and that prisoners in Kush were bound with gold fetters. Though obviously apocryphal, this statement may imply that ancient Nubian attitudes toward metals differed from attitudes in other societies (Edwards, loc. cit.).

471 Shinnie and Anderson 2004: 73-9; Abdelrahman 2011: 392.

dates back to the very beginning of the city's history.[472] Though iron was produced by the Kushites in large quantities,[473] RIE 189 provides no information as to precisely where the Aksumites found the iron during their campaign against the Noba.[474] C^{14} dates obtained from the furnaces excavated at Meroë indicate that the city's iron industry continued into the fourth century CE,[475] which agrees well with the reference to iron in RIE 189. But with nothing in RIE 189 to link Meroë with the iron seized by 'Ēzānā's forces there is no reason to assume that the city's iron supply was directly affected by the Aksumite invasion. Possibly relevant in this context is the fact that during the late Kushite period iron objects, such as iron-tipped spears and arrows, are commonly found in burials over a wider area than in earlier centuries, a phenomenon which has suggested to some scholars that, as centralized power was eroded during Kush's later years, so too was royal control of the iron industry.[476] In such a situation, iron workers are likely to have taken up residence in provincial areas, including perhaps those areas occupied by the Noba. Finally, the use of camels by

[472] Shinnie and Anderson 2004: 74; Haaland and Haaland 2007: 381. Recent excavations at Tombos, near the third Nile cataract, has pushed the history of Kushite iron working back to the late eighth to early seventh century BCE (Abdelrahman 2011: 395).

[473] The actual quantity of iron produced, as estimated from slag at Meroë, may have been as much as 5000 tons, or 2500 tons of finished objects after forging, representing an annual production of perhaps 5-20 tons of iron objects over a period of five centuries (Haaland and Haaland 2007: 380-1). It has been hypothesized that more northerly towns like Tabo, Kawa, and Napata were also centers of iron production, though the evidence at those sites is less clear (Welsby 1996: 170; Abdu and Gordon 2004: 993; cf. Edwards 1989: 156). Since Lower Nubia lacks good wood for fuel, most iron-smelting would have taken place in Upper Nubia, apparently at places with a significant royal presence (Abdu and Gordon 2004: 992, 993-4). To the south of Meroë, iron slag and evidence of iron working have come to light at the sites of Ḥamādāb, al-Ḥaṣā, and Muways (Abdelrahman 2011: 393).

[474] That relatively few iron objects can be dated to the Kushite period, despite the scale of Meroë's iron industry, might suggest that such objects were made primarily for export (Haaland and Haaland 2007: 379-80; cf. Abdu and Gordon 2004: 979, 994, 995; Abdelrahman 2011: 398-9). If so, it could be that groups like the Noba were among the recipients of such iron, particularly if they were, at least at some point, federates of Kush.

[475] Shinnie and Anderson 2004: 75-6.

[476] Haaland and Haaland 2007: 380, 387. The diffusion of iron workshops seems to have continued after the breakup of the Kushite state (Abdelrahman 2011: 394, 401).

the Noba is worthy of note in that this animal acquired a special status as a symbol of military power in post-Kushite funerary culture.[477] The use of the camel for riding and as a beast of burden is attested in Nubia in earlier times,[478] though its more widespread use from the third century on is often assumed on the basis of the greater mobility of certain groups in the eastern Sudan during that period.[479] Nevertheless, the importance of the camel to the Noba remains a question which records of ʿĒzānā's Nubian campaign do not answer.[480]

4.5.2.3. The Attack on Kush

After his attack on the Noba settlements, ʿĒzānā turned his attention to the territory of the Kushites (*Kāsū*). Now for the first time in RIE 189 we find towns mentioned by name.

> 28.And I reached the Kushites and killed them and took [others] prisoner at the 29.confluence of the Nile and the Takkazē rivers, and on the day after I reached them I sent 30.the Maḥazā division and the division of Ḥarā, Damawa, and Falḥa and Ṣerāʾ on a raid 31.up the Nile against the cities of brick and those of straw; the names of the towns 32.of brick were Alwa and Daro. And they killed and took prisoners and cast [the fallen enemy] into 33.the water, and they returned safe and sound, having struck fear into the enemy and defeated them by the power of Go34.d. And from there I sent the division of Ḥalēn, the division of Lūkēn, and 35.the division of Sabarāt, Falḥa, and Ṣerāʾ down the Nile against the four towns of 36.straw of the Noba: [the town of] Neg^{w}ase; [and] the towns of brick of the Kushites which the Noba had captured, Tabito [and] 37.Fertoti. And they reached the territory of the Red Noba, and my tr38.oops returned safe and sound, having taken prisoners and killed and seized booty by the power of the Lord of Hea39.ven.

477 Manzo 2004: 81.
478 Welsby 1996: 154-5.
479 Manzo 2004: 81.
480 There is no evidence that the Noba knew of, much less used, the camel before reaching the Nile Valley.

(28. *Wa-baṣaḥkū Kāsū 'ənza 'əqattəlōmū wa-'əḍēwōmū ba-* 29. *maẖbarta 'aflāg za-'aflāg za-Sīdā wa-Takkazī wa-ba-sānītā baṣaḥkū fannaw* 30. *kū marāda sarwē Maḥazā wa-sarwē Ḥarā wa-Damawa wa-Falḥa wa-Ṣərā'* 31. *mala'əlta Sīdā 'əhgūra nədq wa-za-ḥaśar 'asmāta 'əhgūrīhū* 32. *za-nədq 'Alwā 1 Darō 1. Wa-qatalū wa-ḍēwawū wa-'aṣdafū wəstēta* 33. *māy wa-dāẖna 'atawū 'afrīhōmū ḍarōmū wa-mawī'ōmū ba-ẖayla 'Əg* 34. *zī'a-bəḥēr wa-'əmmənēhū fannawkū sarwē Ḥalēn wa-sarwē Lūkēn wa-* 35. *sarwē Sabarāt wa-Falḥa wa-Ṣərā' mataḥta Sīdā 'əhgūra Nōbā za-* 36. *ḥaśar 4 Nəgʷasē 1 'əhgūra nadaq za-Kāsū za-Nōbā naś'a Tabītō 1* 37. *Fərtōtī 1. Wa-baṣḥū 'əska dawala Nōbā qayyəḥ wa-dāhna 'atawū 'ə* 38. *ḥzābīya ḍēwəwōmū wa-qatīlōmū wa-mahrīkōmū ba-ẖayla 'əgzī'a sa* 39. *māy.*)[481]

This portion of 'Ēzānā's campaign, then, was a two-stage operation. In the first stage, several Aksumite military units, organized along clan lines,[482] went upriver (*mala'əlta Sīdā*) after reaching the Nile and captured the towns of Alwa and Daro. The units in question comprised the clans of Maḥazā,[483] Ḥarā,[484] Damawa, Falḥa, and Ṣerā'.[485]

[481] RIE 189 (Bernard et al. 1991: 264).

[482] Merid Wolde Aregay 2005: 159-63. On the origin and political status of clans in Aksumite Ethiopia, see De Blois 1984, who argues that royal clans were matrilineal groups. For a different interpretation, see Merid Wolde Aregay (2005: 162).

[483] On the Maḥazā regiment, see ibid.: 161, 181 (n. 12).

[484] De Blois (1985: 10-11) gives numerous attestations of the root √ḥrr in Ethiosemitic, all having the sense of "free." On the basis of Ge'ez *ḥarā* ("troops") he suggests that "a 'freeman' was by definition a clansman, and thus a 'soldier.'" If so, it is likely that Ḥarā is to be understood as a title rather than a clan-name as such, which would support Merid Wolde Aregay's hypothesis that Ḥarā is an honorific name (Merid Wolde Aregay 2005: 161).

[485] Of these, the Ṣerā' recall the Ṣere' mentioned in RIE 263, a fragmentary Ge'ez inscription erected at the Ḥimyarite capital of Ẓafār following Kālēb's second invasion of South Arabia in 525 (Bernard et al. 1991: 350). Alternatively, Ṣere' in RIE 263 might refer to the Romans (Hatke 2011: 359). Having examined the Ge'ez material from 'Ēzānā's reign, the author now considers the possibility that the Ṣerā' of RIE 189 and the Ṣere' of RIE 263 are one and the same, a not inconceivable scenario since Aksumite clans continued in existence for several centuries. As a case in point, a military unit called Dākēn/Dakʷēn in inscriptions from 'Ēzānā's time (RIE 187:21 and RIE 188:10 [Bernard et al. 1991: 256, 260]) appear again in RIE 191 from the reign of Kālēb (RIE 191:15, 16 [Bernard et al. 1991: 272]). The Ḥarā, Damawa,

In the second stage of ‘Ēzānā’s operation, the aforementioned clans of Falḥa, and Ṣerā’, having returned to the confluence of the Nile and Takkazē, were sent down the Nile (*mataḥta Sīdā*) along with the Sabarāt, the Lūkēn,[486] and ‘Ēzānā’s own clan of Ḥalēn,[487] against four “straw towns” of the Noba, of which only one, Negʷasē, is mentioned by name,[488] and against two Kushite towns, Tabito and Fertoti, which the Noba had captured. The Takkazē River was evidently of some strategic importance, as the Noba had earlier felt confident that it was a sufficient barrier between them and the Aksumites. It is not surprising, then, that ‘Ēzānā made the confluence of the Nile and the Takkazē rivers his base and from there sent divisions of his army to secure the regions to the south and north.

There are, however, two ways of interpreting ‘Ēzānā’s claim to have reached the Nile at its confluence with the Takkazē. If the confluence in question is that of the Takkazē and the ‘Aṭbara, the latter being wrongly assumed to be the Nile, the Aksumite army would then have reached what is now the Sudanese province of al-Qaḍārif, well to the southeast of Kush. If, on the other hand, the Aksumites referred to the ‘Aṭbara as the Takkazē—which would have been logical enough given that these two rivers become one in the Sudan—then the confluence of the Takkazē and Nile to which RIE 189 refers would be the confluence of the ‘Aṭbara and the main Nile, some 96 km to the north of Meroë. Since this latter region lay within what was at least nominally Kushite territory we may presume that when ‘Ēzānā claimed to have reached the confluence of the Nile and the Takkazē he was referring to the Nile-‘Aṭbara confluence. There are good grounds for locating the Nubian toponyms mentioned in RIE 189 in this general area. The first of these, Alwa, immediately suggests the name ‘Alwa (علوه) by which Alodia, the southernmost of the three Christian kingdoms of medieval Nubia was known.[489] However, while it is true

and Falḥa also reappear in the sixth century (Merid Wolde Aregay 2005: 162).

[486] On the Lūkēn clan, whose name is also read as Laken, see Merid Wolde Aregay, loc. cit.: 161, 181 (n. 14).

[487] The writing of this name in RIE 189 is inconsistent. It is written Ḥalēn (ሐሌን) here in Line 34 but Ḥalen (ሐለን) in Line 2.

[488] Hintze 2000: 53.

[489] The only difference is that in RIE 189 the toponym Alwa is written አልዋ with an initial glottal stop /’/, whereas a closer equivalent of the Arabic

that Soba, the future capital of Alodia, was occupied during the Kushite period,[490] it need not follow that in ʻĒzānā's time this town bore the name by which Alodia would centuries later be known to the Arabs.[491] Moreover, since Soba is located on the lower Blue Nile c. 22 km south of present-day Khartoum, one would have expected RIE 189 to refer to the confluence of the Blue and White Niles, as it does not.[492] By contrast, there are good reasons for locating Alwa further north. Comparing it with Abale, mentioned in a list of Nubian toponyms in a fragment of Juba's geographical treatise preserved by Pliny the Elder,[493] Priese identifies the Alwa of RIE 189 with the site of al-Muqrin near the mouth of the ʻAṭbara.[494] Whether or not Alwa can be identified with Abale, locating the town in this area receives some support from the close association in RIE 189 of Alwa with Daro, as this latter name designated the region around al-Dāmir, just south of the ʻAṭbara's confluence with the Nile, as late as the seventeenth century.[495] Excavation at the cemetery site of Gabati indicates Kushite occupation in this region as late as the fourth century CE.[496] Far less plausible is Crawford's more southerly location for Daro, which he identifies with the village of Daron mentioned in Ptolemy's *Geographika*.[497] Based on Ptolemy's coordinates for the similarly named Daron,[498] Crawford proposes that the Daro of RIE 189 is to be identified either with Abū

would have been *ዐልዋ with an initial voiced pharyngeal fricative /ʻ/. It is unlikely that the vocalization of Alwa in RIE 189 provides an example of the conflation of these two phonemes observable in Geʻez manuscripts from the medieval period, when the orthography of Geʻez came to be influenced by Amharic pronunciation. Since the pharyngeal fricative is not attested in any Nubian language the ʻAlwa of Arabic sources would instead seem to reflect an Arabization of a Nubian toponym, in which case it cannot predate the Islamic period.

490 Welsby 1999.

491 It is doubtful that Alodia is to be identified with the land of *Arut/Alut (*ʼI-r3-t*) mentioned in an inscription of Nastaseñ, a Kushite king of the second half of the fourth century BCE (Berlin Ägyptisches Museum 2268:16), as believed by some scholars (*Fontes Historiae Nubiorum II* 1996: 498).

492 Cf. Kirwan 1960: 168.

493 Pliny, *Naturalis historia* 6.179 (*Fontes Historiae Nubiorum III* 1998: 805).

494 Priese 1984: 496.

495 Bradley 1984: 249.

496 Edwards 1998.

497 Crawford 1951: 17-18.

498 Ptolemy, *Geographika* 4.7.5 (*Fontes Historiae Nubiorum III* 1998: 928-9).

Ḥarāz at the confluence of the Blue Nile and the Rahad, or with Arbagi a short distance downriver.[499] But since the Noba's aggressions were directed at the peoples of Aksum's northwestern frontier, located in northwestern Eritrea and the neighboring regions of the Sudan's Kasalā Province, it is highly improbable that 'Ēzānā would led his troops southwards towards the upper Blue Nile, far from the Noba's area of operations against Aksum's western frontier, and only afterwards pushed on northwards into the Kushite heartland. Nor is it likely that the Aksumite army, having reached the Takkazē, reached the Blue Nile by way of the Buṭāna, as Hintze argues,[500] for RIE 189 gives a riverine context for the battles against the Noba and says nothing of crossing the steppeland between the Takkazē and the Blue Nile. We can only conclude, then, that Ptolemy was either mistaken in his location of Daron or, more probably, that his Daron is different from RIE 189's Daro. Moreover, Crawford's location of Daro in the upper Blue Nile Valley is hard to reconcile with his suggestion that Alwa in RIE 189 refers to Meroë,[501] particularly when RIE 189 treats the Aksumite attack on Alwa and Daro as a single operation, which could hardly have been the case if Alwa were Meroë and Daro a town on the distant upper Blue Nile. Locating Alwa and Daro in the region of al-Dāmir, however, makes good sense in that the most direct route from Aksum to Nubia leads in a northwesterly direction via the Takkazē to the confluence of the 'Aṭbara with the Nile.[502] In light of this it is proposed here that the confluence of the Nile and Takkazē mentioned in RIE 189 refers to the confluence of the Nile with the 'Aṭbara, and that it was on this spot that 'Ēzānā established his main base for military operations in Nubia.

So much for the towns taken by the striking force of the Maḥazā, Ḥarā, Damawa, Falḥa, and Ṣerā' clans. What of the towns taken in the downriver operation undertaken by the Ḥalēn, Lūkēn, Sabarāt, Falḥa, and Ṣerā' units? These latter towns, as we have seen, were the "brick towns" of Tabito and Fertoti and four "straw towns" of the Noba, of

[499] Crawford 1951: 17-18.
[500] Hintze 2000: 52.
[501] Crawford 1951: 17. This theory is accepted by Kirwan and others (Kirwan 1960: 168).
[502] On this route, see Chittick 1982: 51.

which only Negʷase is named. This Negʷase cannot be identified with any modern toponym, though it may well correspond with the town of Nakis, located by Ptolemy on the east bank of the Nile between Meroë and Napata.[503] Tabito and Fertoti are tentatively identified by Crawford with the islands of Tibet and Birti respectively, the first located at 19.2 N/32.29 E, the second at 18.54 N/32.17 E near the border of the modern Sudanese provinces of Berber and Dongola.[504] In this he may be correct not only given the similarity of the names but also in light of the remains of a stone fort on the west bank facing Tibet and the discovery of Kushite beads at Birti.[505] Excavations in this region will have to be undertaken to confirm these hypotheses, but if 'Ēzānā's troops reached the main Nile near the embouchement of the 'Aṭbara, as seems likely from RIE 189, then Negʷasē, Tabito, and Fertoti would all have been located downriver from Meroë. Hintze notes that the name Fertoti poses a bit of a linguistic problem in that the Meroitic language lacks the phoneme /f/,[506] but since this phoneme is found in Nubian it is possible that this erstwhile Kushite town was renamed by the Noba after they captured it. The Aksumite campaign is said to have reached its limit in the territory of the "Red Noba" (*Nōbā qayyəḥ*). What the epithet "red" connotes in this instance is not clear. Though a conflict between "the blacks and the reds" is alluded to at the beginning of RIE 189, the Semitic habit of pairing of black and red as an idiomatic way of expressing the idea of "everyone" suggests that the allusion to blacks making war on the reds does not refer to a conflict between two different ethnic groups. In fact, the Red Noba are the only ethnic group which RIE 189 specifically associates with a color. Since no corresponding Black Noba are mentioned in the inscriptions it is safe to assume that the Red Noba are not among those involved in the black-versus-red war. References to "red Ethiopians" are attested in Graeco-Roman literature as early as the first century CE,[507] though it

[503] Priese 1984: 496; Ptolemy, *Geographika* 4.7.5 (*Fontes Historiae Nubiorum III* 1998: 928-9). It is hard to accept Crawford's suggestion that Negʷasē has any connection with the Ge'ez word for king, *nəgūś* (Crawford 1951: 19).

[504] Ibid.: 19 (n. 62).

[505] Ibid. Edwards (1989: 84), on the other hand, believes that the extant ruins at the site of Birti are from the Christian period, i.e., post-sixth century.

[506] Hintze 2000: 53.

[507] Snowden 1970: 3.

cannot be assumed that the Red Noba were named thus by the Aksumites on account of their skin color. Color names, particularly red, black, and white, are often applied to inner Asian ethnonyms in Roman and Iranian sources without any association with the physique of such groups,[508] while among the Afar nomads of the Danakil desert social divisions of "noble" and "commoner" are designated by color terms.[509] It could very well be that we have a similar situation with RIE 189's Red Noba.[510] Significantly, RIE 189 makes no mention of Aksumite conflict with the Red Noba but states only that 'Ēzānā's troops "reached the territory of the Red Noba and returned safe and sound" (*baṣḥū 'əska dawala Nōbā qayyəḥ wa-dāẖna 'atawū*). Presumably, then, the Red Noba were a separate group from the Noba who had attacked the Mangurto, Khasa, and Barya, as a result of which 'Ēzānā saw no need to dispatch punitive campaigns against them. Since the military divisions which reached the territory of the Red Noba are said in RIE 189 to have been dispatched downriver by 'Ēzānā, the Red Noba would have lived somewhere beyond the Nile-'Aṭbara confluence. A Ge'ez graffito at Kawa (Temple T)[511] between the third and fourth cataracts of the Nile has been thought to represent the limit of Aksum's penetration into Nubia,[512] but since the graffito is almost completely illegible it is impossible to date it or to determine in what context—military, commercial, or diplomatic—it was left. Kawa is also well beyond the geographic scope of RIE 189,[513] and although we cannot exclude the possibility that the Aksumites reached the town via a direct route across the desert from the bend in the Nile, such an operation cannot be determined on the basis of RIE 189. It may be that the border of the Red Noba territory reached by 'Ēzānā's army lay somewhere below the fourth cataract.[514]

[508] Sinor 1990: 300-1.
[509] Levine 2000: 55.
[510] The theory that the Red Noba were Blemmyes/Beja (Trimingham 1949: 45) is implausible on the grounds that the Aksumites were well acquainted with the Beja and always designated them as such in inscriptions.
[511] Rabin 1949.
[512] Kirwan 1960: 169.
[513] Hintze 2000: 53.
[514] Following the collapse of the Kushite state in the mid-fourth century, a culture with localized characteristics developed in the Dongola Reach (Edwards 2004: 193-5). Could the reference in RIE 189 to the Red Noba as a

In sum, the reconstruction of the Aksumite invasion of Nubia offered here suggests that ʻĒzānā's main base, as well as the area in which his troops operated, lay to the north of Meroë, in which case the theory that ʻĒzānā's goal was to overthrow the kingdom of Kush by attacking its capital is quite untenable. As RIE 189 makes clear, the primary *casus belli* of the Aksumite invasion was aggression on the part of the Noba, specifically their attacks on Aksumite vassals and their breaking of the oaths which they had made with ʻĒzānā. This may explain why Meroë is absent from RIE 189. A badly weathered Geʻez graffito from pyramid Bagrawiyya N 2 at Meroë's royal cemetery[515] and another from Chapel M 292 at Meroë City[516] might seem to suggest otherwise, but since these graffiti are nearly as illegible as the Geʻez graffito from Kawa[517] they provide no information that" might allow us to date them to the period of ʻĒzānā's Nubian campaign. For all we know, the Meroë graffiti might well have been left by an Aksumite soldier or officer in the course of the invasion of Kush described in RIE 286 and SNM 24841. Regarding ʻĒzānā's attack on the Kushites it is worthy of note that, out of the four towns of brick sacked by the Aksumites according to RIE 189, two of them, Tabito and Fertoti, are described as Kushite towns which had already fallen into the hands of the Noba. We may presume, then, that the attack on those towns was part of ʻĒzānā's campaign against the Noba, not the Kushites. There is even some ambiguity surrounding the political status of Alwa and Daro. According to RIE 189, ʻĒzānā first made an attack on the Kushites at the confluence of the Nile and Takkazē (i.e., the ʻAṭbara), and then on the following day sent several divisions of his army on a separate mission against Alwa and Daro, which raises the question as to whether these two towns are to be associated with the Kushites at

distinct group indicate the first stage in the evolution of a new polity? In that case the Red Noba might, as Brakmann (1994: 69) suggests, be identified with the polity which by the sixth century would evolve into the kingdom of Makouria. This is an intriguing possibility, though one which is as yet impossible to prove.

[515] Rabin 1949.

[516] Török 1999: 143 (n. 89).

[517] Of the graffito from Bagrawiyya N 2 only the words *kʷəllō mədra wa-* ("all the land and...") can be made out.

all.[518] Scholars have long associated the brick towns with the Kushites and the straw towns with the Noba,[519] even though RIE 189 refers unambiguously to the Noba living in brick as well as straw towns,[520] and to their possession of temples and storehouses. It is not impossible that Kush had become fragmented by this time. By stating that Aksumite troops reached as far as the domain of the Red Noba, RIE 189 would appear to describe the campaign in terms of the Noba's territorial divisions, as opposed to the boundaries of the Kushite state. This might suggest that Kush was no longer the unrivaled power of the middle Nile. That Meroë was not involved with 'Ēzānā's campaign may indicate that the old Kushite capital had lost control over the regions to the north, which would explain why Kush was unable to prevent the Noba from raiding the Aksumite frontier. If Meroë had lost its hold on the area north of the Nile-'Aṭbara confluence, there is no reason to assume that whatever Kushite elements remained there did not throw in their lot with the Noba, thus prompting a military response from 'Ēzānā.

4.5.2.4. Tallying Up the Spoils of War

The concluding portion of RIE 189 describes the erection of a victory throne in Upper Nubia following the attack on the Red Noba, the tallying up of the prisoners of war and livestock, and the erection of a throne at Aksum which originally bore this text.

> [39.]And I set up a throne at the confluence of the Nile and [40.]Takkazē rivers facing the town of brick which was in the middle of that island. The male prisoners which the L[41.]ord of Heaven gave me: 214; the female prisoners: 415; the total: 629. [42.]The men killed: 602; the women and children killed: 156; the total: 7[43.][58]. The total of prisoners and dead [together]: 1387. The booty: 10,5[44.]60 cows and 51,050 sheep. And I set up here at Śadō a throne by the pow[45.]er of the Lord of Heaven, He who aided me and gave me the kingdom. May the L[46.]ord of Heaven

[518] This point further calls into question Hintze's identification of Alwa with Meroë (Hintze 2000: 52).
[519] Kirwan 1960: 166.
[520] §4.5.2.2.

> strengthen my kingdom, and as He has on this day defeated for me my enemies [47.]may He defeat [them] for me wherever I go, just as He has on this day defeated and subjugated my ene[48.]mies for me with justice and righteousness, for I do not deal unjustly with people. And I have entrust[49.]ed this throne which I have set up to the care of the Lord of Heaven who has made me king. And if there be one who removes the earth [50.]that supports it and destroys it and tears it down, he and [51.]his kinfolk shall be uprooted and eradicated; from the land will he be uprooted. And I have set up this th[52.]rone through the power of the Lord of Heaven.
>
> ([39.]*Wa-takalkū manbara wəstēta mah̲barta 'aflāg za-Sīdā wa-*[40.]*za-Takkazī 'anṣāra hagara nədq za-wəsṭa zā-dassēt. Za-wahabanī 'Ǝ*[41.]*gzī'a samāy ḍēwā ʻəd 214 ḍēwā 'anəst 415 kōna 629.* [42.]*Wa-qətla ʻəd 602 qətla 'anəst wa-daqīq 156 kōna 7*[43.][58] *wa-kōna ḍēwā wa-qətl 1387. Wa-məhrəkā lahm 10,5*[44.]*60 wa-baggəʻ 51,050. Wa-takalkū manbara ba-zəyya ba-Śadō ba-h̲ay*[45.]*la 'əgzī'a samāy za-wə'ətū 'arda'anī wa-wahabanī mangəśta. 'ə*[46.]*gzī'a samāy yāṣnəʻ mangəśtəya wa-kama yōm mō'a līta ḍarəya* [47.]*la-yəmā' līta wa'əda ḥōrkū kama yōm mō'a līta wa-'agnaya līta ḍa*[48.]*rəya ba-ṣədq wa-ba-rətʻ 'ənza 'ī-'əʻēməḍ 'əḥzāba. Wa-'amaḥḍa*[49.]*nkū za-manbara za-takalkū la-'əgzī'a samāy za-'angaśanī. Wa-la-mə*[50.]*dr za-yəṣawwərō la-'əmma-bō za-naqalō wa-'amāsanō wa-naśatō wə'ətū wa-*[51.]*zamadū yəśśarraw wa-yətnaqqal 'ə[m]-bəḥēr yəśśarraw. Wa-takalkū za-ma*[52.]*nbara ba-h̲ayla 'əgzī'a samāy.*)[521]

RIE 189 was thus, like other Aksumite royal inscriptions, erected as part of a symbolic throne. The location of this throne is said to have been a place called Śadō. This was evidently a spot of some importance, for RIE 188, dating from ʻĒzānā's pre-Christian days and recording his campaigns against the tribes of Saʻnē, Ṣawantē, Gēmā, and Zaḥtan,[522] was also erected on a throne at Śadō.[523] The *Maṣḥafa*

[521] RIE 189 (Bernard et al. 1991: 264-5).
[522] Presumably tribes living somewhere in the Ethiopian Highlands.
[523] RIE 188:24 (Bernard et al. 1991: 260).

'Aksūm, dating from the seventeenth century but incorporating earlier material,[524] mentions a place called Sōdō in the Walda 'Akrōsdam quarter of Aksum with which 'Ēzānā's Śadō is probably to be identified.[525] In addition to the throne at Śadō, 'Ēzānā erected a throne at the confluence of the Nile and Takkazē rivers where his army had first entered Nubia proper. The name of this town of brick is not given. RIE 189 is a bit ambiguous as to whether this throne was set up on the opposite bank facing the town on the island, or was located on the island itself in front of the town. However, given the location of SNM 24841 along a processional way leading to Meroë's Temple KC102, one would expect 'Ēzānā's inscription at the Nile-Takkazē confluence to have been similarly located at a prominent spot as close as possible to the unnamed town to which RIE 189 refers. Thus it is likely that his throne was erected on the island and not across the river where it would not have been easily visible from the town. Sayce believed that he had indeed found the remains of the site of 'Ēzānā's throne at the southern end of 'Aṭbara Island, located at the mouth of the 'Aṭbara River.[526] At that spot he excavated a platform of unshaped stones protected by a stone embankment, though with no trace of any throne or inscription.[527] Such an inscription would no doubt have given yet another account of 'Ēzānā's Nubian campaign, presumably in Greek like the other public inscriptions erected by the Aksumites in Nubia.[528]

RIE 189 reveals that the spoils of war favored by the Aksumites were both human and animal. In the case of the former, it is noteworthy that the number of women prisoners of war (415) is almost twice that of men (214), while the number of men killed in battle (602) is nearly four times that of fallen women and children combined (156).[529] No distinction is made between the Noba and Kushites here. It

[524] Lusini 2003.
[525] Huntingford 1989: 55 (n. 1).
[526] Sayce 1923: 352-3.
[527] Ibid. On this site, see Edwards 1989: 67.
[528] In contrast to these public inscriptions, the graffiti left by the Aksumites at Kawa's Temple T and Bagrawiyya N 2 were written in Ge'ez. Since Greek was an international language it was the Aksumites' preferred medium when addressing a foreign audience.
[529] To be sure, due caution is in order when dealing with tallies of prisoners, fallen enemies, and booty, particularly when ancient sources are prone to inflate numbers. That said, there is no reason to think that the capture of a

need hardly be stressed that since the men fought in war they would naturally have died in far greater numbers than those (namely women and children) who did not. A possible explanation for the predominance of females among the prisoners of war is that many of the women captured by the invaders ended up as domestic servants and/or concubines at the royal residence at Aksum, while others were given to the Aksumite generals and perhaps also to rank and file of the Aksumite army, again as concubines. We are poorly informed on the African slave trade during this period, though it is also possible that some of the Nubians captured by ʻĒzānā's army were later sold by the Aksumites as slaves. The *Periplus of the Erythraean Sea* testifies to the exportation of slaves from the Horn of Africa and the East African coast as early as the first century CE,[530] and a late sixth-century contract from Egypt, drawn up for the sale of a slave girl from Alodia (Papyrus Strassburg Inv. Nr. 1404), provides evidence of the trade in Nubian slaves in later times.[531] While we do not know how this particular slave girl reached Egypt,[532] the possibility that some of this trade was handled by Aksumites deserves consideration.[533]

What is particularly striking, though, is that the number of Nubian prisoners of war taken during ʻĒzānā's campaign is considerably smaller than the number of Beja captured in battle by the king's brothers Śeʻāzānā and Ḥadefā on an earlier campaign and then resettled *en masse* in Ethiopia along with their chieftains.[534] The invocation of the pagan deities ʻAstar, Medr, and Maḥrem in the Geʻez

total of 629 men and women was beyond the capacity of the Aksumite army, in addition to which 629 and the total number of dead (758) are not the sort of neat, round numbers that one might expect in cases of hyperbole. These numbers of dead and captured enemies may thus be accurate.

530 *Periplus* 8.3.32; 13.5.4-5.

531 Pierce 1995.

532 Pierce (ibid.: 150) suggests that she was brought overland by way of the oases of the Western Desert.

533 On the Nubian slave trade in antiquity, see Burstein 1995.

534 RIE 185 II:5-9 (Bernard et al. 1991: 243). For a translation of the passage, see Huntingford 1989: 48. The Beja chieftains, of whom there are said to have been six, are called "kings," *ngśt* (=**nagaśt*), in the inscription. Rodinson (1981) suggests that the Beja were resettled by the Aksumites in Bagēmder to the west of Aksum, though his attempt to interpret the name of that region as "Beja-land" (**Bəgā-mədr*) is not convincing.

inscription recording this campaign (RIE 185 I+II),[535] and the invocation of Ares in the Greek (RIE 270)[536] leaves no room for doubt that it predates the Nubian expedition launched by ʿĒzānā in 360, as the records of the latter contain language reflecting the king's conversion to Christianity. According to RIE 185 II, RIE 185*bis* II, and RIE 270 some 4400 Beja[537] were resettled in Ethiopia,[538] i.e. seven times the number of Nubian captives (629) recorded in RIE 189.[539] Relocating 4400 prisoners of war in a country with as difficult a terrain as Ethiopia's would have been a major undertaking, and given the vast quantities of bread, drink, and cattle given by ʿĒzānā to the Beja chieftains for the support

[535] RIE 185 I:20-1, cf. RIE 185: II: 21 (Bernard et al. 1991: 243). The text survives in two versions, both in Geʿez, the first in South Arabian *musnad* with mimation (RIE 185 I), the second in unvocalized *fidal* (RIE 185 II).

[536] RIE 270:5, 27, 31, 37 (Bernard 2000: 6).

[537] RIE 185 II:8-9 (Bernard et al. 1991: 243); RIE 185*bis* II:9-11 (ibid.: 247); RIE 270:19 (Bernard 2000: 6); RIE 270*bis*:15 (ibid.: 12; *Fontes Historiae Nubiorum III* 1998: 1095, 1096). The number given in RIE 270*bis* might also read 4420, according to the reading offered in *Fontes Historiae Nubiorum III* 1998: 1096 (n. 689).

[538] Huntingford (1989: 48) translates the unvocalized word *sb'* (=**sab'*) of the Geʿez inscriptions as "men," in which case the number 4400 would refer only to the male prisoners of war, not counting their children and women (*dqq*^{m} *w-'nst*^{m}=**daqīq wa-'anəst*) whom the inscription includes among the captives a few lines earlier (RIE 185 I: 5-6=RIE 185 II: 7-8 [Bernard et al. 1991: 242, 243]). Though Huntingford does not develop this idea further, his interpretation has significant implications for our understanding of the scale of ʿĒzānā's resettlement program, for if one assumes that every man had a wife and one child, the figure of 4400 men would imply a total of 13,200 Beja men, women, and children. This would not be an implausible estimate if one allows both for unmarried men among the Beja as well as for men who had several children, a common phenomenon in pre-industrial societies. However, the Geʿez plural *sab'* can mean not only "men" but "people" more generally. Since RIE 270 makes no claim that the relocated Beja comprised only men, "people" would be a much more appropriate translation of *sab'* than Huntingford's "men."

[539] Once again one must view such neat, round numbers with a bit of skepticism. However, 4400, even if rounded off, seems much more credible as a number of captured Beja than 15,200, which an Egyptian inscription from the reign of Amūnḥotep II (c. 1425-1400 BCE) gives as the number of captured Shasū, a nomadic people like the Beja (Spalinger 2005: 144-5). There are, of course, no census records for the Beja from any period before the modern era, but if the number of 500,000 estimated for the Beja population of the Sudan's Kasalā Province in the 1970s (Morton 1989: 66 [n. 9]) is in any way indicative of the demographic capacity of just one portion of the larger Beja region in antiquity, it is perfectly credible that over 4000 Beja were resettled by ʿĒzānā in Ethiopia.

of their people,[540] the logistical demands of the resettlement project would have been heavy for the Aksumite state. Only a serious political and military threat would have called for such pains to be taken. Moreover, if ʻĒzānā sought to keep closer watch on the Beja by resettling in Ethiopia not only large numbers of their men, women, and children but also six of their chieftains, the fact that this same policy was not repeated with Nubia suggests that the Beja posed if not a greater threat to Aksum than the Noba then at least a different sort of threat that called for a different policy.

If the war-spoil tally is any indication, it would seem that livestock was a far more sought-after commodity than human captives. 10,560 cows and 51,050 sheep are reported in RIE 189 to have been captured in the course of ʻĒzānā's Nubian campaign—numbers which, even if exaggerated, far exceed the number of prisoners of war captured by the Aksumite troops. Regarding the people from whom these cattle and sheep were seized no distinction is made between the Noba and the Kushites any more than such a distinction is made regarding the ethnicity of the prisoners of war. Evidently ʻĒzānā was concerned solely with quantity when it came to tallying up the results of his campaign. To place the scale of ʻĒzānā's Nubian campaign in broader historical context it might be instructive to compare the numbers of the cattle and sheep captured by his troops with the quantity of booty recorded in an inscription erected by the Kushite king Nastaseñ in the second half of the fourth century BCE (Berlin Ägyptisches Museum 2268), which records a series of military victories over the peoples somewhere on the frontier of Kush. In a campaign against the land of Mekhindekennete, Nastaseñ is said to have seized no fewer than 209,659 head of long-horned oxen, together with 505,349 head of generic livestock.[541] Then in a campaign against the rebels of Rebala and Akulakuro some 203,216 long-horned oxen and 603,107 head of livestock were captured.[542] In further campaigns 22,120

[540] Said to be 22,000 loaves of wheaten bread and 4190 head of cattle to each of the six Beja chieftains (thus 25,140 head in total), together with enough meat, beer, and wine for four months (RIE 185 II:12-13, 16-18 [Bernard et al. 1991: 243=Huntingford 1989: 48-9]).
[541] *Fontes Historiae Nubiorum II* 1996: 488.
[542] Ibid.: 489.

long-horned oxen and 55,200 head of livestock were seized from the land of Mahae;[543] 203,146 long-horned oxen and 33,050 head of livestock from the land of Makhsherkharta;[544] and 35,330 long-horned oxen and 55,526 head of livestock from the land of Mayokue.[545] The countries mentioned in Nastaseñ's inscription cannot be identified with any certainty, particularly since many of them are not attested in any other text. But even allowing for what may be a great deal of hyperbole, the fact that such a vast quantity of livestock was conceivable by the Kushites as booty captured in the course of Nastaseñ's campaigns suggests that many if not most of the rebel lands named in the inscription are to be located within the belt of annual rainfall that extends southwards from the 'Aṭbara's confluence with the Nile and provides sufficient grazing land for large herds. Since paleoclimatic studies indicate that the climate of the northern Sudan was much the same during the Kushite period as it is today,[546] this same rainfall pattern would have prevailed during both the fourth century BCE and the fourth century CE. What is immediately noticeable is how vastly larger the number of cattle and other livestock captured by Nastaseñ is in comparison with that captured by 'Ēzānā. Clearly the Aksumites were either dealing with enemy peoples who had far less booty to offer than their counterparts in Nastaseñ's time, or else had undertaken a military which had far less of an impact than that of Nastaseñ. Also striking in RIE 189's record of livestock captured by the Aksumites is the fact that sheep outnumber cows by a ratio of nearly 5:1. One might explain this phenomenon by positing that a change in pastoral habits, whereby sheep came to be favored over cattle, occurred in Upper Nubia between Nastaseñ's time and 'Ēzānā's, or perhaps that the Aksumites simply preferred sheep when selecting livestock to take back with them to Ethiopia. Neither of these explanations seems plausible, however. More probably we are dealing here with a simple fact of geography and climate. According to the interpretation proposed in the present study 'Ēzānā's Nubian campaign would have affected only the northernmost fringe of the

543 Ibid.: 490.
544 Ibid.
545 Ibid.: 491.
546 Ahmed 1984: 13.

Sudanese rain-belt. Since sheep can tolerate drier conditions than cattle, one would expect sheep to play a more important role in the economy of the region north of the 'Aṭbara's confluence with the Nile.[547] Whatever the case, livestock seems to have been the limit of the Aksumites' interest in Nubia's resources. Since 'Ēzānā's troops are said to have simply tossed the confiscated grain, copper, iron, and cotton into the Nile, as opposed to carrying it back with them to Ethiopia, it would appear that these particular items counted for little as far as the Aksumites were concerned. Indeed the treatment meted out to the Noba's grain and raw materials is described in RIE 189 exactly like the treatment of their idols: they are simply cast into the river, so useless to the Noba in the face of the Ethiopian invaders. That iron was dealt with in this fashion may also reflect an effort on the Aksumites' part to deprive the Noba of a material used to manufacture weapons that might conceivably be used against Aksum and its subject peoples.[548]

4.5.3. A Third Account of the Nubian War: RIE 190

RIE 190, our third and final source for 'Ēzānā's invasion of Nubia is by far the most fragmentary and in many ways raises more questions than it answers. The inscription was found in the 'Enda Sem'ōn quarter in Aksum in 1959 and was published by Schneider in 1974 together with inscriptions of the sixth-century kings Kālēb and Wa'zeb (RIE 191 and RIE 192 respectively).[549] A second article, devoted solely to RIE 190, was published by Schneider two years later, with several photographs of the inscription and an improved reading of the text.[550] A newer edition is provided in the *Recueil des inscriptions de l'Éthiopie* published by Bernard, Drewes, and Schneider.[551] Like Ousanas' RIE 186, RIE 190 is written in Sabaicizing Ge'ez using the unvocalized *musnad* script of

[547] Zooarchaeological studies of Meroë suggest a greater proportion of cattle relative to caprovines, though the special status of Meroë as the capital of Kush might have led to a pattern of consumption that differed from other sites in the region (Ahmed 1984: 92).

[548] Aksum appears to have possessed a viable iron industry of its own during the fourth century, as indicated by an analysis of archaeometallurgical remains from the site of Aksum, dating from 325 CE (Severin et al. 2010). This being the case, 'Ēzānā may have had little need of Nubian iron.

[549] Schneider 1974.

[550] Idem 1976.

[551] Bernard et al. 1991: 268-71.

South Arabia, complete with mimation.[552] Indeed, although RIE 190 preserves no royal name or title, the fact that it is carved on the back of the Greek account of ʿĒzānā's Nubian war (RIE 271)[553] strongly suggests that it too dates from that king's reign. In addition, although it is hardly a word-for-word copy of either of the other two inscriptions recording ʿĒzānā's activities in Nubia, RIE 190 has enough thematic similarities with these to warrant its attribution to ʿĒzānā. The fact that the *musnad* script, on which *fidal* is ultimately based, is employed in RIE 190 can in no way be taken as palaeographic evidence for the inscription's date, given that *musnad* was a deliberately anachronistic script in fourth-century Aksum and was resurrected simply to serve a symbolic function in inscriptions. Indeed, the inscriptions of Kālēb and his son Waʿzeb (RIE 191 and RIE 192 respectively), though dating some two hundred years after ʿĒzānā's inscriptions, both use *musnad* rather than the vocalized *fidal* that was developed during ʿĒzānā's reign.[554] Another valuable clue to the date of RIE 190 is the name of the monotheistic deity 'Egzīabḥēr (*'gz'bḥr*[m]), which appears in several places in the text.[555] Since this divine name is not used in any pre-Christian inscriptions, RIE 190 cannot predate ʿĒzānā's conversion to Christianity, and can therefore be associated with the Nubian campaign of 360. While what little can be understood of the badly eroded text differs somewhat in content from RIE 189, the differences are no greater than those between RIE 189 the Greek account of ʿĒzānā's Nubian campaign (RIE 271). RIE 190 must therefore represent a third version of the account of this campaign.

Given the damaged state of RIE 190 and the ambiguities inherent in the unvocalized *musnad* script, much of the extant text is amenable to alternative readings. That the word *bšy*[m] in Line 1[556] might also be

[552] RIE 190 is by no means the only inscription from ʿĒzānā's reign in which Geʿez is written—anachronistically—in the *musnad* script. The Geʿez records of ʿĒzānā's campaign against the Beja (RIE 185 I and RIE 185*bis* I) also employ the *musnad* script, together with the mimation typical of Sabaic—but foreign to Geʿez.

[553] Bernard et al. 1991: 268.

[554] *fidal*, the vocalized Ethiopian script based on a syllabic system, appears for the first time in RIE 187 and RIE 188, both of which date from the pre-Christian period of ʿĒzānā's reign.

[555] RIE 190:8, 9 (Face A), 3-4 (Face B) (Bernard et al. 1991 : 269, 270).

[556] Ibid.: 269.

read *bry*^{m},[557] suggestive of the Barya people mentioned in RIE 189 and RIE 271,[558] is a case in point. In Lines 2-6, however, we find a complete passage which, according to the edition in the *Recueil*, may be read as *'mnh*^{m} *'z*^{m} *ybl*^{m} *wʿn*^{m} *w-'zḏn*^{m} *b-z*^{m} *'nbr*^{m} *w-šrʿkw*^{m} *b-z*^{m} *ynbš̌*^{m} *w-whbkw*^{m} *ml'k*^{m} *w-nbšt*^{m} *w-'zḏkw*^{m} *yʿn*^{m} *Nb*^{m} *w-šrʿkw*^{m} *ygbr*^{m} *ṣyḥ*^{m} *w-ẖḏd*^{m} *w-ytkl*^{m} *'byt*^{m} *ngš*^{m} *wśt*^{m} *bḥš̌*^{m} *w-tšr*^{ʿm}.[559] Among the emendations suggested by the authors of the *Recueil* for these lines is that *ynbš̌*^{m} in Line 3 be read as *ynbr*^{m}, *nbšt*^{m} in Line 4 as *nbrt*^{m}, and *bḥš̌*^{m} in Lines 5-6 as *bḥr*^{m}.[560] Bearing these (admittedly hypothetical) emendations in mind, one might further suggest that *'z*^{m} in Line 2 be emended to *'nz*^{m}, the omission of *n* being attested in the later inscription of Kālēb from Aksum.[561] If these emendations are correct, Lines 2-6 of RIE 190 might be vocalized as ... **'əmmənēhū 'ə[n]za yəbal w[?]ʿ[?]n wa-'azazanī ba-zə 'ānbərō wa-śaraʿkəwwō ba-zə yənbar wa-wahabkəwwō mal'aka wa-nabarta wa-'azazkəwwō yəʿēn Nōbā wa-śaraʿkəwwō yəgbar ṣəyyāḥa wa-ẖ[?]ḏ[?]d wa-yətkal 'abyāta nəgūś wəsta bəḥēr wa-taśarʿa*. Bearing in mind that this is a very tentative—and in places incomplete—reading, this passage may then be translated as: "...from Him, saying, "[...];"[562] and He commanded me to settle them [there]. So I established them that they might reside there and I sent unto them a messenger and garrisons and set them in order to keep an eye on the Noba. And I decreed that they make a road and a [...][563] and erect royal houses in the land, and it was set in order [thus]."

A few points must be made to justify this reading. First, the fact that the Aksumite king is said to receive commands would suggest that only a power which he regarded as higher than himself, namely God, can be the subject of the verb *'azaza* ("he commanded') and probably *yəbal* ("he says," "saying") as well. Secondly, the letters *w* and *y* are best treated as consonants here because long vowels are often not indicated

557 Ibid.: 271.
558 Schneider 1974: 769; idem 1976: 112.
559 Bernard et al. 1991: 269.
560 Ibid.: 271.
561 *W-'brn wst mnbr 'bwy* (RIE 191:5 [Bernard et al. 1991: 272]). Schneider (1976: 772) is almost certainly correct in reconstructing *'brn* as *'nbrn* (=**'anbaranī*) hence **wa-'anbaranī wəsta manbara 'abawəya*, "and He placed me on the throne of my fathers."
562 Reading uncertain.
563 Reading uncertain.

in the orthography of Aksumite inscriptions in *musnad*.[564] Thus *šr'kw* can conceivably be read as **śara'kəwwō* ("I established him/it") rather than **śara'kū* ("I established"). Thirdly, since groups are often treated as collective nouns—and thus grammatically singular—in 'Ēzānā's inscription in vocalized Ge'ez (RIE 189),[565] the use of the masculine third person singular in RIE 190 in object pronouns (-*ō*) and verbs (**yəgbar*, **yətkal*) can also theoretically be translated as plural forms. If so, and if *bšy*^{m} in Line 1, for which no meaning presents itself, can be read as *bry*^{m} and thus interpreted as a reference to the Barya people, then there could be grounds for seeing in RIE 190 as a record of Barya involvement in 'Ēzānā's frontier defenses. The recruitment of locals to perform some sort of service on the frontier is conceivable enough, though with so much of the text missing or illegible, the nature of the Barya's (possible) involvement must remain for now a matter for speculation. Reading *ygbr*^{m} *ṣyḥ*^{m} in Lines 4-5 as **yəgbar*[*ū*] *ṣəyyāḥa* "that [they] make a road" invites comparison with Lines 15-16 of RIE 186 from the reign of Ousanas, as well as the concluding portion of *Monumentum Adulitanum II*, in which we are informed of the construction of roads by Aksumite kings following military victories. If RIE 190 does in fact document 'Ēzānā's efforts to strengthen his western frontier by stationing garrisons there and perhaps also by enlisting help from the Barya in keeping a close watch on the Noba, it might provide a context for the Noba attacks on the Barya and their neighbors described in RIE 189. The "royal houses" (*'byt*^{m} *ngš*^{m}=**'abyāta nəgūś*), literally "houses of the king," were presumably lodges at which 'Ēzānā intended to reside during tours of the frontier. That such structures were erected in the first place suggests that he planned to spend a fair amount of time on his frontier, and it may have been at one such lodge that he made the pacts with the Noba to which RIE 189 refers. As the Latin graffito from Muṣawwarāt al-Ṣafrā' indicates, it was not uncommon for rulers to receive foreign envoys at a temporary residence in a frontier region.

[564] Note, however, *ṣyḥ*^{m} in RIE 186:15 (Bernard et al. 1991: 252) as the *musnad* rendering of the verb *ṣēḥa*, "to make level," "to pave a road," "to build a road."

[565] §4.5.2.1.

We have seen that in RIE 186 Ousanas claims to have used the road he built to procure food for his subjects and his army, and if the construction of a similar road is among the activities described in Lines 2-6 of RIE 190, it is likely that ʻĒzānā would have used this road to facilitate the transport of supplies and foodstuffs to his army. This hypothesis is supported by an apparent reference to provisions in Lines 6-11: *w-kmz*^{m} *bṣḥkw*^{m} *ḏ*^{m} *d*^{m} *w-b-hy*^{m} *'zḏnh*^{m} *l-śrwt*^{m} *ymṣ*^{m} *šnq*^{m} *l-ʻlt*^{m} *ʻšr*^{m} *b-t'mn*^{m} *'gz'bḥr*^{m} *w-b-tblt*^{m} [..^{m}] *w-ẖlfn*^{m} *'mḏ*^{m} *b-z*^{m} *'gz'bḥr*^{m} *mrḥn*^{m} [..]*wl.*^{m} *ẖdgn*^{m} *nwṣ*^{m} *ḥrn*^{m} *w-wʻln*^{m} *w-ḥ[rn]*^{m} *w-btn*^{m} *w-qtln*^{m} [...][566] Transcribed into vocalized Geʻez, this passage can be tentatively read as follows: **wa-kama-zə baṣāḥkū za-d[awala?]*[567] *wa-ba-həyya 'azaznā la-sarāwīt yāmṣā['ū]*[568] *śanaqa la-ʻəlat ʻaśūr wa-ba-ta'amnōta 'Əgzī'abḥēr wa-ba-tanābəlt* [..?] *wa-ẖalafna 'əm-zə ba-zə 'Əgzī'abḥēr maḥarana [ba-da]wal(?) ẖadīgana nūṣā['ō]*[569] *ḥōrna wa-waʻalna wa-ḥōrna wa-batanna wa-qatalna...* "And thus I reached this country(?) and there we commanded the army divisions to bring provisions for ten days by the faith [in] God and with the envoys [..?]. We departed from there while God guided us [through the re]gion(?). He having allowed us to defeat them, we went forth by day. And we went forth and scattered and killed..." The remaining course of the narrative is impossible to follow, though its military context is clear from the number of times the verbs "to kill" (*qtl*^{m}=**qatala*)[570] and "to take prisoner" (*ḍww*^{m}=**ḍēwawa*)[571] are used throughout the inscription. The related word *ḍw*^{m} appears in Lines 33,

[566] RIE 190:6-11 (Bernard et al. 1991: 269, with modifications).

[567] The inscriptions gives us only *d*^{m}, representing the vowel /d/ with mimation. This is meaningless in Geʻez unless we take it as an orthographic error on the part of the Aksumite scribe. Since a foreign campaign is described in RIE 190, it is tempting to reconstruct *d*^{m} as **dwl*^{m} (=*dawal*). In support of this emendation one may note that *Mḍ* (Greek Μάτλια), the territory in which ʻĒzānā settled the defeated Beja earlier in his reign is called a *dwl* in RIE 185I:15 and RIE 185 II:16 (Bernard et al. 1991: 242, 243). The Greek account of ʻĒzānā's campaign against the Beja (RIE 270:21) gives τόπος ("place") as the equivalent of the Geʻez *dwl* (*Fontes Historiae Nubiorum III* 1998: 1095).

[568] The final letter /'/ is missing in the original text, but the imperfect of *'amṣə'a*, "to bring," fits perfectly here. The text is emended accordingly.

[569] Reading dubious.

[570] RIE 190:10, 16, 18, 32, 41 (Bernard et al. 1991: 269-70).

[571] RIE 190:13, 15, 16, 18, 20 (ibid.).

36, and 38[572] as a quantified noun and is probably to be read as *ḍəwā*, "prisoner." Men (*‘d*^{m}=**‘əd*), women (*’nst*^{m}=**’anəst*), and children (*dq*^{m}=**daqq*) figure as both casualties and prisoners of war,[573] as are officials (*mgbt*^{m}=**magabt*).[574] Quite probably these last are none other than the Danokwe, Dagale, Anakwe, and Ḥaware whose demise at the hands of the Aksumite troops is recorded in RIE 189.

Given its damaged state, the extant text of RIE 190 is predictably sparing in information on ethnic groups and toponyms. In addition to the reference to them in Line 4, the Noba are also mentioned in a fragmentary passage in Line 23: ...]^{m} *t‘ynt*^{m} *w-’md̲*^{m} *w-b*^{m} *Nb*^{m} (=*[?] *tə‘əyyənt wa-’əmzə wa-bō’a Nōbā*),[575] "...the troops, and after this the Noba entered." No reference to the Kushites is to be found in the inscription, though with so much of the text illegible it would be hazardous to read too much into their apparent absence. The geographical context of RIE 190 would seem to be the same as that of RIE 189 given the reference to the Takkazē (*Tkd̲*^{m}) in Line 22.[576] That the armed conflict recorded in the inscription took place in the Nile Valley and its eastern watershed is indicated by the mention of a river (*flg*^{m}=**falag*) in Line 24.[577] The passage in RIE 189 in which ‘Ēzānā casts the Noba's grain, copper, iron, and cotton into the Nile, after which the Noba themselves perish in the river while fleeing before the Aksumite invaders, comes to mind. As is so often the case, however, it is impossible to make any coherent sense of what might be the corresponding passage in RIE 190.

Regrettably this group of fragmentary passages represents the extent of the meaningful historical information furnished by RIE 190. This does not, however, diminish the importance of this inscription, for if the interpretation of the text proposed above is accepted, RIE 190 would add several important details to what we know about ‘Ēzānā's Nubian campaign and the background of Aksum's conflict with the Noba. Fearing the growing power of the Noba and perhaps skeptical of Kush's ability to contain this group, ‘Ēzānā stationed garrisons along

[572] Ibid.: 270.
[573] RIE 190:32, 33, 36, 38 (ibid.: 269-70).
[574] RIE 190:12, 25 (ibid.: 269).
[575] Bernard et al. 1991: 269.
[576] Ibid.
[577] Ibid.

his kingdom's western frontier. If *bry*^{m} is to be read in place of *bšy*^{m} in Line 1, it is possible that the Barya people mentioned in RIE 189 and RIE 271 were somehow involved with this development, though it is impossible to tell in what capacity. The development of local infrastructure, most notably the construction of a road and seasonal residences for the king, indicates that Aksum's western frontier came to receive greater attention during 'Ēzānā's reign, and that the king himself anticipated spending prolonged periods of time there. If the threat posed by the Noba was never enough to warrant an undertaking as massive as the large-scale resettlement of the Beja earlier in his reign, this might be a reflection of the latter's closer proximity to the Aksumite heartland. On the other hand, establishing garrisons and building roads and royal lodges were significant undertakings in their own right, in which case one might argue that 'Ēzānā simply adopted different policies towards the Noba and the Beja, without necessarily regarding either group as a greater threat than the other. This brings us back to the question of the scale of 'Ēzānā's Nubian campaign. While the spoils of war seized by 'Ēzānā's troops in Nubia are modest when compared with the vast quantity of livestock seized centuries earlier by the Kushite king Nastaseñ, it could be that 'Ēzānā was less interested in Nubia's economic potential than in simply making a show of force there.

4.6. Assessing the Impact of Aksum on Nubia in the Fourth Century

Exactly how serious the impact of the Aksumite invasions were on Upper Nubia is hard to say. While RIE 189 provides numbers of the prisoners of war, the archaeological evidence is ambiguous and sheds little if any direct light on the matter. Tempting though it is to identify invasions in the archaeological record based on traces of destruction at a given site, one must in such circumstances prove that the destruction was deliberate, and even if this can be demonstrated it is often unclear whether such signs of violence can be attributed to an invasion from without or to internal upheaval. As for the textual evidence regarding Aksum's wars with Nubia, we are totally reliant on Aksumite sources. No Kushite—much less Noba—account of the conflict survives, and despite some progress towards its decipherment in recent years the

Meroitic language is still imperfectly understood.[578] Thus, should a Kushite inscription recording either of the two Aksumite invasions of Nubia be discovered at some point in the future, the problem of understanding the language would still remain.

4.6.1. The Archaeological Evidence

Bearing in mind the inherent ambiguities of such archaeological evidence as conflagration, we will begin our discussion of the long-term Aksumite impact on Kush with a look at the traces of destruction at several temples at Meroë, dating from the latter part of the city's history. The temples in question, built in the first century CE as determined by C^{14} dating, were in several cases occupied by squatters during their later phases. According to Shinnie and Anderson, several of these temples "were destroyed by fire and showed signs of having undergone a deliberate destruction that marked the end of squatter occupation."[579] Thus in the case of Temple KC100, a thick, hard burn layer of charcoal, reddened earth, and ash 3-5 cm thick sealed the entire site of the temple.[580] Four cracks radiating out from the center of the temple's sandstone altar, together with fragments of the altar found scattered throughout the structure, are interpreted by Shinnie and Anderson as evidence of deliberate destruction.[581] Temples KC104 and M720 were also destroyed by fire, and the fragments of statues found within the mix of ash and charcoal in the former have been interpreted as further evidence of intention destruction.[582] Much though this evidence recalls 'Ēzānā's claim in RIE 189 to have destroyed the idols in the Noba's temples, we are still faced with the absence of Meroë from that inscription, in addition to which it is not clear whether all of the statue fragments found in Temple KC104 actually originated in the temple or came from elsewhere.[583] Whether the earlier Aksumite invasion recorded in Greek in RIE 286 and SNM 24841 was responsible for the destruction of these temples is certainly

[578] For a thorough and up-to-date study of the Meroitic language, see Rilly 2007.
[579] Shinnie and Anderson 2004: 64.
[580] Ibid.: 20.
[581] Ibid.
[582] Ibid.: 35-6, 62.
[583] Ibid.: 62.

possible, but no more so than their destruction at the hands of the Noba. Meanwhile, such temples at Meroë as KC101 and M282 revealed no trace of deliberate destruction at all,[584] and while some blackening by fire was noted in the latter structure it was limited to a small area.[585] Given the association of burned animal bones with charcoal in Temple M282,[586] it is likely that this fire was lit by the squatters to prepare food. Similar activities are attested at Structure KC103, possibly another temple, in the form of fragments of animal bones associated with charcoal, together with two cooking pots and a bowl.[587] Thus, while it is not impossible that the destruction of several of Meroë's temples can be attributed to an attack on the city—whether by the Aksumites or the Noba—it is equally conceivable that at least some of the conflagration noted at the temples was accidental, caused perhaps by cooking-fires lit by squatters which got out of hand. That Temples KC 100, KC101, KC104, and M282 were occupied by squatters in the first place indicates that these structures had long ceased to serve their religious and economic function, in which case they would hardly have been attractive targets for foreign invaders intent on seizing booty.

Moving down the Nile, we find further signs of destruction by fire at the Kushite sites of Jabal Barkal, Sanam, Kawa, and Tabo. The conflagrations at the first three sites were initially associated by Reisner and Griffith with the Roman invasion of Nubia in 24 BCE,[588] but were later identified by Kirwan with destruction by 'Ēzānā's army.[589] Edwards has challenged Kirwan's claim that the Aksumite army ever operated this far north, but concedes that "a sudden, catastrophic episode" does seem to have marked the last use of Kawa's temple.[590] As for the destruction of much of the Jabal Barkal complex, Edwards concurs with the original theory proposed by Reisner and Griffith, regarding the Roman invasion a much likelier explanation than

[584] Ibid.: 44, 51.
[585] Ibid.: 51.
[586] Ibid.
[587] Ibid.: 55.
[588] On this invasion, see Török 1997: 451-4.
[589] Edwards 1989: 172.
[590] Ibid.

'Ēzānā's campaign.[591] In light of the Ge'ez graffito from Kawa, Edwards' reservations about an Aksumite presence in that region must be qualified, but as stated above the context in which this graffito was left is uncertain. In the case of the temple at Tabo, Edwards argues that the burning there occurred after a period of abandonment, and that there was nothing to show a violent end to the use of the temple.[592] Attributing the conflagration to an Aksumite invasion is therefore dubious.

It is not suggested here that we should doubt 'Ēzānā's claims to have destroyed the temples and storehouses of the Noba and burned their towns of brick and straw. Rather, we should exercise caution in attributing traces of destruction at Upper Nubian sites to Aksumite attacks, all the more so given that RIE 189 records violent destruction at only some of the towns in the region, of which those that are named, even if correctly identified, have yet to be excavated. The straw towns burned by the Aksumites are in any event unlikely to have left easily detectable traces in the archaeological record, though a much-needed archaeological survey of the bend in the Nile between Meroë and Napata may well shed light on the matter.

In any assessment of Aksum's impact on fourth-century Nubia it must also be remembered that invasions tell us only part of the story. As is evident from the royal titles of Ousanas and 'Ēzānā, the Aksumites regarded Kush as a vassal state. This would in theory imply that Kush paid regular tribute to Aksum, as argued by Burstein on the basis of RIE 286. It could be that so long as tribute was paid the Aksumites saw no need to maintain a permanent military or administrative presence in Nubia. As for what form Nubian tribute took, and for how long it was paid, neither the archaeological nor the epigraphic evidence provides an answer. Since no royal inscriptions have been identified for the period of almost two hundred years between 'Ēzānā and Kālēb, it is impossible to tell whether 'Ēzānā's immediate successors continued to lay claim to Kush, much less effectively ruled Nubia. Furthermore, what precious little Aksumite material has come to light in Nubia only emphasizes the region's isolation from Aksum's political

[591] Ibid. Whether the Roman army reached Napata is questioned by Török 1997: 453-4.
[592] Edwards 1989: 172.

and economic orbit. A case in point is a copper coin of an anonymous Aksumite king found at Meroë. The coin was first published by Shinnie and Bradley in their excavation report, in which they date it to the mid-fourth century,[593] thus making the coin roughly contemporary with the two Aksumite invasions of Nubia launched by Ousanas and 'Ēzānā respectively. This date, however, is contested by Török, who notes that the obverse of the coin shows a royal bust with the inscription ΒΑCΙΛΕΥC ("king"), while the reverse features a "Maltese" cross within a wreath with the inscription ΤΟΥΤΟ ΑΡΕΣΕ ΤΗ ΧΩΡΑ ("may this please the country").[594] Since, Török argues, this type of cross appears for the first time on obverses of mints of Theodosius II (408-450), no Aksumite coin imitating this particular Roman obverse type could have been issued before the end of the first quarter of the fifth century.[595] The coin, then, is much too late to have any connection with the Aksumite military operations in Nubia during the fourth century. Moreover, since no further Aksumite coins have come to light in Nubia it would be hazardous to take this isolated fifth-century coin as evidence of a permanent Aksumite presence at Meroë following these operations. How the coin reached Meroë in the first place is not clear. Though copper coins were minted by the Aksumites primarily for domestic use, as indicated by discovery of significant numbers of such coins at Aksumite domestic occupation sites dating to the fifth and sixth centuries,[596] the discovery of a few Aksumite copper coins in India[597] suggests that some were used abroad for small transactions. While the anonymous Aksumite coin found by Shinnie's team could have reached Meroë in this manner, the city itself was at most occupied by squatters during the fifth century and was thus hardly a center for trade, in which case it is unlikely that the coin could have come with Aksumite merchants. On the other hand, imitations of Aksumite copper coins are attested at numerous sites in Egypt—some 70 copper Aksumite imitations have been found at the Christian

[593] Shinnie and Bradley 1980: 185, 211 (Fig. 76).
[594] Török 1985: 22.
[595] Ibid.
[596] Phillipson 2009b: 364.
[597] Metlich 2006: 102.

pilgrimage site at Abū Mīnā (45 km south of Alexandria) alone[598]—and could conceivably have found their way south. If so, it is not impossible that the single Aksumite coin from Meroë has no direct connection with Aksum at all.

4.6.2. The Graeco-Roman Textual Evidence

What if anything the Roman world knew about Aksumite relations with, and activities in, Nubia, remains an open question. Dating as it does from the late third or early fourth century, the tantalizingly laconic Latin graffito from Muṣawwarāt al-Ṣafrā' indicates that the Kushites had the opportunity to discuss these matters with Roman diplomats at about the time that their Aksumite neighbor was expanding to the west and the north. If so, such a discussion has left no trace in the historical record. In the *Vita Constantini* of Eusebius of Caesarea (d. 339) we are told that an embassy of Blemmyes, Ethiopians, and Indians paid their respects to Constantine I in 336[599]—an intriguing report indeed if, following late antique habit,[600] we are to understand the "Ethiopians" as Nubians and the "Indians" as Aksumites.[601] Of these peoples Eusebius says only that they brought gifts to the Roman emperor, and that some were "honored with Roman posts of dignity."[602] Significantly, since he makes a distinction between the Beja, Kushites, and Aksumites it would seem that in 336 Kush was independent of Aksum and that whatever authority Ousanas might have hoped to establish over Kush had come to an end. 'Ēzānā's claim to Kush, as expressed in his royal title in those inscriptions of his predating his Nubian campaign of 360, would thus be a political fiction.

The only Graeco-Roman source that refers directly to Aksumite relations with Kush is the *Aithiopika* of Heliodorus,[603] a fictional story of an Ethiopian princess and priestess of Apollo who falls in love with, and eventually ends up marrying, a Thessalian nobleman. In the course of the novel we are told of the kingdom of Meroë and its

598 Noeske 1998: 257.
599 Eusebius, *Vita Constantini* 4.7 (*Fontes Historiae Nubiorum III* 1998: 1079-81).
600 Mayerson 1993.
601 *Fontes Historiae Nubiorum III* 1998: 1081; Török 2011: 523.
602 *Fontes Historiae Nubiorum III* 1998: 1081.
603 Heliodorus 1935-43.

successful efforts to fend off an invasion by the Achaemenid Persians. Although Herodotus' account of the ill-fated Nubian campaign of Cambyses (530-523 BCE)[604] is the source of this part of the story, the Aksumites (Αὐξωμιτῶν) make an anachronistic cameo appearance when, following his defeat of the Persians, the king of Meroë receives representatives from his allies and well-wishers.[605] For their part the Aksumites bring what seems to be a giraffe as a gift.[606] That Aksum should figure in a story set in the sixth century BCE is a testament to its author's inventive use of information about Africa in a fictional setting.[607] That aside, the Aksumite reference invites speculation as to what the author of the *Aithiopika* might have known about the politics of northeast Africa. Of Heliodorus himself we know next to nothing. Hailing from Emesa (modern Ḥimṣ in western Syria), his claim to descent from "the race of the sun" indicates clearly that he was a pagan and, judging from his name, a devotee of the Helios cult in Emesa.[608] But if Heliodorus gives no information about himself that would shed light on when exactly he lived, his *Aithiopika* can be assigned to sometime in the second half of the fourth century CE in light of its account of a siege of Syene (=Aswān) by the Achaemenids, which seems to be based on a description by Ephraem the Syrian of the Sāsānid Persians' siege of Nisibis in 350.[609] If so, then Heliodorus would have been writing at about the time of the Aksumite campaigns in Nubia, though whether or not some historical kernel can be detected in his novel is quite another matter.

As Heliodorus explains in the *Aithiopika*, the Aksumites who paid their respects to the Kushites "were not tributaries but were friends and allies of the [Kushite] king."[610] Burstein sees in this an allusion to peaceful relations between Aksum and Kush which, while totally out of place in a sixth-century BCE context, might reflect a real friendship between Aksum and Meroë at the time when Heliodorus was writing.[611]

[604] Herodotus 3.17-25.
[605] Heliodorus, *Les Éthiopiques* 10.27.1.
[606] Ibid.
[607] On this point, see Morgan 1982.
[608] Giangrande 1970: 493.
[609] Bowersock 1994: 44-8.
[610] Heliodorus 1943: III: 107-8.
[611] Burstein 1981: 48.

To take Burstein's theory a step further one might even posit some relationship based on gift-exchange between the two kingdoms. As has been argued in this study, Aksumite claims to Kush more often than not reflected an ideal rather than a reality, so it is not impossible that the political rhetoric of Aksumite rule of Kush conceals what was in fact some system of diplomatic gift-exchange. Against this, however, one may note that in Heliodorus' *Aithiopika* it is the Aksumites who bring a gift to the Kushites, with no mention of the Kushites giving anything in return. There is even reason to doubt whether the *Aithiopika* is a trustworthy source on which to base theories about Aksumite relations with Kush in the first place, as Heliodorus mentions the presence, side by side with the Aksumites, of envoys sent not only from the Troglodytes and Blemmyes but also, most implausibly, the South Arabians and Seres (=Chinese), on the occasion of the Kushite victory over the Persians.[612] A similar conjunction of Aksumites, South Arabians, Blemmyes, and Chinese at Aurelian's triumphal procession in 274—albeit as prisoners and accompanied by a host of other peoples from Asia and Europe—is described in the *Historia Augusta*, another fourth-century work.[613] In light of this, the *Aithiopika*'s reference to Aksumite envoys visiting the Kushite king, like the description of the siege of Syene, may be nothing more than an extraneous topos grafted onto a Nubian setting for no other purpose than its exoticizing effect. In fact, it has even been argued that the *Historia Augusta*'s mention of an Aksumite presence at Aurelian's victory celebrations is itself not historical at all but is rather the product of a later emendation of the *Historia Augusta*.[614] Therefore, given the spurious, second-hand nature

[612] Heliodorus 10.25-26.

[613] *Historia Augusta* 33.4-5; Bowersock 1994: 49. Although the *Historia Augusta* presents itself as the work of no fewer than six authors writing between the reigns of Diocletian (284-305) and Constantine (306-337)—the "Life of Aurelian" which concerns us at present being attributed to Flavius Vopiscus —text-critical studies suggest that the *Historia* is in fact the work of a single author, and that it was written between 395 and 399 (Barnes 1978: 13-18).

[614] Hohl (1985: 401 [n. 204]) believes that the passage about the foreign presence in Aurelian's procession has been tainted by an ahistorical insertion of the name of the Aksumites in place of the broader category of "Ethiopians" which, as we have seen, did not come to refer to the Aksumites until the mid-fourth century, when it appears in ʿĒzānā's Greek inscription RIE 270*bis* as the equivalent of the *Ḥbšt/Ḥbśt* of his Geʿez inscriptions RIE 185*bis* I and RIE 185*bis* II (see §3.3.2). For his part, Hartmann (2008: 319 [n.

of Heliodorus' information on Aksum and Kush alike, it seems best to reject the *Aithiopika* as a source from which we can derive any useful information about relations between the two kingdoms.

4.6.3. The Fall of Kush: Was Aksum to Blame?

Thus far it has been argued that Aksum was directly involved with Nubian political affairs at least as early as the reign of Ousanas, and that this involvement initially took the form of a military campaign against Meroë itself. Aksum at this stage seems to have required little of Kush apart from tribute—however that might have been perceived by the Kushites—and in light of the growing power of the Noba during this period it is probable that the extension of Aksumite political influence to the middle Nile Valley was strategic rather than economic in nature. That Aksum and Kush never appear to have vied for control of each other's trade routes supports the contention of the present study that Aksumite intervention in Nubia was not primarily motivated by economic concerns. By the time Ousanas' son 'Ēzānā came to power, the Noba had reached Aksum's western frontier and Kush was incapable of doing anything about it. Although 'Ēzānā did take up arms against the Kushites, these last were of only secondary importance in his Nubian campaign and the exact nature of their relationship with the Noba is not altogether clear. Based on archaeological evidence, most notably the cessation of royal burials at Meroë sometime in the middle of the fourth century and the rapid decay of the city itself from that point on, it is clear that Kush as a political entity collapsed around that time. Since this is about the time at which Aksum invaded Nubia, the question then arises as to whether the fall of Kush can be attributed to Aksumite invasions.

Before answering this question a clarification of what is meant by the Kushite decline is in order. As noted above,[615] Kush maintained commercial and political ties to the Roman world into the fourth

69]) regards as "zweifellos unhistorisch" the entire description of the royal spectacle with its animals and foreign peoples bringing gifts. The participation of foreigners in the spectacle—moreover as captives—seems to reflect an idealized image of the Roman emperor as the ruler of the entire world. This same idea is expressed later on in the *Historia Augusta* (41.10-11), where we are told that the Saracens, Blemmyes, Aksumites, Bactrians, Seres, Hibernians, Albanians, Armenians, and Indians revered Aurelian as a god!

[615] §3.3.4.

century, and was even at that late period in firm control of Lower Nubia. Such decline as took place cannot therefore be seen as a long-term process lasting several centuries. Rather it would appear that Kush came to an end in a relatively swift collapse. As for when this might have occurred, we have Török's argument for dating the Kushite collapse to c. 360-370, the evidence for which, specifically the funerary equipment of Bagrawiyya W 130, has been discussed above.[616] Whether Bagrawiyya W 130 can be dated this precisely may in fact prove not to be as significant as Török makes it out to be, for the cessation of pyramid building at Meroë need not imply the end of the Kushite state itself, but rather shift in the cultural values of the Kushite elite.[617] Highly suggestive in this regard is a large tumulus grave surrounded by an enclosure found by Lepsius at Meroë in 1844, recalling the tumulus burials of rulers at the very beginning of Kushite history at al-Kurrū.[618] Based on excavations at sites in Lower Nubia it is known that tumulus burials were the standard for royalty and commoner alike in post-Kushite times,[619] in which case the large tumulus at Meroë may mark a reversion to earlier types of royal burial at the very end of Kushite history.[620] To this one might add the tumulus at El Hobagi, though the Kushite identity of its occupant has yet to be decisively proven. Since the Meroë tumulus is no longer visible and its location is uncertain, we are deprived of insight into what may be the burial of one of the last rulers of Kush.[621] As further evidence for the survival of the Kushite capital into the second half of the fourth century one could cite the *Res Gestae* of Ammianus Marcellinus, which names Meroë as a city of the "Ethiopians" (i.e., Kushites).[622] While it is not impossible that this reference to Meroë is an anachronistic detail culled from earlier sources, the fact that Ammianus made a journey to Egypt at some

[616] §4.5.1.
[617] Welsby 1996: 199-200.
[618] Ibid.: 200.
[619] Ibid.: 201.
[620] That the tumulus at Meroë cannot itself be a tomb from the early Kushite period like those at al-Kurrū is clear from the fact that the earliest graves at Meroë post-date the tumulus-burials at al-Kurrū by several centuries.
[621] Welsby 1996: 200.
[622] Ammianus Marcellinus, *Res Gestae* 22.15.2 (*Fontes Historiae Nubiorum III* 1998: 1113).

point between 371 and 378 raises the possibility that he had access there to more up-to-date information about the regions to the south.[623] That said, the mere existence of Meroë in the 370s is not in itself proof that a kingdom of Kush still existed at that time.

All things considered, then, it seems best to avoid assigning a fixed date to the fall of Kush. Without such a date, the solution to the question of Aksum's role in Kush' demise can only rely on the epigraphic material. In this study it has been argued that none of 'Ēzānā's inscriptions say anything about Meroë, and it has been argued as well that the geographical details provided by these inscriptions suggest that the Aksumite king's invasion of Nubia targeted the region to the north of the Kushite capital. Since 'Ēzānā's campaign was primarily a punitive expedition against the Noba, the at best secondary role of the Kushites in the conflict is not surprising. Furthermore, in contrast to the earlier Aksumite invasion of Nubia, launched—so it has been argued in this study—in Ousanas' reign and recorded in Greek in RIE 286 and SNM 24841, 'Ēzānā's Nubian campaign does not appear to have involved a confrontation with a ruler of Kush, if only because no such ruler is mentioned in any of 'Ēzānā's inscriptions. Could it be, then, that it was not 'Ēzānā's invasion of Nubia but rather that launched by Ousanas which dealt the final blow to Kush? On the whole this seems improbable, for RIE 286 mentions the imposition of tribute, presumably on the Kushites given that the inscription was erected at Meroë, and the Aksumites could hardly have been expected Kush to pay tribute if they had already destroyed it outright. If during 'Ēzānā's reign there were still some elements in Kush who regarded Aksum as their protector and/or sovereign, it comes as no surprise that the region of Meroë was not attacked by 'Ēzānā's army. But since RIE 189 records a punitive expedition against the Kushites it would appear that such a pro-Aksumite attitude was far from universal in Kush—if indeed it existed at all. Either Meroë's central authority had lost its ability to enforce a consistent policy of vassalage to Aksum in the more northerly regions of Kush, or else Kush itself had become politically fragmented. That some Kushites decided to throw in their lot with the Noba is quite possible in such a scenario, which may explain 'Ēzānā's

[623] Török 1988: 32; idem *Fontes Historiae Nubiorum III* 1998: 1114.

punitive expedition against the Kushites to the north of Meroë, described in RIE 189. Significantly, while RIE 189 reports that the Kushite towns of Tabito and Fertoti were captured by the Noba, it gives no indication as to whether the takeover was violent or peaceful.

A full discussion of the reasons for the collapse of the Kushite state is beyond the scope of this study and is in any event in need of further research. There were undoubtedly numerous causes of the Kushite collapse. One of these causes seems to have been political fragmentation, the effects of which may be observed in the abandonment of Meroë's royal pyramid cemetery at Bagrawiyya North around the middle of the fourth century and the development of tumulus cemeteries with high-status burials all over Kushite territory beginning in the second half of that century.[624] In light of the cultural continuities between the Kushite and post-Kushite periods such fragmentation is likely to have been internally generated.[625] However, although the Aksumite invasions in the reigns of Ousanas and ʿĒzānā and the consequent seizure of booty and prisoners of war could only have had an adverse effect on Upper Nubia, none of the extant inscriptions indicate that Aksum was responsible for overthrowing the entire Kushite state. As Edwards cautions, discussions of the so-called "fall of Meroë" have for too long been modeled on the fall of the Roman Empire and have consequently laid too much emphasis on specific events such as foreign invasions.[626] This being the case, scholars must resist the temptation to assign a precise date to the fall of Kush on the basis of Aksumite inscriptions, for the chronology of Aksum's campaigns against Nubia and the chronology of the final years of Kush are two separate issues entirely. If the lack of evidence for any Aksumite invasion of Nubia after ʿĒzānā's reign is any indication, it would seem that once ʿĒzānā had dealt with the Noba threat there was no need for further intervention in Nubia and the region was left to its own devices. If lack of documentation from fifth-century Aksum is any indication,[627] the Ethiopian kingdom was either

[624] Török 2011: 519-20, 522.
[625] Edwards 2011: 509-10.
[626] Ibid.: 503.
[627] The only historical material from fifth-century Aksum is coinage, which provides little more than the names of Aksumite kings during that period.

too weak to enforce its authority in Nubia or felt that the possible benefits of doing so would not have repaid the effort. All the same, the experience of fourth-century Aksumite rule in Nubia, however ephemeral, left an indelible mark on Aksumite royal propaganda, such that the fiction of Kushite vassalage was maintained some two centuries later in the reigns of Kālēb and his son and successor Wa'zeb, long after the kingdom of Kush itself had ceased to exist.

5. After Kush: Aksum and Nubia in the Sixth Century CE

An able and powerful ruler, Kālēb (c. 510-540) compares favorably with ʻĒzānā as one of Aksum's greatest military leaders. By far the most significant development in his reign was the conquest of the South Arabian kingdom of Ḥimyar, the successor to Saba' and the polity which since the early fourth century had enjoyed uncontested dominion over South Arabia from the Tihāma to the Ḥaḍramawt. In 518, an invasion force sent by Kālēb against South Arabia brought to power a Christian Ḥimyarite potentate named Maʻdīkarib Yaʻfur, who ruled the region as Aksum's client. A rebellion led by one Yūsuf 'As'ar Yath'ar (c. 522-525), a Ḥimyarite Jew, brought an end to this client regime. The Christian community of South Arabia, comprising not only local converts but also a significant Ethiopian minority at the Ḥimyarite capital of Ẓafār and the Red Sea port of al-Mukhā', was massacred by Yūsuf's troops, resulting in a second Aksumite invasion in the spring of 525, this time led by Kālēb in person. After Kālēb's victory over Yūsuf power was once again entrusted to a Ḥimyarite Christian, in this case a recent convert by the name of Sumūyafaʻ 'Ashwaʻ, who ruled with the assistance of Aksumite officials appointed by Kālēb.[628] It was only when 'Abrehā, a general in the Aksumite army stationed in Ḥimyar, rebelled at some point after 531[629] that Aksum lost direct control of South Arabia, though after two failed attempts by Kālēb to depose him 'Abrehā agreed to pay tribute to Kālēb's successor Waʻzeb (c. 540-560).[630] Well documented though Kālēb's activities in

[628] For a detailed discussion of Kālēb's invasions of Ḥimyar, see Hatke 2011.

[629] The first epigraphically dated mention of 'Abrehā is in a Sabaic inscription dated Dhū-Qiyāẓ$^{\bar{a}n}$ 657 (June 547), and though 'Abrehā undoubtedly came to power before this date, he could not have done so before 531, when we last hear of Sumūyafaʻ 'Ashwaʻ in connection with a Roman diplomatic mission to Ḥimyar (Gajda 2009: 116).

[630] Procopius, *De Bell. Pers.* 1.20.4-8. In this source 'Abrehā is given as Abramos, while Kālēb is referred to as Hellestheaeus, a corruption of the king's alternative name 'Ella-'Aṣbeḥā (literally, "he who has brought the dawn"). Waʻzeb is not mentioned by name by Procopius, but it is obvious that the anonymous successor of "Hellestheaeus" to whom Procopius refers is to be identified with him, since Waʻzeb refers to himself as the son of 'Ella-'Aṣbeḥā (*wld 'l-'ṣbḥ=*walda 'Ella-'Aṣbeḥā*), i.e. Kālēb, in his inscription from Aksum (RIE 192:7 [Bernard et al. 1991: 275]).

South Arabia are, however, the extent and nature of Aksumite relations with Nubia during his reign and the period thereafter are obscure. The evidence for such relations, all of it dating from the sixth century, is limited to Kālēb's title in his inscription from Aksum (RIE 191) and the Greek *Martyrium Arethae*, while for period after Kālēb we find mention of Aksumite contact with Nubia in the ecclesiastical history of John of Ephesus. In our survey of this material, all of which dates from the sixth century, we will begin with the Nubian references in Kālēb's title, which represent an intriguing mixture of both anachronistic and innovative elements.

5.1. Kālēb and Nubia: RIE 191

In RIE 191, written in Ge'ez but employing the same form of unvocalized *musnad* script used in the fourth-century inscriptions of Ousanas and 'Ēzānā, Kālēb proudly styles himself "King of Aksum and Ḥimyar and D̲h̲ū-Raydān and Saba' and Salḥīn and Ṭawd^{um} and Yamānāt and Tihāma and Ḥaḍramawt and all of their Arabs and the Beja and the Noba and Kush and Ṣēyāmō and *DRBT*" (*ngš 'ksm w-Ḥmr w-z-Rydn w-Sb' w-Slḥn w-Ṭd^{m} w-z-Ymnt w-Thmt w-Ḥḍrmwt w-kl 'rbm w-z-Bg w-Nb w-z-Ks w-Ṣym w-z-Drbt=*nəgūśa 'Aksūm wa-Ḥəmēr wa-Raydān wa-Saba' wa-Salḥīn wa-Ṭōd wa-Yamānāt wa-Tihāmāt wa-Ḥaḍramawt wa-k^{w}əllū 'Arabōmū wa-za-Bəgā wa-Nōbā wa-za-Kāsū wa-Ṣəyāmō wa-za-DRBT*).[631] Most of the military operations recorded in RIE 191 were mounted against African peoples, such as the 'Ag^{w}ēzāt (*'gzt*) of northern Ethiopia,[632] who had already clashed with Aksumite forces in 'Ēzānā's reign.[633] None of Kālēb's African campaigns seem to have extended as far as Nubia, which apart from the references to Noba and Kush in the king's title is never mentioned in the inscription. Though none of these African campaigns can be cross-referenced with dated references to northeast African affairs in Graeco-Roman sources, an approximate date can be established for RIE 191 on the basis of the allusions to South Arabian events towards the end of the inscription. Only one invasion of Ḥimyar is mentioned, and since this is stated to have been led by one Ḥayyān

[631] RIE 191:8-10 (Bernard et al. 1991: 272).
[632] RIE 191: 12 (ibid.).
[633] RIE 187: 9-12 (ibid.: 256).

Salabān[634] (*Ḥyn Slbn*),[635] who is undoubtedly the *ḤYWN'* known from the Syriac *Book of the Ḥimyarites* as the commander of the Kālēb's first Ḥimyarite campaign in 518, but not of his second in 525, RIE 191 can be dated to sometime between 518 and 525.[636] As the Ḥimyarite campaign and the construction of a church in Ḥimyar in its immediate aftermath are the last events mentioned in RIE 191, it is likely that this inscription dates from shortly after the first invasion of Ḥimyar, most likely c. 519.

As we have seen, it is most improbable that Ousanas and 'Ēzānā ever ruled South Arabia, the inclusion of Ḥimyar and Saba' in their lists of vassals notwithstanding. On the other hand, their claims of sovereignty over Kush, superficial and ephemeral though this may have been, are supported by the epigraphic record of Aksumite military operations in Nubia during the mid-fourth century. With Kālēb's reign we find the exact opposite situation in that there exists abundant documentation of Aksumite activity in South Arabia[637] but a total absence of similar documentation regarding Nubia. From Greek, Syriac, and Sabaic sources it is well known that Kālēb had appointed client-kings of his choosing to rule on his behalf in Ḥimyar, a fact which clearly indicates the establishment of Aksumite suzerainty in South Arabia.[638] Independently of each other, Syriac and Sabaic sources also refer to an Ethiopian community in South Arabia that numbered in the hundreds,[639] a claim that receives support from the discovery of Aksumite domestic pottery at Qāni' on Yemen's southern coast, which the site's excavator Alexander Sedov suggests may be evidence of Aksumite settlement.[640] To this we must add the hoards of Aksumite

[634] *Slbn*<Tha'labān?

[635] RIE 191: 34-5 (Bernard et al. 1991: 273).

[636] On the name and identity of Ḥayyān Salabān and the significance of this individual for the chronology of Kālēb's wars against Ḥimyar, see Hatke 2011: 124-36. There is no evidence that Ḥayyān took part in either of Kālēb's failed attempts to depose 'Abrehā in Ḥimyar, and according to Procopius (*De Bell. Pers.* 1.20.5) the first of these was led by a relative of Kālēb—something which Ḥayyān, who seems to have been a South Arabian, was not.

[637] Hatke 2011.

[638] Ibid.: 166-76, 216-17, 250, 299-311, 333-4, 347-8.

[639] Ibid.: 196, 200-3.

[640] Sedov 1996: 22; idem 2007: 85.

gold coins that have come to light in Yemen.[641] We also have direct references in foreign sources, as well as in RIE 191, to the effect that Kālēb established churches throughout South Arabia.[642] Other churches referred to in South Arabian inscriptions in connection with Yūsuf 'As'ar Yath'ar's attacks on Ḥimyar's Ethiopian community in 522/3[643] may have been built by Ethiopian expatriates in the period following Kālēb's first invasion of South Arabia in 518. Finally, there are the Aksumite inscriptions in Ge'ez from Yemen which record Kālēb's victory over Yūsuf's forces in 525.[644] Of Aksumite activities on this scale in sixth-century Nubia there is simply no evidence. In light of the Aksumite trade with Sasu described by Cosmas Indicopleustes, contact between Aksum and the kingdom of Alodia to the west of Sasu during the sixth century might be expected. Confirmation of such contact does indeed survive in the form of two fragments of Soba Ware, typical of Alodia, which have been found at Aksum and which probably date from the sixth century.[645] Indirect evidence for trade between Nubia and Aksum from roughly the same period may also survive in the form of a fragment of a footed bowl from a site near Heis on the northern Somali coast.[646] This sherd is thought to have been manufactured either at Aswān c. 300-500 CE or, more probably, in Lower Nubia c. 500-600 CE.[647] It is more likely that this item reached Somalia by sea than by

[641] Munro-Hay 1989a; Hahn 2000. A sixth-century letter in Greek from Gabalayn, deriving from the Blemmyan community in Upper Egypt, mentions the receipt of eight gold *solidi*, which are described as Νουβαρ[...] (Török 1988: 66). Though this curious word has been interpreted as "Nobadian," Török is undoubtedly correct that the scribe either misunderstood something or rendered it unintelligible, for the existence of Nobadian currency is quite improbable (ibid.). Likewise, the absence of Aksumite gold coins in Nubia militates against any suggestion that the *solidi* referred to in the letter from Gabalayn were Aksumite gold coins. To the extent that foreign currency was known at all in Nubia, it functioned not as currency but rather as a type of bullion which could be traded like other rare items imported from abroad (Gradel 2007: 145).

[642] Hatke 2011: 137-46, 272, 349.

[643] Ibid.: 217-19.

[644] Bernard et al. 1991: 284-8, 349-3. For a detailed discussion of this epigraphic material and its historical significance, see Hatke 2011: 355-84.

[645] Phillips 1997: 455; idem 2003a: 440.

[646] Chittick 1982: 53.

[647] Ibid.

land,[648] and since Nubia, in contrast to Aksum, had no seafaring tradition, the bowl may well have arrived as cargo on an Aksumite ship. That the ship may have been from Roman Egypt is, however, also possible. Whatever the case, there are no grounds for supposing the existence of particularly intensive trade between Nubia and Aksum, even if the Soba sherds from Aksum do demonstrate the maintenance of commercial ties between the northern Ethiopian Highlands and the middle Nile in the sixth century. All the same, such material can hardly be used as evidence of Aksumite rule in Nubia during that period. Quite apart from the spuriousness of Kālēb's claim to Nubia in the first place, there is the obvious anachronism of Kush's presence in his list of vassals in RIE 191, dating as it does from nearly two centuries after the collapse of the kingdom of Kush.[649]

[648] Ibid.

[649] Only in a few isolated instances was "Kush" used as a name for Nubia after the fourth century. Among these is the ffth-century Meroitic inscription of the Nobadian king Kharamadoye from Kalabsha, in which we find a reference to Kush (*Qes*), though as a geographical, rather than a political, term (*Fontes Historiae Nubiorum III* 1998: 1104, 1107; Török 2011: 517). In foreign sources from Late Antiquity "Kushite" would appear to have become largely divorced from any memory of the kingdom of Kush. Thus in fifth-century Coptic texts the term is employed in a generalized manner as an alternative for "Blemmyan" or "barbarian" (Török, loc. cit.: 524), while in the *Edessene Apocalypse*, a Miaphysite text in Syriac dating from c. 691/2, we are told that Alexander the Great was given an Ethiopian consort named Kūshyaṯ "by the king of Kush, and they are called Nub[ians]" (*men malkā ḏ-Kūš w-hennōn meṯqrēn Nūḇ*) (*Edessene Apocalypse*=Nau 1917: 432-3 [Syriac text]). While this text would seem to preserve a vague memory of a Nubian kingdom called Kush, the term *Kūšāyē* had by this time become so widely accepted in Syriac-speaking circles as a generic term for black Africans—to the extent that even the Aksumites were called *Kūšāyē*—that some qualification was needed when the anonymous author of the *Edessene Apocalypse* used the term to refer to Nubians. An Old Nubian graffito of medieval date from Jabal Abū Nagīla in northern Kordofan has long been thought to contain an illusion to Kush. When first read, this graffito was taken to refer to a man named Anena who came "from Kush when Aaron was king" (Arkell 1951). Although the graffito itself bears no date it was confidently assigned to the Nubia's Christian period in light of the cross that accompanies the text, as well as the use of Old Nubian, which was not written before Nubia's conversion to Christian in the second half of the sixth century, and which fell out of use as a written language after the Islamization of Nubia during the later Middle Ages. In light of a more recent reading of the Abū Nagīla graffito, however, this apparent reference to Kush is untenable (Ochała 2011). Far from referring to a man from Kush, the graffito instead mentions one Siti, a Christian Nubian king known to have

Easy though it is to dismiss the mention of Kush in Kālēb's list of vassals in RIE 191 as a political fiction created by copying parts of the titles borne by Ousanas and 'Ēzānā, Kālēb's title, whatever the dubious historicity of some of its claims, is of interest in that it contains several innovative features that set it apart from those of the king's fourth-century predecessors. The innovations are most noticeable in the list of Arabian vassals in RIE 191, which include not only the kingdoms of Ḥimyar and Saba' with their respective royal citadels of Dhū-Raydān at Ẓafār and Salḥīn at Mārib, but also several other South Arabian regions not mentioned in fourth-century Aksumite inscriptions but regularly used in the titles borne by Ḥimyarite kings from the mid-fifth century on.[650] The regions in question are the Tihāma (corresponding to Arabia's Red Sea coast and its immediate hinterland),[651] Ṭawd (probably Najd and Yamāma, perhaps including part of the Ḥijāz as well),[652] Yamānāt (probably the southern coast of Yemen along the Gulf of Aden),[653] and Ḥaḍramawt (the easternmost region of Yemen and

reigned in the 1330s, whose precise relationship with Anena remains obscure (ibid.: 151-5). This medieval Nubian presence in northern Kordofan may reflect a growing interest on the part of Christian Nubians in regions to the west of the Nile during the late Middle Ages, which would explain the remains of a Christian Nubian monastery at Jabal al-'Ayn just north of the modern boundary between the Kordofan and Shamāliyya provinces (Eger 2011). Needless to say, nothing could be further removed from the ancient kingdom of Kush! (The author wishes to thank Grzegorz Ochała for bringing Eger's article to his attention.)

[650] Hatke 2011: 122-3. Kālēb's list of Arabian vassals is based on what Robin designates the "titulature très longue 2" (TTL 2), which appears for the first time in an inscription of the Ḥimyarite king Ḥaśśān Yuha'min (c. 440-448) and his brother Shuraḥbi'īl Ya'fur and reads thus: *mlk S¹b' w-d̲-Ryd^n w-Ḥḍrmwt w-Ymnt w-ʿʿrb-hmw Ṭwd^m w-Thmt* (Robin 1996: 683, 685).

[651] Zwettler 2000: 253 (n. 55).

[652] Gajda 1996: 69; Zwettler 2000: 239 (n. 30).

[653] Zwettler (1996: 102) contends that Yamānāt designates "(the rest of the) South/(the whole) South/(the) South (in general)," though it seems unlikely that the Ḥimyarites would have used a geographical term in such a vague, imprecise manner, particularly when the corresponding "north" (*s²'mt*), while attested epigraphically, is not used in royal titles as a counterpart to Yamānāt. Since the root √*ymn* in Arabic can have the sense of "south" (see for example *shām^an wa-yaman^an*, "to the north and the south"), a sense retained in Yemeni Arabic (Piamenta 1991: II: 537), Yamānāt undoubtedly does refer to some southern region. Rather than taking it to refer to a generic "south," however, Yamānāt is best understood as denoting the southern coast of Yemen, extending perhaps as far as Ẓufār and possibly including the Yemeni island of Soqotra. For a list of similar theories, see

once a kingdom in its own right).[654] An ethnic group, the Arabs, also make an appearance in Kālēb's title in connection with the aforementioned regions, hence the category of "all of their Arabs" (*kl 'rbm=*k*^{w}*əllū 'Arabōmū*; cf. Sabaic *kl 'rb-hmw*). Similarly the list of Kālēb's African vassals in RIE 191, though loosely based on fourth-century precedents, is not a slavish copy of its counterpart in the titles of Ousanas and 'Ēzānā, for the Noba and the as yet unidentified *DRBT* people in Kālēb's title are not attested in earlier Aksumite royal titles. As we have seen, the Noba were a serious threat to Aksum's western frontier in the reign of 'Ēzānā. Since 'Ēzānā describes his suppression of the Noba in great detail in his inscriptions, the fact that he does not include them in the list of vassals in his royal title suggests that they were simply subsumed under the category of "Kush." That 'Ēzānā probably did not recognize the legitimacy of the Noba's regime might even have made them unworthy for inclusion in his royal titles.[655] The political topography of Nubia in Kālēb's day was a bit more complex, as the area of the old kingdom of Kush had by this point given way to three kingdoms (See Map 3). From north to south these were Nobadia, located between the first and third Nile cataracts, whose name is clearly derived from that of the Noba; Makouria, located between the third and fifth cataracts; and Alodia, extending southwards from the fifth cataract as far as the lower Blue Nile.[656] All three kingdoms would eventually be converted to Christianity by Roman missionaries in the second half of the sixth century.[657] In his *Chronographia* John Malalas, a

Zwettler 1996: 99.

[654] On the Ḥimyarite conquest of Ḥaḍramawt, see Robin 2005.

[655] See §4.5.2.1.

[656] Welsby 2002: 24-8; Edwards 2004: 194-5, 202.

[657] Kirwan 1937; idem 1994; Richter 2002; Dijkstra 2008: 282-304. Even before Christianity became the state religion of the three Nubian kingdoms there appears to have been a Christian presence in Nubia, for fifth-century Nobadian chieftain named Abourni had a son who bore the Christian name Mouses, while one fifth-century monk from Philae corresponded in a Christian-style letter with the Nobadian chief Tantani (Dijkstra, loc. cit.: 294; Török 2011: 529). Cosmas Indicoplesutes mentions bishops of Nubia in the third book of his *Christian Topography* (*Top. Chr.* 3.66.5). Since Cosmas was in the process of writing the sixth book of this treatise in 547, at which point he records two eclipses in that year (ibid.: 6.3), his references to bishops in Nubia in the third book must therefore reflect conditions in the 540s at the latest. The empress Theodora, wife of Justinian, is known to have sent a

Syriac-speaking author writing in Greek in the mid-sixth century, seems to allude to this political division in his description of the "seven empires of the Indians," four of which he says belonged to the Ethiopians,[658] by which he probably means Aksum and the three kingdoms of Nubia. That Kālēb preferred the anachronistic "Kush" over the names of the Kushites' heirs in Nubia may reflect his desire to give a certain historical depth to his claim to Nubia, a deliberate archaism reminiscent of his use of the same fourth-century form of the South Arabian *musnad* script employed by Ousanas and 'Ēzānā in their inscriptions. On the other hand, Kālēb's innovative inclusion of the Noba in his royal title as an independent group among the vassals of Aksum, listed separately from Kush, hints at an attempt on his part to "update" his title, perhaps in light of new political developments in Nubia.

The consolidation of the three kingdoms of Nubia by the sixth century may well have been one of these developments. As part of this process, a Nubian king named Silko conquered the regions of Lower Nubia which had been occupied by the Blemmyes since the late fourth century[659] and in a record of his victory, written in Greek on the walls of the temple of Kalabsha, styles himself "King of the Nobades and all the Ethiopians" (βασιλίσκος Νουβάδων καὶ ὅλων τῶν Αἰθιόπων).[660] Silko's campaign is also alluded to in a Greek letter from Qaṣr Ibrīm, sent by the Blemmyan king Phonen to the Nobadian king Abourni,[661]

Miaphysite mission to Nubia in 543, though on the basis of the history of John of Ephesus it would seem that the first bishop of the Nobades was not appointed until 566 (Török 2011: 516).

[658] Malalas 18.15 (transl. Jeffreys et al. 1986: 251).

[659] A demotic graffito from Philae indicates that the Blemmyes had already made inroads into Lower Nubia as early as 372-4, following the fall of Kush and with it the collapse of centralized control of Lower Nubia from Meroë. On this text, see *Fontes Historiae Nubiorum III* 1998: 1110-12; Török 1999: 148. By 394 the Blemmyes had come to occupy the whole of the Dodekaschoinos (*Fontes Historiae Nubiorum III* 1998: 1115-18; Török, loc. cit.).The Meroitic inscription from Kalabsha naming the Nobadian king Kharamadoye and believed to date from the beginning of the fifth century may belong to the final period of Blemmyan occupation in Lower Nubia before the Nobadian takeover under Silko. On this inscription, see *Fontes Historiae Nubiorum III* 1998: 1103-7. On the identity of Kharamadoye, see Török 1999: 152-3.

[660] *Fontes Historiae Nubiorum III* 1998: 1149 (Greek text), 1150 (English translation).

[661] Ibid.: 1158-65.

who appears to have been Silko's successor.[662] Phonen's letter has been dated to the mid-fifth century on the basis of the style of the script,[663] thus providing a *terminus ante quem* of c. 450 for Silko's inscription from Kalabsha.[664] Despite attempts by Phonen to seek compensation for his people on account of Silko's excesses, Blemmyan rule seems to have been pushed back to the Eastern Desert from the mid-fifth century on.[665] By contrast, the state established by Silko survived into the medieval period as the kingdom of Nobadia.[666] Such a development could hardly have passed unnoticed in Aksumite circles, significant as Silko's conquests were both for the Aksumites' Roman trading partners and for their Blemmyan neighbors. It is curious that a ruler claiming dominion over "all the Ethiopians," i.e., all the Nubians, should have contented himself with the title of βασιλίσκος, "kinglet," when the more grandiose Βασιλεύς would seem to have been more appropriate. In 'Ēzānā's Greek inscription recording his victory over the Beja (RIE 270*bis*), the Beja chieftains are referred to as βασιλίσκοι,[667] as befitting their status as vassals of Aksum. If Silko, on the other hand, was answerable to any higher authority it would have been the Romans, not the Aksumites, who granted him status as a semi-autonomous federate. This is supported by studies of late Roman titles, which demonstrate that the term βασιλίσκος always appears as a title for rulers who had some relationship with the Roman emperor.[668] In contrast to the relative abundance of textual material for fifth-century Nubian history, the fifth century is a historical blank as far as Aksum is concerned, and while its kings continued to mint coins throughout this period, there is no evidence of far-flung military campaigns that could have re-established Aksum's sphere of influence as far afield as Nubia. Thus we again find that Kālēb's inclusion of the Noba in his royal title reflects nothing more than a political fiction. But contrived though this claim to Noba territory was, the fact that Kālēb saw the

[662] Ibid.: 1148.
[663] Skeat 1977: 159 (n. 3).
[664] *Fontes Historiae Nubiorum* III 1998: 1148.
[665] Török 1988: 62.
[666] Welsby 2002: 21-2.
[667] RIE 270*bis*: 25 (*Fontes Historiae Nubiorum III* 1998: 1095 [Greek text], 1096 [English translation]; cf. Bernard 2000: 12).
[668] Török 1999: 136 (n. 28).

need to "update" his title in this manner might suggest awareness on his part of the rise to political prominence of the Noba's northern cousins, the Nobades, following Silko's conquest of Lower Nubia. The *Martyrium Arethae*, our second source for Aksumite relations with Nubia in Kālēb's reign, further indicates that the Nobades lay within the Roman, as opposed to the Aksumite, sphere of influence, but that they were nevertheless considered as potential mercenaries in Aksumite warfare.

5.2. The Nobades and Blemmyes: Would-be Mercenaries of Aksum?

The *Martyrium Arethae*, a sixth-century Greek text documenting the Aksumite invasion of Ḥimyar in 525,[669] quotes what purports to be the transcript of a letter which the Roman emperor Justin I (518-527) urged Timothy III, the Coptic archbishop of Alexandria (517-535), to write on his behalf to Kālēb, promising logistical aid to the Aksumites in the invasion.[670] At one point in the letter, mention is made of the dispatch of mercenaries recruited from the Nobades and Blemmyes as part of this aid: "For our part we will send, from Coptos, Berenike, and [the territory] of the men called Blemmyes and Nobades, a large army: our troops, by pushing through your lands, will reduce the entire country of the Ḥimyarite (i.e., Yūsuf 'As'ar Yaṯ'ar), and he himself, to utter desolation and anathema."[671] Since nothing further is said of

[669] On the date of this work, see Detoraki 2007: 98.

[670] The Coptic patriarchate continued to claim ecclesiastical jurisdiction over Aksum well into the Middle Ages. Thus the patriarch Markos III (1166-1189) is called "the great Archbishop of the city of Alexandria and the city of Babylon and Nobadia and Arouda and Makour[ia] and Dalmatia and Aksum" in the Greek subscript of a Coptic transcript of a letter from Qaṣr Ibrīm, the original draft of which was sent to Alexandria by King Moses George of the late medieval Nubian kingdom of Dotawo (Adams 1996: 228-9). Alexandria continued to send Coptic archbishops to Ethiopia as late as the 1950s, though Markos' claim to jurisdiction over Aksum reflects that town's importance as a religious — rather than a political — center during the Middle Ages.

[671] *Martyrium Arethae* 27.19-22. Beaucamp (ibid. 2007: 258) notes that the syntax of the passage referring to the movement of the Blemmyes and Nobades through Kālēb's territory poses several difficulties of interpretation. In Detoraki's edition of the text, the entire passage is given as follows: Καὶ ἡμεῖς δὲ διὰ Κόπτου καὶ Βερονίκης καὶ τῶν λεγομένων Βλεμμύων καὶ Νοβάδων πλῆθος στρατευμάτων ἐκπέμψαντες παρόδῳ χρησάμενα τὰ στρατόπεδα ἡμῶν διὰ τῆς γῆς σου πᾶσαν συτρίψωσιν τὸν δὲ Ὁμηρίτην καὶ τὴν χώραν αὐτοῦ εἰς τέλειον ἀφανισμὸν καὶ ἀνάθεμα

these mercenaries in the *Martyrium*, it would seem that Justin failed to keep his promise, with the result that Kālēb was obliged to recruit instead some 15,000 "Barbaroi" Ethiopians,[672] from Somalia. This, too, was a futile endeavor, for all of the Barbaroi perished in the "waterless, inaccessible mountains" before reaching Arabia.[673]

It is worthy of note that the letter quoted in the *Martyrium* implies that it was Justin, not Kālēb, who was to provide mercenaries from among the Blemmyes and Nobades to augment the Aksumite invasion force. That Kālēb was not expected to undertake the task of recruiting from these two groups may be further evidence—albeit indirect—of how limited Aksum's political influence to the west and north of the Ethiopian Highlands was during the sixth century. This would in turn support the argument presented above[674] that Kālēb's claim to the land of the Noba in his royal title is nothing more than a political fiction. Additionally, even if some of the more southerly tribes of the Beja/Blemmyes were still vassals of Aksum at this time, the fact that Kālēb did not himself impress these into military service suggests that he did not regard them as a viable military force. Even from the Roman side, it is not at all clear how Justin intended to send Nobadian mercenaries to Aksum, as the territory of the Nobades lay beyond the jurisdiction of sixth-century Roman Egypt. As for the Blemmyes at this time, some still resided not only in close proximity to Rome's southern frontier but also within Roman Egypt proper, as Eastern Desert Ware

καταστήσωσιν. Beaucamp translates the problematic passage as "nos troupes, en se frayant un passage à travers tes terres, les ruineront toutes et réduiront l'Homérite et tout son pays à une disparition complète et à l'anathème" (ibid.). She notes, however, that a variant recension of the *Martyrium* reads πᾶσαν τὴν χώραν τοῦ Ὁμηρίτου καὶ αὐτὸν εἰς τέλειον ἀφανισμὸν καταστήσωσιν ("ils réduiront tout le pays de l'Homérite, ainsi que lui-même, à une disparition complète"), of which she says that "la menace que fait peser Justin sur l'Éthiopie est ainsi effacée du texte" (ibid.: 258, n. 168). One is inclined to favor this latter recension, which is adopted in the present study, given that Justin, by sending the Blemmyes and Nobades to aid Aksum in the war against Ḥimyar, would, in the interest of diplomacy, have wanted to avoid any collateral damage to Aksumite territory.

[672] *Martyrium Arethae* 29.11.

[673] Ibid.: 29.14-17.

[674] §5.1.

has been found in the latest levels of the site of Berenike,[675] the very port from which the mercenaries were to be sent to Kālēb. In addition, documentary evidence of a Blemmyan presence in Upper Egypt during the early sixth century is provided by a series of letters in Greek and Coptic found at Gabalayn, recording the affairs of the local Blemmyan community.[676] But even if some Blemmyes did reside within Roman territory, it need not follow that the Romans enjoyed anything like a stable relationship with Blemmyes elsewhere—much less with the Nobades. In fact during the first half of the sixth century the Romans had to pay both groups in gold to prevent them from raiding Egypt.[677] It is difficult to imagine that groups who had to be paid just to keep the peace would have warmed to the idea of military service in distant South Arabia—and this on behalf of an Aksumite king to which they owed no allegiance. This, more than anything, explains why Justin failed, or was unable, to keep his promise to send Blemmyan and Nobadian troops to Kālēb. Moreover, whatever significance the political fiction of ruling the Noba might have had for Kālēb would appear to have died with him, for the title of his son and successor Wa'zeb, as preserved in inscription RIE 192 from Aksum, is for the most part a direct copy of the antiquated titles borne by Ousanas and 'Ēzānā, still including Kush in the list of Aksum's vassals, but with none of the innovative features introduced by Kālēb.[678] Gone are the Noba, whose place in Aksum's imagined empire was no longer judged important enough for inclusion in a royal title, leaving only the anachronistic Kush as a reminder of fourth-century Aksumite campaigns in Nubia.

[675] See §3.3.1.

[676] *Fontes Historiae Nubiorum III* 1998: 1196-1216; Török 1988: 64-9.

[677] Dijkstra 2008: 283.

[678] In his inscription Wa'zeb styles himself simply "King of Aksum and Ḥimyar and Raydān and Saba' and Salḥīn and *SLF* and the Beja and Kush and Ṣeyāmō and *WYTL*" (*ngš 'ksm w-ḏ-Ḥmyr*^{m} *w-ḏ-Rydn w-ḏ-Sb' w-ḏ-Slf w-ḏ-Bg w-ḏ-Ks w-ḏ-Ṣym w-ḏ-Wytl=*nəgūša 'Aksūm wa-za-Ḥəmēr wa-za-Raydān wa-za-Saba' wa-za-SLF wa-za-Bəgā wa-za-Kūs wa-za-Ṣəyāmō wa-za-WYTL*) (RIE 192: 5-7 [Bernard et al. 1991: 275]). Who the *SLF* and *WYTL* were is impossible to ascertain, as these peoples are referred to only in this inscription. In Line 5 Wa'zeb claims to have made war on the latter, stating: *ḍb'k Wytl* (=**ḍabā'kū Wytl*), "I fought *WYTL*" (ibid.). Judging from their placement in the list of vassals in the king's title, it is probable that the *SLF* and *WYTL* were African peoples.

5.3. Longinus' Mission and the Aksumite Presence in Alodia

Even though sixth-century Aksumite claims to Nubia are a political fiction, and even though the Nobadian and Blemmyan mercenaries which Justin promised to send to Kālēb never materialized, there is one bit of textual data indicating that Aksum remained in direct contact with Nubia until the late sixth century. But as always, due caution is needed in interpreting this data. The text in question is the *Ecclesiastical History* of John of Ephesus (c. 507-586/8).[679] Writing in Syriac of the evangelization of Nubia,[680] John notes that, in the course of his travels in Upper Nubia c. 580, the Roman missionary Longinus encountered in the kingdom of Alodia "men from the Aksumites[681] who had fallen into the disease of Julian's fantasy and said that Christ endured neither suffering nor mortality in body" (*nāšē g̱ēr men Aḵsīmīṭōn da-ḇ-kurhānā ḏ-panṭasīya ḏ-Yulīyānā npīlīn w-āmrīn da-ḇ-pag̱rā lā ḥāšūšā w-lā māyūṯā ḥašš Mšīḥā*).[682] Though the Alodian capital of Soba is not mentioned in the text, the town was already in existence by this time[683] and, given that the passage in question deals with Longinus' conversion of the Alodian royal house, it is not impossible that Longinus met the Aksumite contingent at Soba. The "disease of Julian's fantasy" is a polemical allusion to aphthartodocetism, a doctrine most famously propounded by the Miaphysite bishop Julian of Halicarnassus (d. post 527), which held that Christ's body was incorruptible not only after resurrection but from the very moment of his conception. Thus the suffering of Christ, Julian argued, was contrary to the nature of his body but nevertheless occurred miraculously through his will. Though Julian was condemned as a heretic during his lifetime, aphthartodocetism enjoyed a brief period

[679] On John's background and the writing of his history, see Dijkstra 2008: 276-79, 282-92.

[680] On Roman missionary efforts in Nubia, see Kirwan 1937; idem 1994.

[681] The *Ecclesiastical History* of John of Ephesus is the only Syriac source in which the Aksumites are given a gentilic derived from the name of their kingdom rather than the generic epithet *Kūšāyē*. Even then, John's term for them, *Aḵsīmīṭōn* (ܐܟܣܝܡܝܛܘܢ), is a calque on the Greek Ἀξωμιτῶν—the correct plural form would have been **Aḵsīmāyē* < *Aḵsūmāyē* according to the rules of Syriac morphology—which suggests that the "Aksumite" was a rather unfamiliar term in Syriac tradition.

[682] John of Ephesus 1853: 290 (Syriac text).

[683] Welsby 1998: 272; idem 1999: 666.

of official support in the mid-sixth century, when Justinian (527-565) saw it as a means of promoting doctrinal unity among his Christian subjects.[684] If some Aksumites had adopted Julian's doctrine during this period, perhaps as a result of contact with Egypt, where Julian had fled in 518, the death of Justinian in 565 spelled the end of imperial endorsement of the doctrine, a development which Longinus was quick to exploit in his dealings with the Aksumite aphthartodocetists whom he met in Alodia. We are informed of these matters in a letter preserved by John of Ephesus, purporting to have been sent by Longinus himself to the Nobatian king Urepeyula (ܐܘܪܦܝܘܠܐ)[685] with a request that it be forwarded to Alexandria. In this letter Longinus claims to have rectified the Aksumites' religious views, saying: "We taught them the true faith and demanded that they anathematize the heresy in writing, and we [then] accepted them through [their] written confession" (*awdaʿn ennōn ḥattīṯūṯā ḏ-haymānūṯā wa-ṯḇaʿn d-ḇa-ḵṯīḇāṯā naḥrmūn l-heresīs wa-ḇ-līḇlōn qabbeln ennōn*).[686]

Thus we find definitive proof in the *Ecclesiastical History* of John of Ephesus of Aksumite contact with Upper Nubia during the sixth century. The nature and extent of this influence, however, is not clear from the text. As it stands, the passage regarding the Aksumite presence in Alodia is quite opaque, and since John's history has for the most part been studied by Nubiologists through secondary sources rather than in the original text, the Syriac author's intentions have often been misconstrued. Hence the attempts by some scholars to see in the above-cited passages evidence of an Aksumite agenda to convert Alodia to Christianity,[687] when in fact John of Ephesus says nothing of any official Aksumite mission to Alodia, nor states that the Aksumites in Alodia were interested in converting the local population at all. The most he tells us is that Longinus met with some Aksumite Christians in Alodia and persuaded them to abandon their aphthartodocetist beliefs. Whether such beliefs had any impact on the Alodians, either through the Aksumites or through some other source, remains a matter for

[684] On Julian and his religious teachings, see Gregory 1991a and idem 1991b.
[685] Payne Smith (1860: 320) regards this name as a corruption of the Greek Eurypylus.
[686] John of Ephesus 1853: 290 (Syriac text).
[687] Phillips (2003a: 440) calls the Aksumites in Alodia "missionaries."

speculation. Furthermore, John gives no details about the profession of the Aksumite visitors to Alodia, and it cannot be excluded they were simply merchants[688] by whose activities in Alodia the sherds of Soba Ware found in sixth-century contexts at Aksum might be explained. Seen in this light, the *Ecclesiastical History* of John of Ephesus tells us only what we already know, to wit that in the sixth century as at most other times, Aksum maintained limited, small-scale contact with Nubia, without exerting any political or cultural influence on the region.

5.4. Into the Middle Ages: Ḥaḍānī Dāne'ēl and Aksum's Western Neighbors

One final set of texts worth considering in light of Aksumite relations with regions to the west of Ethiopia is RIE 193 I+II+III, a series of inscriptions from the reign of one Dāne'ēl found at Aksum at the turn of the twentieth century.[689] Though none of these inscriptions mention Nubia *per se*, a number of scholars have seen in RIE 193 I references to the Barya people, as well as to the town of Kasalā in the eastern Sudan, in which case a discussion of Dāne'ēl's inscriptions is not without relevance for the history of Aksumite relations with Nubia. In the case of RIE 193 I+II+III we are dealing with an epigraphic corpus that differs considerably from the Aksumite texts hitherto examined in this study. While all of the latter are inscribed on stelae made specifically for the purpose, those of Dāne'ēl are crudely scratched on the base of a stone throne,[690] indicating that they are secondary features added to an older monument. In RIE 193 I Dāne'ēl bears the title *ḥaḍānī*, which can refer to a tutor or guardian of children but which in this case might mean something more along the lines of "guardian of the state."[691] No coins minted in the name of this king have ever been found, and in light of the atypical nature of RIE 193 I's execution it is likely that Dāne'ēl was not a ruler of Aksum's royal line at all. In fact the second inscription in Dāne'ēl's name (RIE 193 II), inscribed on the left-hand side of the same throne-base,[692] was

[688] As suggested by Török (1988: 71).
[689] For a critical edition of these texts with bibliography see Bernard et al. 1991: 278-80.
[690] Ibid.: 279.
[691] Munro-Hay and Nosnitsin 2005: 84.
[692] Bernard et al. 1991: 279.

interpreted by Littmann as a record of a campaign against Aksum itself,[693] though a more recent edition of the text calls Littmann's reading into question.[694] The third text (RIE 193 III) on the front of the throne-base is undoubtedly related to the previous two, though apart from a single word, *ngs* (=**nəgūs<nəgūś*), meaning "king," nothing more than disjointed letters can be made out.[695] While Aksumite royal inscriptions conventionally name the king's father and clan, RIE 193 I+II give only Dāne'ēl's title, *ḥaḍānī*, and a rather cryptic reference to his being the "son of the monastery of Ferēm" (*walda dabra Fərēm*).[696] The latter may be an allusion to a monastery dedicated in honor of the evangelizer of fourth-century Aksum Frumentius (Ge'ez *Fərēmnaṭōs*), perhaps attached to the ancient church of Ferēmōnā located 6 km to the south of Adwā, and therefore close to the town of Aksum.[697] If so, Dāne'ēl could have been raised in the monastery as a boy, or else spent the earlier part of his life there as a monk.[698] With no chronological context for RIE 193 I+II+III, the dates suggested for Dāne'ēl range from the seventh century to as late as the twelfth,[699] which would place him after the collapse of the Aksumite state in the seventh century[700] or perhaps at the very end of the Aksumite period if one accepts the earliest possible date for RIE 193 I+II+III. That he bore the title *ḥaḍānī*, however, supports the hypothesis of a post-Aksumite context for his reign, as this title is only attested during the post-Aksumite period. In

[693] Littmann 1913: 45-6.
[694] Bernard et al. 1991: 280, 282.
[695] Ibid.: 279, 282.
[696] RIE 193 I: 4-5; RIE 193 II: 4-5 (ibid.: 279).
[697] Munro-Hay and Nosnitsin 2005: 84.
[698] Ibid.
[699] Ibid.
[700] Among the evidence for the decline of Aksum in the seventh century is the cessation of coinage, the abandonment of palatial structures at Aksum by c. 650, and the abandonment of entire sites, such as Matarā and Adulis, around the same time (Finneran 2007: 212-13). Ecological decline may have played a role in the downfall of the Aksumite state by weakening its agricultural base (ibid.: 210-11). On the final years of the Aksumite kingdom, see Munro-Hay 1991: 89-94, 258-62. That Aksumite forms remained popular in early medieval church architecture in Ethiopia suggests some degree of cultural continuity between the kingdom of Aksum and its successors further to the south-east (Finneran 2007: 212, 214-24). Whether there existed any political continuity remains to be proven.

external sources it appears for the first time in the treatise of the tenth-century Arab geographer Ibn Ḥawqal, who refers to the Ethiopian king of his day as *ḥaḍānī*.[701] The title *ḥaḍānī* is also borne by the late twelfth-/early thirteenth-century king Lālībalā of the Zāg^{w}ē Dynasty.[702] Dāne'ēl, then, can be assigned with reasonable confidence to the post-Aksumite period, the Aksumite provenance of his inscriptions being simply a reflection of Aksum's continued importance as a religious center during the Middle Ages.

If Dāne'ēl was not an Aksumite king in the first place, any military activities on his part belong to a very different political environment than the one with which we have dealt thus far. As for the oft-repeated claim that he made war on Kasalā and the Barya,[703] this too, based as it is on Littmann's original reading of RIE 193 I, is questionable. Reading a line of text in Lines 14-15 of the inscription as *'awfarū Kasalā*, Littmann translates "[sie] zogen nach Kasalā."[704] Then in Lines 17-19 he reconstructs the text as *wa-'agatkū za-baṣ[ḥa] Kasalā* [...]*hābāyāta* [.] *wa-ḥayada Bāryā*, translating this as "und ich.....die nach Kasalā kamen.....................und sie plünderten (?) die Bāryā."[705] As we have seen, Ethiopia was in contact with the eastern Sudan throughout antiquity, but since Dāne'ēl's inscriptions are extremely difficult to read,[706] they raise more questions than they answer. Thus, while the Barya people are attested in Aksumite inscriptions from 'Ēzānā's time, as well as in the works of medieval Arab authors, the fact that Kasalā was only founded in 1834[707] makes it a chronologically impossible fit for a town mentioned in RIE 193 I. Clearly, whatever contact Aksum's successors

701 Munro-Hay and Nosnitsin 2005: 84.
702 Ibid.
703 Littmann 1913: 43-4; Kobishchanov 1979: 120, 157; Munro-Hay 1991: 262 (with reservations); al-Nūr 2004; Munro-Hay and Nosnitsin 2005: 84.
704 Littmann 1913: 43.
705 Ibid.
706 A more recent (and more conservative) reconstruction of the relevant portion of Lines 14-15 by Bernard et al. (1991: 280) reads simply *wa*[...]*r : b-.-.- :*, that of Lines 17-19 *wa.-t-k- : zab-*[*ṣ-*]*.-.-m-ku*[...]*b-y-t- : ...*]*b-.-y- :*. Needless to say, no sense can be made of any of this, though it is quite possible that weathering of the stone in the decades following Littmann's initial study of the inscriptions is in part responsible for the much more fragmentary reconstruction proposed by Bernard et al.
707 Salih 2007: 354.

might have maintained with Nubia, Dāne'ēl's inscriptions shed no light on it.[708]

[708] The nature of Nubian-Ethiopian contact during the Middle Ages remains obscure, and what evidence we have dates mostly from the late medieval period; see, for example, Ceccarelli-Morolli 1998.

6. Conclusion

What have we learned of Aksumite-Nubian relations? In fact, very little. For the period before the rise of Aksum, there is indeed good evidence of commercial and even political contact between Nubia and the Horn of Africa. By the turn of the first millennium BCE, however, the two regions seem to have gravitated toward two different axes: a Nile Valley axis in the case of Nubia and an Ethiopian Highlands–Red Sea axis in the case of Ethiopia. Thus for the Nubian kingdom of Kush, the most obvious point of contact with the outside world was Egypt, which had long ruled Nubia but which, for a few decades beginning in the late eighth century BCE, came to be ruled *by* Nubia. In later times Egypt continued to provide a cultural model for the Kushite ruling elite. For its part, Ethiopia, having long interacted with its Arabian neighbors across the Red Sea and having already adopted the Semitic speech of the latter, borrowed many aspects of South Arabian culture, such as writing, art, and monumental architecture, in the first half of the first millennium BCE. With the development of a maritime route linking the Mediterranean with the Indian Ocean by way of the Red Sea shortly before the turn of the Common Era, Ethiopia's ties to the Red Sea—as opposed to its ties to the Nile Valley—were reinforced, the Aksumites deciding that trade by sea with the Roman Empire, South Arabia, and India was more profitable than overland trade with the middle Nile.

It is hardly satisfying to the student of history to learn that two ancient states were merely aware of each other's existence but, apart from some small-scale trade, a few isolated incidents of armed conflict, and interregional travel by private individuals, never interacted much. But this is precisely how the history of Aksumite contact with Kush from the first to fourth century CE can best be summarized, and there is no indication that Aksumite relations with Kush's successors in the middle Nile Valley in the sixth century changed this. Having examined in detail the archaeological, epigraphic, and literary evidence for Ethio-Nubian relations in antiquity, several important points do, however, suggest themselves. The first point is that ancient northeast

Africa was not an integrated region politically, economically, or culturally. The Nubians were indeed involved with trade between Punt and the Nile Valley, modest trade goods did pass between Nubia and Ethiopia, and Aksum did indeed invade Nubia twice in the fourth century CE. But none of these factors were the bases for an interregional commonwealth, and so long as Nubia remained oriented towards the Nile Valley and Ethiopia towards the highlands of the Horn of Africa and the Red Sea, neither had reason to infringe on the other's territory or vie for control of the other's trade routes. Only when Kush began to falter in the mid-fourth century CE did Aksum intervene in Nubia. Judging from the records of ʻĒzānā's invasion of Nubia, a weak Kush meant an unprotected western frontier for Aksum. The second point is that political fictions played an important role in Aksumite royal ideology. No matter how tenuous Aksum's political links with Nubia may have been even in periods following military intervention, the consistency with which Kush was named as a vassal in royal titles indicates that it had to have meant something to Aksum, if only as a symbolic western counterbalance to the South Arabian territories claimed by Aksum. There is nevertheless a disparity between South Arabia's place in Aksumite royal ideology and Nubia's place. Thus, while several Aksumite kings erected inscriptions in a script imitating South Arabian *musnad*, no Aksumite inscription takes Kushite monumental culture as a model. There is, for example, no Geʻez inscription written in the Meroitic script or in hieroglyphics. The third and final point is that, although the most important records for Aksumite relations with Nubia are royal inscriptions, it need not follow that Aksum's invasions of Nubia in the fourth century were the end result of political relations at the highest level gone bad. During ʻĒzānā's reign at least, it was not conflict between the ruling elites of Aksum and Kush, but rather conflict between the peoples living in the frontier region separating the two states, that brought about war.

Since the dearth of Nubian material in Ethiopia and Ethiopian material in Nubia is indeed striking it may be asked whether analogous situations exist elsewhere in the ancient world. In fact the Late Bronze Age Mediterranean (late ffteenth-late thirteenth century BCE) provides us with one such analogy. In one study of trade in this region,

Cline draws attention to the extreme paucity of Aegean objects in the Hittite realm and the parallel paucity of Hittite objects in the Aegean, and attributes this phenomenon to a Hittite economic embargo against the Mycenaeans.[709] Despite the potential which this model might be thought to have for the interpreting the history of Aksumite-Nubian relations, one must be careful not to uncritically apply Cline's theory of an official trade embargo to ancient northeast Africa, whose economies operated quite differently from those of the Late Bronze Age Mediterranean. Moreover, the foundations of Cline's theory have been called into question by recent studies of Hittite-Aegean interaction which suggest that, rather than maintaining an embargo on Mycenaean trade, the Hittites preferred to obtain Aegean products through Syro-Palestinian intermediaries.[710] But even if one rejects Cline's theory of a Hittite embargo on Mycenaean trade, his conclusion, based on archaeological evidence, that the Hittite and Mycenaean realms had little contact with each other still stands.[711] That it does has significant implications for the present study in that, when viewed from the perspective of Hittite-Mycenaean relations, it is evident that the phenomenon of two neighboring polities coexisting with little interaction is not limited to Aksumite-Nubian relations but has a parallel with other regions in the ancient world.

But if the dearth of evidence for Aksumite-Nubian contact cannot be explained as the result of an official policy of isolationism, what, then, of smaller-scale, private interaction between Aksum and Kush? A relationship of this type, based as it would have been on commerce in humbler, utilitarian goods and raw materials, is admittedly difficult to identify in the historical and archaeological record. Certainly, products of this type neither involved nor interested merchants from the Mediterranean world, with the result that they never merited mention in Graeco-Roman writings on northeast Africa. For their part neither the Aksumites nor the Kushites were in the habit of recording

[709] Cline 1991. More recently, Genz (2011: 303-9) has drawn attention to the dearth of Hittite objects, or even evidence of Hittite influence, to the west of central Anatolia. He also notes that Mycenaean pottery is known from only three sites in the Hittite heartland (ibid.: 309).
[710] Bryce 2010: 48.
[711] Ibid.

commercial transactions, the documentary evidence left by both groups tending instead to focus on military matters. The problem is compounded by the fact that the origin of the utilitarian goods and raw materials which turn up during archaeological excavations, and which might allow us to reconstruct interregional trade networks, is often difficult to identify—and this when such material leaves trace in the archaeological record at all.[712] All the same, absence of evidence is not evidence of absence, and there is no reason why trade in humbler —and often perishable—items should not have taken place, even if the Red Sea, rather than overland routes to Nubia, remained Aksum's key outlet to the foreign world. As Crone's studies of pre-Islamic trade in the Ḥijāz have shown,[713] leather was in high demand in military circles and to that end was transported over long distances, and it is easy to conceive of a similar trans-regional trade in leather goods in ancient northeast Africa.[714] To give another example, incense was in demand for use in cultic and funerary rituals[715] in Nubia during Kushite and post-Kushite times, and it is quite likely that much of it came from the Horn of Africa by way of Aksum.[716] One need not assume the direct involvement of the state in such trade, for while Aksum acquired gold from Sasu through state-sponsored commercial expeditions headed by the Aksumite governor of the Agaw, trade in non-luxury items need not have warranted state control. In this connection it must not be forgotten that, for all the attention they receive in literature, aromatic spices like frankincense and myrrh were not regarded as luxury items in antiquity.[717] It is quite probable that peddlers and agro-pastoral groups traveled back and forth between Aksum and Nubia just as their modern-day counterparts cross the border between Ethiopia and the Sudan.[718] To be sure, small-scale commerce in non-luxury goods did on

[712] Obsidian is one of the few exceptions (§1.1).
[713] Crone 1987; idem 2007.
[714] On the importance of leather products in Aksum, see Hatke 2011: 419.
[715] Lenoble and Sharif 1992: 634; Edwards 1994: 173, 174, 176; Welsby 1996: 93. A systematic study of the use of incense in ancient Nubia has yet to be undertaken but would certainly repay the effort.
[716] There is to date no evidence of direct Kushite trade with South Arabia, which also produced incense.
[717] Fitzpatrick 2011: 33-4.
[718] The role of pastoralists in long-distance exchange networks in ancient northeast Africa has also been noted by Fattovich (2009: 284).

occasion take on great importance in antiquity, and for that reason the famous Tax Law of Palmyra, dating from 137 CE, focuses on trade in utilitarian goods to the exclusion of luxury items.[719] Since small-scale commerce in utilitarian goods did not, however, have an impact on the political sphere, we should dispense with the notion of a political conflict between Aksum and Kush born of commercial rivalry. One way in which the circulation of trade goods could, however, have had an impact on political relations was through gift-exchange between ruling elites. Conceivably what the Aksumites regarded as Kushite tribute was in fact nothing more than gifts sent by Kush to curry favor with Aksum. What if anything the Aksumites gave in exchange is impossible to say, and while Heliodorus' *Aithiopika* hints at their dispatch of animals as gifts to Kush, the spuriousness of this work makes speculation a hazardous undertaking. One can easily imagine one kingdom sending foodstuffs to the other, whether in time of need or simply to maintain good relations, but without archaeological or textual evidence, the political importance of such transactions remains a moot point.

Finally, some cautionary remarks regarding the nature of the archaeological evidence are also in order. If a regular, albeit informal, trade in non-luxury items was conducted by the frontier communities of Aksum and Kush, we should not expect to find much in the archaeological record that can be traced to a specific region. Thus, whereas Soba Ware is easy enough to spot at Aksum, the origin of leather cannot be pinpointed. To this we should add that archaeologists are still only beginning a proper study of the Ethiopian-Sudanese borderlands, where traces of these small-scale, informal commercial exchanges between the peripheral communities of Aksum and Nubia are likely to be found. Excavations at Tabot, as well as at sites in the Gash Delta, raise intriguing possibilities of finding further evidence of such exchanges and it may be the case that some of the hypotheses put forth in this study will in due course require revision. Perhaps by that time a more complete history of Aksumite relations with Nubia can be written.

[719] Matthews 1984: 172.

Bibliography

Abdu, B. and Gordon, R. (2004) "Iron artifacts from the land of Kush." *Journal of Archaeological Science* 31: 979-98.

Abdelrahman, M. F. (2011) "A New Study Concerning Kushite and Post-Meroitic Objects." In *La pioche et la plume: autour du Soudan, du Liban et de la Jordanie: hommages archéologiques à Patrice Lenoble*. V. Rondot, F. Alpi, and F. Villeneuve (dir.). Paris: Presses de l'université Paris-Sorbonne: 391-402.

Adams, N. K. (1987) "Textile Remains from a Late Temple in Egyptian Nubia." *Ars Textrina* 8: 85-124.

Adams, W. Y. (1977) *Nubia: Corridor to Africa*. Princeton: Princeton University Press.

-----. (1996) *Qaṣr Ibrîm: The Late Mediaeval Period*. London: Egypt Exploration Society.

Ahmed, K. A. (1984) *Meroitic Settlement in the Central Sudan: An Analysis of Sites in the Nile Valley and the Western Butana*. Oxford: BAR.

Alexander, J. (1988) "The Saharan divide in the Nile Valley: the evidence from Qasr Ibrim." *African Archaeological Review* 6 (1): 73-90.

Álvarez-Mon, J. (2010) *The Arjān Tomb: At the Crossroads of the Elamite and the Persian Empires*. Leuven: Peeters.

Anfray, F. (1981) "The civilization of Aksum from the first to the seventh century." In *General History of Africa. II: Ancient Civilizations of Africa*. G. Mokhtar (ed.). Paris: Unesco: 362-80.

Apologia=Athanasius of Alexandria (1987) *Deux apologies à l'empereur Constance pour sa fuite*. J. M. Szymusiak (ed. and transl.). Paris: Editions du Cerf.

Appleyard, D. L. (1996) "Ethiopian Semitic and South Arabian: Towards a Re-examination of a Relationship." *Israel Oriental Studies* 16: 203-28.

-----. (2004) "Beja as a Cushitic Language." In *Egyptian and Semito-Hamitic (Afro-Asiatic) Studies: in memoriam W. Vycichl*. G. Takács (ed.). Boston: Brill: 175-94.

Arkell, A. J. (1944) "Cosmas and the Gold Trade of Fazoqli." *Man* 44: 30-1.

-----. (1951) "An Old Nubian Inscription from Kordofan." *American Journal of Archaeology* 55 (4): 353-4.

-----. (1961) *A History of the Sudan: from the earliest times to 1821*. 2nd ed. London: University of London, Athlone Press.

Barnard, H. (2002) "Eastern Desert Ware, a first introduction." *Sudan & Nubia* 6: 53-7.

-----. (2005) "Sire, il n'y a pas de Blemmyes. A Re-evaluation of Historical and Archaeological Data." In *People of the Red Sea: Proceedings of Red Sea Project II, held in the British Museum, October 2004*. J. C. M. Starkey (ed.). Oxford, England: Archaeopress: Hadrian Books: 23-40.

-----. (2008) "Suggestions for a *Chaîne Opératoire* of Nomadic Pottery Sherds." In *The Archaeology of Mobility: Old World and New World Nomadism*. H. Barnard and W. Wendrich (eds.). Los Angeles: Cotsen Institute of Archaeology, University of California: 413-39.

Barnes, T. D. (1978) *The Sources of the Historia Augusta*. Bruxelles: Latomus.

-----. (1993) *Athanasius and Constantius: Theology and Politics in the Constantinian Empire*. Cambridge: Harvard University Press.

Becchaus-Gerst, M. (1984-5) "Sprachliche und historische Rekonstruktionen im Bereich des Nubischen unter besonder Berücksichtigung des Nilnubischen." *Sprache und Geschichte in Afrika* 6: 7-134.

-----. (1996) *Sprachwandel durch Sprachkontakt am Beispiel des Nubischen in Niltal: Möglichkeiten und Grenzen einer diachronen Soziolinguistik*. Cologne: Rüdiger Köppe Verlag.

-----. (2004) "Beja Idenity in Tu Beɖawiɛ." In *Egyptian and Semito-Hamitic (Afro-Asiatic) Studies: in memoriam W. Vycichl*. G. Takács (ed.). Boston: Brill: 195-204.

Beeston, A. F. L. (1980) "The Authorship of the Adulis Throne Text." *Bulletin of the School of Oriental and African Studies* 43 (3): 453-8.

Bender, M. L. (1968) "Analysis of a Barya Word List." *Anthropological Linguistics* 10 (9): 1-24.

Bernard, E. (1982) "Nouvelles versions de la campagne du roi Ezana contre les Bedja." *Zeitschrift für Papyrologie und Epigraphik* 45: 105-14.

-----. (2000) *Recueil des inscriptions de l'Éthiopie des périodes pré-axoumite et axoumite. Tome III: Traductions et commentaires, A. Les inscriptions grecques*. Paris: Diffusion de Boccard.

Bernard, E., Drewes, A. J., and Schneider, R. (1991) *Recueil des inscriptions de l'Éthiopie des périodes pré-axoumite et axoumite. Tome I: Les documents*. Paris: Diffusion de Boccard.

Black, S. L. (2008) ""In the Power of God Christ": Greek inscriptional evidence for the anti-Arian theology of Ethiopia's frst Christian king." *Bulletin of the School of Oriental and African Studies* 71 (1): 93-110.

Blench, R. (1999) "The westward wanderings of Cushitic pastoralists: Explorations in the Prehistory of Central Africa." In *L'homme et l'animal dans le bassin du lac Tchad: actes du colloque du Réseau Méga-Tchad, Orléans, 15-17 octobre 1997*. C. Baroin and J. Boutrais (eds.). Paris: Editions IRD, Institut de recherche pour le développement: 39-80.

Blois, F. de (1984) "Clan-names in ancient Ethiopia." *Die Welt des Orients* 15: 123-5.

-----. (1985) "'Freemen' and 'nobles' in Iranian and Semitic languages." *Journal of the Royal Asiatic Society* 17: 5-15.

-----. (2002) "Naṣrānī (Ναζωραῖος) and ḥanīf (ἐθνικός): studies on the religious vocabulary of Christianity and of Islam." *Bulletin of the School of Oriental and African Studies* 65 (1): 1-30.

Boivin, N., Blench, R., and Fuller, D. Q. (2009) "Archaeological, Linguistic and Historical Sources on Ancient Seafaring: A Multidisciplinary Approach to the Study of Early Maritime Contact and Exchange in the Arabian Peninsula." In *The Evolution of Human Populations in Arabia: Paleoenvironments, Prehistory and Genetics*. M. D. Petraglia and J. I. Rose (eds.). Dordrecht: Springer: 251-78.

Boivin, N. and Fuller, D. Q. (2009) "Shell Middens, Ships, and Seeds: Exploring Coastal Subsistence, Maritime Trade and the

Dispersal of Domesticates in and Around the Arabian Peninsula." *Journal of World Prehistory* 22: 113-80.

Bowersock, G. W. (1994) "The *Aethiopica* of Heliodorus and the *Historia Augusta*." In *Historiae Augustae Colloquium Genevense*. Bari: Edipuglia: 43-52.

Bradley, R. J. (1984) "Summary of Discussion." In *Meroitische Forschungen 1980: Akten der 4. Internationalen Tagung für meroitische Forschungen vom 24. Bis 29. November 1980 in Berlin*. F. Hintze (ed.). Berlin: Akademie-Verlag: 247-52.

Brakke, D. (2000) "Athanasius." In *The Early Christian World*. P. F. Esler (ed.). London and New York: Routledge: Vol. 2: 1102-27.

Brakmann, H. (1994) *ΤΟ ΠΑΡΑ ΤΟΙϹ ΒΑΡΒΑΡΟΙϹ ΕΡΓΟΝ ΘΕΙΟΝ: Die Einwurzelung der Kirche im spätantiken Reich von Aksum*. Bonn: Borengässer.

Browne, E. G. (2004) "Blemmyes and Beja." *The Classical Review* (New Series) 54: 226-8.

Bryce, T. (2010) "The Hittite Deal with the Ḫiyawa-Men." In *Pax Hethitica: Studies on the Hittites and their Neighbours in Honour of Itamar Singer*. Wiesbaden: Harrassowitz: 47-53.

Buffa, V. (2007) *Ma'layba et l'âge du bronze du Yémen*. Deutsche Archäologisches Institut Ṣan'ā'. Wiesbaden: Reichert Verlag.

Bukharin, M. D. (2011) "The notion τὸ πέρας τῆς ἀνακομιδῆς and the location of Ptolemais of the Hunts in the Periplus of the Erythraean Sea." *Arabian Archaeology and Epigraphy* 22: 219-31.

Burstein, S. M. (1981) "Axum and the Fall of Meroe." *Journal of the American Research Center in Egypt* 18: 47-50.

-----. (1995) "The Nubian Slave Trade in Antiquity: A Suggestion." In Burstein, S. M. *Graeco-Africana: Studies in the History of Greek Relations with Egypt and Nubia*. New Rochelle: Aristide D. Caratzas: 195-205.

-----. (1998) "The Roman Withdrawal from Nubia: A New Interpretation." *Symbolae Osloenses* 73: 125-32.

-----. (2008) "Trogodytes=Blemmyes=Beja? The Misuse of Ancient Ethnography." In *The Archaeology of Mobility: Old World and New World Nomadism*. H. Barnard and W. Wendrich (eds.). Los

Angeles: Cotsen Institute of Archaeology, University of California: 250-63.

-----. (2009) *Ancient African Civilizations: Kush and Axum*. New ed. Princeton: Markus Wiener Publishers.

Carter, P. L. and Foley, R. (1980) "A Report on the Fauna from the Excavations at Meroe, 1967-1972." In Shinnie, P. L. and Bradley, R. J. *The Capital of Kush 1: Meroe Excavations 1967-1972*. Berlin: Akademie-Verlag: 298-312.

Casson, L. (1989) *The Periplus Maris Erythraei*. Princeton: Princeton University Press.

-----. (1993) "Ptolemy II and the Hunting of African Elephants." *Transactions of the American Philological Association* 123: 247-60.

Ceccarelli-Morolli, D. (1998) "Un interessante brano di un manoscritto etiopico del XVI sec. concernente la Nubia." In *Actes de la VIIIe Conférence internationale des études nubiennes: Lille, 11-17 septembre 1994. III—Études*. Villeneuve d'Ascq: Université Charles de Gaulle-Lille III : 67-72.

Chatterji, S. K. (1968) *India and Ethiopia from the Seventh Century B.C.* Calcutta: Asiatic Society.

Chittick, H. N. (1982) "Ethiopia and the Nile Valley." In *Meroitic Studies: Proceedings of the Third International Meroitic Conference, Toronto 1977*. N. B. Millet and A. L. Kelly (eds.). Berlin: Akademie-Verlag: 50-4.

Chowdhury, K. A. and Buth, G. M. (1971) "Cotton seeds from the Neolithic in Egyptian Nubia and the origin of Old World cotton." *Biological Journal of the Linnean Society* 3 (4): 303-12.

Cline, E. (1991) "A Possible Hittite Embargo against the Mycenaeans." *Historia: Zeitschrift für Alte Geschichte* 40 (1): 1-9.

Connah, G. (1987) *African Civilizations: Precolonial Cities and States in Tropical Africa: An Archaeological Perspective*. Cambridge: Cambridge University Press.

----- (2001) *African Civilizations: An Archaeological Perspective*. 2nd ed. Cambridge: Cambridge University Press.

Contenson, H. de (1963) "Les fouilles de Haoulti en 1959." *Annales d'Éthiopie* 5 (5): 41-86.

Crawford, O. G. S. (1951) *The Fung kingdom of Sennar; with a geographical account of the middle Nile region*. Gloucester: J. Bellows.

Crone, P. (1987) *Meccan Trade and the Rise of Islam*. Princeton: Princeton University Press.

----- (2007) "Quraysh and the Roman Army: Making sense of the Meccan leather trade." *Bulletin of the School of Oriental and African Studies* 70: 63-88.

Curtin, P. D. (1984) *Cross-cultural Trade in World History*. Cambridge: Cambridge University Press.

Cuvigny, H. and Robin, C. J. (1996) "Des Kinaidokolpite dans un ostracon grec du désert oriental (Égypte)." *Topoi* 6/2: 697-720.

Davies, V. (2003) "Sobeknakht of Elkab and the coming of Kush." *Egyptian Archaeology* 23: 3-6.

Desanges, J. (1978) *Recherches sur l'activité des méditerranéens aux confins de l'Afrique, VIe siècle avant J.-C.-IVe siècle après J.-C.* Rome: École française de Rome.

Detoraki, M. (2007) "Première partie: la genèse du texte." In *Le martyre de Saint Aréthas et de ses compagnons (BHG 166)*. J. Beaucamp (ed. and transl.). Paris: Association des amis du Centre d'histoire et civilisation de Byzance: 13-99.

Dihle, A. (1965) *Umstrittene Daten: Untersuchungen zum Auftreten der Griechen am Roten Meer*. Cologne and Opladen: Westdeutscher Verlag.

-----. (1989) "L'ambassade de Théophile l'indien ré-examinée." In *L'Arabie préislamique et son environnement historique et culturel: actes du Colloque de Strasbourg, 24-27 juin 1987*. T. Fahd (ed.). Leiden: E. J. Brill: 461-8.

Dijkstra, J. H. F. (2008) *Philae and the End of Ancient Egyptian Religion: A Regional Study of Religious Transformation (298-642 CE)*. Leuven and Dudley: Peeters; Departement Oosterse Studies.

Dimmendaal, G. J. (2007) "Eastern Sudanic and the Wadi Howar and Wadi el Milk Diaspora." *Sprache und Geschichte in Afrika* 18: 37-67.

Dixon, D. M. (1963) "A Meroitic Cemetery at Sennar (Makwar)." *Kush* 11: 227-34.

Drewes, A. J. (1962) *Inscriptions de l'Éthiopie antique*. Leiden: E. J. Brill.

-----. (1980) "The Lexicon of Ethiopian Sabaean." *Raydān* 3: 35-54.

-----. (2002-2007) "La question de 'Ezânâ, roi d'Axoum." *Semitica* 52-53: 125-38.

Edessene Apocalypse (1917) = Nau, F. "Révélations et legends: Methodius —Clement—Andronicus." *Journal Asiatique* 9: 415-52.

Edwards, A. B. (1877) *A Thousand Miles up the Nile*. London: Longmans, Green & Co.

Edwards, D. N. (1989) *Archaeology and Settlement in Upper Nubia in the 1st Millennium A.D.* Oxford: B.A.R.

----- (1994) "Post-Meroitic ('X-Group') and Christian Burials at Sesibi, Sudanese Nubia. The Excavations of 1937." *Journal of Egyptian Archaeology* 80: 159-78.

-----. (1998) *Gabati: A Meroitic, Post-Meroitic and Medieval Cemetery in Central Sudan*. Oxford: Archaeopress.

-----. (2004) *The Nubian Past: An Archaeology of the Sudan*. London and New York: Routledge.

-----. (2011) "From Meroe to "Nubia": Exploring Culture Change without the "Noba"." In *La pioche et la plume: autour du Soudan, du Liban et de la Jordanie: hommages archéologiques à Patrice Lenoble*. V. Rondot, F. Alpi, and F. Villeneuve (dir.). Paris: Presses de l'université Paris-Sorbonne: 501-14.

Eger, J. (2011) "Ein mittelalterliches Kloster am Gebel al-Ain?" *Mitteilungen der Sudanarchäologischen Geselschaft zu Berlin e.V*. 22: 115-20.

Ehret, C. (2002) *The Civilizations of Africa: A History to 1800*. Charlottesville: University Press of Virginia.

Eigner, D. (2004) "Archaeological Research Conducted by the German Archaeological Mission to Eritrea." In *Neueste Feldforschungen im Sudan und in Eritrea: Akten des Symposiums vom 13. bis 14. Oktober 1999 in Berlin*. S. Wenig (ed.). Wiesbaden: Harrassowitz: 103-29.

Falk, H. (2001) "The *yuga* of Sphujiddhvaja and the era of the Kuṣâṇas." *Silk Road Art and Archaeology* 7: 121-36.

-----. (2004) "The Kaniṣka era in Gupta records." *Silk Road Art and Archaeology* 10: 167-76.

Fattovich, R. (1990) "Remarks on the Pre-Aksumite Period in Northern Ethiopia." *Journal of Ethiopian Studies* 23: 1-33.

-----. (1995) "The Origins of the Kingdom of Kush: Views from the African Hinterland." *Archéologie du Nil moyen* 7: 69-78.

-----. (2004) "The 'Pre-Aksumite' state in northern Ethiopia and Eritrea reconsidered." In *Trade and Travel in the Red Sea Region: Proceedings of Red Sea Project I held in the British Museum, October 2002*. P. Lunde and A. Porter (eds.). Oxford: Archaeopress: 71-7.

-----. (2009) "Reconsidering Yeha, c. 800-400 BC." *African Archaeological Review* 26: 275-90.

Fattovich, R. and Bard, K. (2001) "The Proto-Aksumite Period: An Overview." *Annales d'Éthiopie* 17: 3-24.

Fauvelle-Aymar, F.-X. (2009) "Les inscriptions d'Adoulis (Érythrée): Fragments d'un royaume d'influence hellénistique et gréco-romaine sur la côte africaine de la mer Rouge." *Bulletin de l'institut français d'archéologie orientale* 109: 135-60.

Fernandez, G. (1989) "The Evangelizing Mission of Theophilus "The Indian" and the Ecclesiastical Policy of Constantius II." *Klio* 71 (2): 361-6.

Fiaccadori, G. (1992) *Teofilo Indiano*. Ravenna: Mario Lapucci.

-----. (2004) "Sembrouthes 'gran re': (DAE IV 3 = RIÉth 275). Per la storia del primo ellenismo Aksumita." *La Parola del Passato* 59: 103-57.

Finneran, N. (2007) *The Archaeology of Ethiopia*. Routledge: London and New York.

Fitzpatrick, M. P. (2011) "Provincializing Rome: The Indian Ocean Trade Network and Roman Imperialism." *Journal of World History* 22 (1): 27-54.

Fontes Historiae Nubiorum (1994-2000) *Fontes Historiae Nubiorum: textual sources for the history of the middle Nile region between the eighth century BC and the sixth century AD*. T. Eide et al. (eds.). 4 vols. Bergen: University of Bergen, Dept. of Classics.

Frantsouzoff, S. A. (2006) "South Arabian Miniscule Writing and Early Ethiopian Script of Pre-Aksumite Graffiti: Typological Resemblance or Genetic Interdependence?" In *Proceedings of the XVth International Conference of Ethiopian Studies, Hamburg, July 20-25, 2003*. S. Uhlig (ed.). Wiesbaden: Harrassowitz: 572-86.

Frézouls, E. (1989) "Cosmas Indicopleustes et l'Arabie." In *L'Arabie préislamique et son environnement historique et culturel: Actes du Colloque de Strasbourg 24-27 juin 1987*. T. Fahd (ed.). Leiden: Brill: 441-60.

Fuller, D. Q. (2008) "The spread of textile production and textile crops in India beyond the Harappan zone: an aspect of the emergence of craft specialization and systematic trade." In *Linguistics, Archaeology and the Human Past*. T. Osada and A. Uesugi (eds.). Kyoto: Indus Project, Research Institute for Humanity and Nature: 1-26.

Fuller, D. Q., Boivin, N., Hoogervorst, T., and Allaby, R. (2011) "Across the Indian Ocean: the prehistoric movement of plants and animals." *Antiquity* 85: 544-58.

Gajda, I. (1996) "Ḥuğr b. 'Amr roi de Kinda et l'établissement de la domination ḥimyarite en Arabie centrale." *Proceedings of the Seminar for Arabian Studies* 26: 65-73.

-----. (2009) *Le royaume de Ḥimyar à l'époque monothéiste: l'histoire de l'Arabie du sud ancienne de la fin du IVe siècle de l'ère chrétienne jusqu'à l'avènement de l'Islam*. Paris: Académie des inscriptions et belles-lettres.

Genz, H. (2011) "Foreign Contacts of the Hittites." In *Insights into Hittite History and Archaeology*. H. Genz and D. P. Mielke (eds.). Leuven, Paris, and Walpole: Peeters: 301-23.

George, A. (n.d.) "What's new in the Gilgamesh epic?" (http://eprints.soas.ac.uk/3251/1/GilgameshWhat'sNew.pdf). Accessed April 30, 2011.

Gervers, M. (1992) "Cotton and Cotton Weaving in Meroitic Nubia and Medieval Ethiopia." In *Orbis Aethiopicus: Studia in honorem Stanislaus Chojnacki natali septuagesimo quinto dicata, septuagesimo septimo oblate*. P. O. Scholz (ed.). Albstadt: K. Schuler: Vol. I: 13-29.

Giangrande, G. (1970) "Heliodorus." In *The Oxford Classical Dictionary*. 2nd ed. N. G. L. Hammond and H. H. Scullard (eds.). Oxford: Oxford Clarendon Press: 493-4.

Glaser, E. (1895) *Die Abessinier in Arabien und Afrika, auf Grund neuentdeckter Inschriften*. Munich: Hermann Lukaschik.

Gradel, C. (2007) "Deux monnaies romaines découvertes à Saï (Soudan)." In *Mélanges offerts à Francis Geus: Egypte-Soudan*. B. Gratien (ed.). Villeneuve d'Ascq: Université Charles de Gaulle-Lille: 141-9.

Gradel, C., Letellier-Willemin, F., and Tallet, G. (*in press*) "«Une laine bien plus belle et douce que celle des moutons» à el-Deir (oasis de Kharga, Égypte): le coton au cœur de l'économie oasienne à l'époque romaine." In *D'Afrique et d'Egypte. Relations et échanges entre les espaces au sud de la Méditerranée à l'époque romaine, Actes du colloque international de l'U. de Limoges*. S. Guédon (ed.). Bordeaux: Ausonius.

Gragg, G. (1997) "Ge'ez (Ethiopic)." In *The Semitic Languages*. R. Hetzron (ed.). London and New York: Routledge: 242-60.

Gregory, T. E. (1991a) "Aphthartodocetism." In *The Oxford Dictionary of Byzantium*. A. P. Kazhdan (ed.). New York and Oxford: Oxford University Press: Vol. 1: 129.

-----. (1991b) "Julian of Halikarnassos." In *The Oxford Dictionary of Byzantium*. A. P. Kazhdan (ed.). New York and Oxford: Oxford University Press: Vol. 2: 1080.

Griffith, F. Ll. (1911) "The Inscriptions from Meroë." In Garstang, J. *Meroë, the city of the Ethiopians; being an account of a first season's excavations on the site, 1909-1910*. Oxford: Clarendon Press: 57-80.

Griffith, F. Ll. and Crowfoot, G. M. (1934) "On the Early Use of Cotton in the Nile Valley," *Journal of Egyptian Archaeology* 20 (1/2): 5-12.

Grimal, N. (1992) *A History of Ancient Egypt*. I. Shaw (transl.). Oxford, United Kingdom; Cambridge, Massachusetts: Blackwell.

Haaland, G. and Haaland, R. (2007) "God of war, worldly ruler, and craft specialists in the Meroitic kingdom of Sudan: Inferring social identity from material remains." *Journal of Social Archaeology* 7 (3): 372-92.

Hackl U., Jenni, H., and Schneider, C. (2003) *Quellen zur Geschichte der Nabatäer: Textsammlung mit Übersetzung und Kommentar*. Freiburg: Universitätsverlag Freiburg.

Hägg, T. (2004) "Axumite Inscription in Greek 6164 (SNM 24841)." In *The Capital of Kush 2: Meroë Excavations 1973-1984*. Wiesbaden: Harrassowitz Verlag: 106-8.

Hahn, W. (1989) "A numismatic contribution to the dating of the Aksumite king Sembrouthes." In *Proceedings of the Eighth International Conference of Ethiopian Studies*. Taddese Beyene (ed.). Addis Ababa: Institute of Ethiopian Studies; Frankfurt am Main: Frobenius Institut, Johann Wolfgang, Goëthe (sic) Universität: Vol. 2: 11-13.

-----. (2000) "Aksumite numismatics: a critical survey of recent research." *Revue numismatique* 6 (155): 281-311.

Hartmann, U. (2008) "Claudius Gothicus und Aurelianus." In *Die Zeit der Soldaten-Kaiser: Krise und Transformation des Römischen Reiches im 3. Jahrhundert n. Chr. (235-284)*. K.-P. Johne (ed.). Berlin: Akademie Verlag: Vol. 1: 297-323.

Hatke, G. (2011) *Africans in Arabia Felix: Aksumite Relations with Ḥimyar in the Sixth Century C.E.* Ph.D. diss. Princeton: Princeton University, Department of Near Eastern Studies.

Haycock, B. G. (1967) "The Later Phases of Meroïtic Civilization." *Journal of Egyptian Archaeology* 53: 107-20.

-----. (1971) "The Place of the Napatan-Meroitic Culture in the History of the Sudan and Africa." In *Sudan in Africa: Studies presented to the first international conference sponsored by the Sudan Research Unit, 7-12 February, 1968*. Y. F. Ḥasan (ed.). Khartoum: Khartoum University Press: 26-41.

Heliodorus (1935-43) *Les Éthiopiques (Théagène et Chariclée)*. J. Maillon (transl.). 3 vols. Paris: Société d'édition «Les Belles lettres».

Herodotus (1987) *The History*. D. Grene (transl.). Chicago and London: University of Chicago Press.

Hintze, F. (2000) "Meroe and the Noba." *Mitteilungen der Sudanarchäologischen Geselschaft zu Berlin e.V.* 10: 49-55.

Historia Augusta=The Scriptores Historiae Augustae (1921-32). D. Magie (transl.). 3 vols. Cambridge: Harvard University Press; London: William Heinemann.

Höfner, M. (1965) "Die semiten Äthiopiens." In *Götter und Mythen in vorderen Orient*. H. W. Haussig (ed.). Stuttgart: Ernst Klett Verlag: 553-67.

Hohl, E. (1985) *Historia Augusta: römische Herrschergestalten*. Vol. 2. Zürich and Munich: Artemis-Verlag.

Huntingford, G. W. B. (1989) *The Historical Geography of Ethiopia from the First Century AD to 1704*. Oxford: Published for the British Academy by Oxford University Press.

Ibn Ḥawqal, Abū l-Qāsim (1938-9) *Kitāb Ṣūraᵗ al-Arḍ* (*=Opus geographicum, auctore Ibn Ḥauḳal*). J. H. Kramers (ed.). 2 vols. Leiden: Brill.

Ibn Sa'īd, 'Alī b. Mūsā (1970) *Kitāb al-jug͟hrafiyya*. I. al-'Arabī (ed.). Beirut: al-Maktab al-Tijārī lil-ṭibā'a wal-nas͟hr wal-tawzī'.

Inizan, M.-L. and Francaviglia, V. M. (2002) "Les périples de l'obsidienne à travers la mer Rouge." *Journal des Africanistes* 72 (2) : 11-19.

al-Iryānī, M. 'A. (1973) *Fī Tarīk͟h al-Yaman: S͟harḥ wa-ta'līq 'alā nuqūs͟h lam tuns͟har: 34 naqs͟hᵃⁿ min majmū'aᵗ 'Alī 'Abd Allāh al-Kahālī*. Ṣan'ā': Markaz al-Dirāsāt al-Yamaniyya.

Jakobi, A. (1993) "The State of Research on Nubian Languages and the Contribution of Linguistics to the Study of Nubian Origins." In *Perspectives and Challenges in the Development of Sudanese Studies*. I. H. Abdalla (ed.). Lewiston, Queenston, and Lampeter: The Edwin Mellen Press: 59-73.

Jesse, F. (2009) "An den Grenzen der Macht—Die Festung Gala Abu Ahmed in der Wüste des Wadi Howar. Ein erster Arbeitsbericht aus einem neuen Forschungsprojekt." http://www.uni-koeln.de/phil-fak/praehist/africa/fst-afrika/deu/sudan/kurier.pdf. Accessed March 12, 2011.

John of Ephesus (1853) *The Third Part of the Ecclesiastical History of John, Bishop of Ephesus*. W. Cureton (ed.). Oxford: Oxford University Press.

Kaplan, S. (1982) "Ezana's Conversion Reconsidered." *Journal of Religion in Africa* 13 (2): 101-9.

Kelly, J. N. D. (1958) *Early Christian Doctrines*. New York: Harper & Brothers.

Kendall, T. (1989) "Ethnoarchaeology in Meroitic studies." In *Studia Meroitica 1984: Proceedings of the Fifth International Conference for Meroitic Studies, Rome 1984*. S. Donadoni and S. Wenig (eds.). Berlin: Akademie-Verlag: 625-745.

-----. (1997) *Kerma and the Kingdom of Kush, 2500-1500 B.C.: The Archaeological Discovery of an Ancient Nubian Empire*. Washington, D.C.: National Museum of African Art, Smithsonian Institution.

-----. (2007) "Evidence for a Napatan Occupation of the Wadi Muqaddam: Excavations at Al-Meragh in the Bayuda Desert (1999-2000)." In *Mélanges offerts à Francis Geus: Egypte-Soudan*. B. Gratien (ed.). Villeneuve d'Ascq: Université Charles de Gaulle-Lille: 197-204.

Khalidi, L. (2009) "Holocene Obsidian Exchange in the Red Sea Region." In *The Evolution of Human Populations in Arabia: Paleoenvironments, Prehistory and Genetics*. M. D. Petraglia and J. I. Rose (eds.). Dordrecht: Springer: 279-91.

Kirwan, L. (1937) "A Contemporary Account of the Conversion of the Sudan to Christianity." *Sudan Notes and Records* 20: 289-95.

-----. (1957) "Tanqasi and the Noba." *Kush* 5: 37-41.

-----. (1960) "The Decline and Fall of Meroë." *Sudan Notes and Records* 8: 163-73.

-----. (1972) "An Ethiopian-Sudanese Frontier Zone in Ancient History." *Geographical Journal* 138: 457-65.

-----. (1994) "Christianity in the Central Sudan: The Byzantine Mission and Nubian Alwa." In *Hommages à Jean Leclant. Volume 2: Nubie, Soudan, Ethiopie*. C. Berger, G. Clerc, and N. Grimal (eds.). Cairo: Institut français d'archéologie orientale du Caire: 245-9.

Kitchen, A., Ehret, C., Shiferaw Assefa, Mulligan, C. J. (2009) "Bayesian phylogenetic analysis of Semitic languages identifies an Early Bronze Age origin of Semitic in the Near East." *Proceedings of the Royal Society B: Biological Sciences* 276: 2703-10.

Kitchen, K. A. (1990) "Further thoughts on Punt and its neighbours." In *Studies on Ancient Egypt in Honour of H. S. Smith*. A. Leahy and J. Tait (eds.). London: Egypt Exploration Society: 173-8.

-----. (1994-2000) *Documentation for Ancient Arabia*. 2 vols. Liverpool: Liverpool University Press.

-----. (2004) "The elusive land of Punt revisited." In *Trade and Travel in the Red Sea Region: Proceedings of Red Sea Project I held in the*

British Museum, October 2002. P. Lunde and A. Porter (eds.). Oxford: Archaeopress: 25-31.

Klemm, D. *et al.* (2001) "Gold of the Pharaohs—6000 years of gold mining in Egypt and Nubia." *African Earth Sciences* 33: 643-59.

Knauf, E. A. (1988) "The West Arabian Place Name Province: Its Origin and Significance." *Proceedings of the Seminar for Arabian Studies* 18: 39-49.

Kobishchanov, Y. M. (1979) *Axum*. J. W. Michels (ed.); L. T. Kapitanoff (transl.). University Park: Pennsylvania State University Press.

Łajtar, A. and van der Vliet, J. (2006) "Rome-Meroe-Berlin: The Southernmost Latin Inscription Rediscovered ("CIL" III 83)." *Zeitschrift für Papyrologie und Epigraphik* 157: 193-8.

Lassányi, G. (2008) "Tumulus burials and the nomadic population of the Eastern Desert in Late Antiquity." In *Between the Cataracts: Proceedings of the 11^{56} International Conference for Nubian Studies, Warsaw University, 27 August-2 October 2006*. PAM Supplement Series 2.2/2. Warsaw: Warsaw University Press: 595-606.

Leclant, J. (1961) "Découverte de monuments égyptiens ou égyptisants hors de la vallée du Nil, 1955-60." *Orientalia* 30: 391-406.

Lenoble, P. and Sharif, N. M. (1992) "Barbarians at the gates? the royal mounds of El Hobagi and the end of Meroë." *Antiquity* 66: 626-35.

Leslau, W. (1991) *Comparative Dictionary of Ge'ez (Classical Ethiopic).* Wiesbaden: Otto Harrassowitz.

Levine, D. (2000) *Greater Ethiopia: The Evolution of a Multiethnic Society*. 2nd ed. Chicago: University of Chicago Press.

Liszka, K. (2011) "'We have come from the well of Ibhet': Ethnogenesis of the Medjay." *Journal of Egyptian History* 4: 149-71.

Littmann, E. (1913) *Deutsche Aksum-Expedition: Sabäische, Griechische, und Altabessinische Inschriften*. Deutsche Aksum-Expedition, Band IV. Berlin: G. Reimer.

Littmann, E. and Meredith, D. (1954) "An Old Ethiopic Inscription from the Berenice Road." *Journal of the Royal Asiatic Society of Great Britain and Ireland* 3/4: 119-23.

Lohwasser, A. (2008) "Das meroitische Reich und die Blemmyer." In *Die Zeit der Soldatenkaiser: Krise und Transformation des Römischen*

Reiches im 3. Jahrhundert n. Chr. (235-284). K.-P. Johne (ed.). Berlin: Akademie Verlag: Vol. 1: 571-80.

Lucas, A. (1927) "Copper in Ancient Egypt." *Journal of Egyptian Archaeology* 13 (3/4): 162-70.

Lusini, G. (2003) "Aksum: Mäṣḥafä Aksum." In *Encyclopaedia Aethiopica*. S. Uhlig (ed.). Wiesbaden: Harrassowitz: Vol. 1: 185-6.

Magid, A. A. (2004) "The Site of Tabot: An Old Waystation in the Southern Red Sea Hills, Sudan." In *Neueste Feldforschungen im Sudan und in Eritrea: Akten des Symposiums vom 13. bis 14. Oktober 1999 in Berlin*. S. Wenig (ed.). Wiesbaden: Harrassowitz Verlag: 155-89.

Magnavita, C. (2006) "Ancient Humped Cattle in Africa: A View from the Chad Basin." *African Archaeological Review* 23: 55-84.

Malalas (1986) *The Chronicle of John Malalas*. E. Jeffreys et al. (transl.). Melbourne: Australian Association for Byzantine Studies; Sydney: Department of Modern Greek, University of Sydney.

Manzo, A. (1997) "Les tessons «exotiques» du groupe du Gash: un essai d'étude statistique." In *Actes de la VIIIe Conférence internationale des études nubiennes: Lille, 11-17 septembre 1994. Vol. II: Découvertes archéologiques*. Villeneuve d'Ascq: Université Charles de Gaulle-Lille III: 77-87.

-----. (2004) "Late Antique Evidence in Eastern Sudan." *Sudan & Nubia* 8: 75-83.

-----. (2005) "Aksumite Trade and the Red Sea Exchange Network: A View from Bieta Giyorgis (Aksum)." In *People of the Red Sea: Proceedings of the Red Sea Project II, held in the British Museum, October 2004*. J. C. M. Starkey (ed.). Oxford: Archaeopress: 51-66.

-----. (2009) "*Capra nubiana* in *Berbere* Sauce? Pre-Aksumite Art and Identity Building." *African Archaeological Review* 26: 291-303.

-----. (2010) "Nubian Pottery and Ceramics from Southern Regions of the Red Sea." In *Mersa/Wadi Gawasis 2009-2010*. K. A. Bard and R. Fattovich (eds.). http://www.archaeogate.org/storage/15_article_1331_1.pdf. Accessed May 23, 2011.

Maraqten, M. (1994) "Typen altsüdarabischer Altäre." In *Arabia Felix: Beiträge zur Sprache und Kultur des vorislamischen Arabien:*

Festschrift Walter W. Müller zum 60. Geburtstag. N. Nebes (ed.). Wiesbaden: Harrassowitz: 160-77.

Marcus, H. G. (1994) *A History of Ethiopia*. Berkeley and Los Angeles: University of California Press.

Marrassini, P. (2003) "The Semites in Abyssinia: Onomastic and Lexicographical Notes." In *Studia Semitica*. L. Kogan (ed.). Moscow: Russian State University for the Humanities: 141-51.

Martyrium Arethae (2007) = *Le martyre de Saint Aréthas et de ses compagnons (BHG 166)*. J. Beaucamp (ed. and transl.). Paris: Association des amis du Centre d'histoire et civilisation de Byzance.

Matthews, J. F. (1984) "The Tax Law of Palmyra: Evidence for Economic History in a City of the Roman East." *Journal of Roman Studies* 74: 157-80.

Mayerson, P. (1993) "A confusion of Indias: Asian India and African India in Byzantine sources." *Journal of the American Oriental Society* 113 (2): 169-74.

Merid Wolde Aregay (2005) "Military Elites in Medieval Ethiopia." In *Land, Literacy and the State in Sudanic Africa*. D. Crummey (ed.). Trenton and Asmara: The Red Sea Press: 159-86.

Metlich, M. A. (2006) "Aksumite gold coins and their relation to the Roman-Indian trade." In *Dal denarius al dinar: l'Oriente e la moneta romana: atti dell'incontro di studio, Roma 16-18 settembre 2004*. Roma: Istituto italiano di numismatica: 99-103.

Mitchell, P. (2005) *African Connections: An Archaeological Perspective on Africa and the Wider World*. Walnut Creek, California: AltaMira Press.

Morgan, J. R. (1982) "History, Romance, and Realism in the Aithiopika of Heliodorus." *Classical Antiquity* 1 (2): 221-65.

Morin, D. (1996) "Y-a-t-il un lexique Beni-Amer?" *Israel Oriental Studies* 16 : 251-67.

-----. (2004) *Dictionnaire historique afar: 1288-1982*. Paris: Karthala.

Morkot, R. G. (2000) *The Black Pharaohs: Egypt's Nubian Rulers*. London: The Rubicon Press.

Morton, J. (1989) "Ethnicity and Politics in Red Sea Province, Sudan." *African Affairs* 88 (350): 63-76.

Müller, W. W. (2010) *Sabäische Inschriften nach Ären datiert: Bibliographie, Texte und Glossar*. Wiesbaden: Harrassowitz Verlag.

Munro-Hay, S. (1981-2) "A Tyranny of Sources: The History of Aksum from its Coinage." *Northeast African Studies* 3 (3): 1-16.

-----. (1989a) "The al-Madhariba Hoard of Gold Aksumite and Late Roman Coins." *Numismatic Chronicle* 149: 83-100.

-----. (1989b) "Aksumite chronology: some reconsiderations." In *Proceedings of the Eighth International Conference of Ethiopian Studies*. Taddese Beyene (ed.). Addis Ababa: Institute of Ethiopian Studies; Frankfurt am Main: Frobenius Institut, Johann Wolfgang, Goëthe (sic) Universität: Vol. 2: 27-40.

-----. (1991) *Aksum: An African Civilisation of Late Antiquity*. Edinburgh: Edinburgh University Press.

-----. (1999) *Catalogue of the Aksumite Coins in the British Museum*. London: British Museum Press.

Munro-Hay, S. and Juel-Jensen, B. (1995) *Aksumite Coinage*. Spink: London.

Munro-Hay, S. and Nosnitsin, D. (2005) "Danə'el." In *Encyclopaedia Aethiopica*. S. Uhlig (ed.). Wiesbaden: Harrassowitz: Vol. 2: 84-5.

Murray, O. (1967) "Review: East of Suez." *The Classical Review* (New Series) 17 (1): 79-81.

Nibbi, A. (1997) "A Note on Atika/Attāka/Tāka and Copper." In Nibbi, A. *Some Geographical Notes on Ancient Egypt: A Selection of Published Papers, 1975-1997*. Oxford: Discussions in Egyptology: 305-12.

Noeske, H.-C. (1998) "Zu den Gußimitationen axumitischer Bronzemünzen in Ägypten und Palästina." In *ΘΕΜΕΛΙΑ: spätantike und koptologische Studien: Peter Grossmann zum 65. Geburtstag*. M. Krause and S. Schaten (eds.). Wiesbaden: Reichert Verlag: 249-62.

Al-Nūr, U. 'A.-R. (2004) "Sharq al-Sūdān: Daltā al-Qāsh fī mā qabl al-tārīkh: lamḥa mūjaza 'an ahamm natā'ij al-baḥth al-maydānī fī sharq al-Sūdān." *Arkamānī* 5 (http://arkamani.com/vol_5/archaeology_5/eastern%20sudan%20and%20south%20arabia.htm). Accessed July 8, 2011.

Ogden, J. (2000) "Metals." In *Ancient Egyptian Materials and Technology*. P. T. Nicholson and I. Shaw (eds.). Cambridge; New York: Cambridge University Press: 148-76.

Ochała, G. (2011) "A King of Makuria in Kordofan." In *Nubian Voices: Studies in Christian Nubian Culture. The Journal of Juristic Papyrology, Supplement XV*. A. Łajtar and J. Van Der Vliet (eds.). Warsaw: Faculty of Law and Administration of the University of Warsaw: 149-55.

Pankhurst, R. (1961) *An Introduction to the Economic History of Ethiopia, from Early Times to 1800*. London: Lalibela House.

-----. (1997) *The Ethiopian Borderlands: Essays in Regional History from Ancient Times to the End of the 18th Century*. Lawrenceville: Red Sea Press.

Payne Smith, R. (1860) *The Third Part of the Ecclesiastical History of John Bishop of Ephesus*. Oxford: University Press.

Peacock, D. and L. Blue (2007) *The Ancient Red Sea Port of Adulis, Eritrea: Results of the Eritro-British Expedition, 2004-5*. Oxford: Oxbow Books.

Piamenta, M. (1990-1) *Dictionary of Post-Classical Yemeni Arabic*. 2 vols. Leiden: Brill.

Phillips, J. (1997) "Punt and Aksum: Egypt and the Horn of Africa." *Journal of African History* 38 (3): 423-57.

-----. (2003a) "Egypt, Nubia and Ethiopia." In *Egyptology at the Dawn of the Twenty-first Century: Proceedings of the Eighth International Congress of Egyptologists, Cairo, 2000. Volume 2: History-Religion*. Z. Hawass (ed.). Cairo and New York: The American University in Cairo Press: 434-42.

-----. (2003b) "Looking Forwards by Looking Backwards: West of Aksum." In *Researching Africa's Past: New Contributions from British Archaeologists: Proceedings of a Meeting held at St. Hugh's College, Oxford, Saturday, April 20th 2002*. P. Mitchell, A. Haour, and J. Hobart (eds.). Oxford : Oxford University School of Archaeology; Oakville: David Brown Book Co.: 69-72.

Phillipson, D. W. (1997) *The Monuments of Aksum: An Illustrated Account*. Addis Ababa: Addis Ababa University Press in collaboration with the British Institute in Eastern Africa.

-----. (1998) *Ancient Ethiopia: Aksum: Its Antecedents and Successors*. London: British Museum Press.

-----. (2009a) "The First Millennium BC in the Highlands of Northern Ethiopia and South-Central Eritrea: A Reassessment of Cultural and Political Development." *African Archaeological Review* 26 (4): 257-74.

-----. (2009b) "Aksum, the entrepot, and highland Ethiopia, 3rd-12th centuries." In *Byzantine Trade, 4th-12th Centuries: The Archaeology of Local, Regional and International Exchange: Papers of the Thirty-eighth Spring Symposium of Byzantine Studies, St John's College, University of Oxford, March 2004*. M. M. Mango (ed.). Farnham and Burlington: Ashgate Publishing Limited: 353-68.

Philostorgius (2007) *Philostorgius: Church History*. P. R. Amidon (transl.). Atlanta: Society of Biblical Literature.

Pierce, R. H. (1995) "A Sale of an Alodian Slave Girl: a Reexamination of Papyrus Strassburg Inv. 1404." *Symbolae Osloenses* 70: 148-66.

Plumley, J. M. and Adams, W. Y. (1974) "Qasr Ibrîm 1972." *Journal of Egyptian Archaeology* 60: 212-38.

Power, T. (2007) "The 'Arabians' of pre-Islamic Egypt." In *Natural Resources and Cultural Connections of the Red Sea*. J. Starkey, P. Starkey, and T. Wilkinson (eds.). Oxford: Archaeopress: 195-210.

Priese, K.-H. (1984) "Orte des mittleren Niltals in der Überlieferung bis zum Ende des christlichen Mittelalters." In *Meroitische Forschungen 1980: Akten der 4. Internationalen Tagung für meroitische Forschungen vom 24. Bis 29. November 1980 in Berlin*. F. Hintze (ed.). Berlin: Akademie-Verlag: 484-97.

Procopius, *De Bell. Pers*. (1914) *History of the Wars*. H. B. Dewing (transl.). Cambridge, Massachusetts and London: Harvard University Press.

Rabin, C. (1949) "Old Abyssinian (?) graffito." In Macadam, M. F. L. *The Temples of Kawa: Oxford University Excavations in Nubia. Vol. 1: The inscriptions.* London: Published on behalf of the Griffith Institute, Ashmolean Museum, Oxford, by Oxford University Press: 117-18.

Rankin, D. (2000) "Arianism." In *The Early Christian World*. P. F. Esler (ed.). London and New York: Routledge: Vol. 2: 975-1001.

Raschke, M. G. (1978) "New Studies in Roman Commerce with the East." In *Aufstieg und Niedergang der Römischen Welt: Geschichte und Kultur Roms im Spiegel der Neueren Forschung*. H. Temporini and W. Haase (eds.). Berlin and New York: Walter de Gruyter: Vol. 2: 604-1361.

Rehren, T. (2001) "Aspects of the production of cobalt-blue glass in Egypt." *Archaeometry* 43 (4): 483-9.

Ricci, L. (1994) "On Both Sides of al-Mandab." In *New Trends in Ethiopian Studies: Papers of the 12th International Conference of Ethiopian Studies, Michigan State University, 5-10 September 1994*. H. G. Marcus (ed.). Lawrenceville: Vol. 1: 409-17.

Richter, S. G. (2002) *Studien zur Christianisierung Nubiens*. Wiesbaden: Reichert Verlag.

Rihani, B. (2004) "Identification of Some Archaeological Nabataean Sites in North-West Saudi Arabia." In *Studies in the Archaeology and History of Jordan*. Amman: Department of Antiquities: Vol. 8: 371-8.

Rilly, C. (2007) *La langue du royaume de Méroé: un panorama de la plus ancienne culture écrite d'Afrique subsaharienne*. Paris: Champion.

-----. (2009) "From the Yellow Nile to the Blue Nile. The quest for water and the diffusion of Northern East Sudanic languages from the fourth to the first millennium BCE." Paper presented at the Third European Conference on African Languages in Leipzig, 4-7 June 2009 (http://www.sfdas.com/blog/wp-content/leipzig-2008-rilly.pdf). Accessed February 24, 2012.

Robin, C. (1989) "La première intervention abyssine en Arabie méridionale (de 200 à 270 de l'ère chrétienne environ)." In *Proceedings of the Eighth International Conference of Ethiopian Studies*. Taddese Beyene (ed.). Addis Ababa: Institute of Ethiopian Studies; Frankfurt am Main: Frobenius Institut, Johann Wolfgang, Goëthe (*sic*) Universität: Vol. 2: 147-62.

-----. (1991) "Quelques épisodes marquants de l'histoire sudarabique." *Revue du Monde Musulman et de la Méditerranée* 61: 55-70.

-----. (1996) "Le royaume hujride, dit « royaume de Kinda », entre Himyar et Byzance." *Comptes-rendus des séances de l'Académie des Inscriptions et Belles-Lettres* 140 (2) : 665-714.

-----. (2005) "Ḥimyar au IVe siècle de l'ère chrétienne: analyse des données chronologiques et essai de mise en ordre." In *Rencontres sabéennes 6: The Periodisation and Chronological Terminology of Ancient Yemen*. Mainz am Rhein: Verlag Philipp von Zabern: 133-51.

Robin, C. and Gajda, I. (1994) "L'inscription de Wadi 'Abadan." *Raydān* 6: 113-37.

Robin, C. and Gorea, M. (2002) "Les vestiges antiques de la grotte de Ḥôq (Suquṭra, Yemen)," *Comptes-rendus des séances de l'Académie des Inscriptions et Belles-Lettres* 146 (2): 409-45.

Robin, C. and Maigret, A. de (1998) "Le Grand Temple de Yéha (Tigray, Éthiopie), après la première campagne de fouilles de la Mission française (1998)." *Comptes-rendus des séances de l'Académie des Inscriptions et Belles-Lettres* 142 (3): 737-98.

Rodinson, M. (1981) "Les nouvelles inscriptions d'Axoum et le lieu de déportation des Bedjas." *Raydān* 4: 97-116.

Roy, J. (2011) *The Politics of Trade: Egypt and Lower Nubia in the 4th Millennium BC*. Leiden: Brill.

Rufinus (1997) *The Church History of Rufinus of Aquileia, Books 10 and 11*. P. R. Amidon (transl.). New York: Oxford University Press.

Salih, M. A. M. (2007) "Kassala." In *Encyclopaedia Aethiopica*. S. Uhlig (ed.). Wiesbaden: Harrassowitz: Vol. 3: 354-5.

Sayce, A. H. (1909) "A Greek Inscription of a King (?) of Axum found at Meroe." *Proceedings of the Society of Biblical Archaeology* 31: 189-90.

-----. (1923) *Reminiscences*. London: Macmillan.

Schmidt, P. R. (2006) *Historical Archaeology in Africa: Representation, Social Memory, and Oral Traditions*. Lanham: AltaMira Press.

Schneider, R. (1974) "Trois nouvelles inscriptions royales d'Axoum." *IV Congresso Internazionale di Studi Etiopici (Roma, 10-15 aprile 1972), Tomo I (Sezione Storica)*. Rome: Accademia Nazionale dei Lincei: 767-86.

-----. (1976) "L'inscription chrétienne d'Ezana en écriture sudarabe." *Annales d'Éthiopie* 10 (10): 109-17.

-----. (1983) "Les origins de l'écriture éthiopienne." In *Ethiopian Studies dedicated to Wolf Leslau on the occasion of his seventy-fifth birthday, November 14th, 1981, by his friends and colleagues*. S. Segert and J. E. Bodrogligeti (eds.). Wiesbaden: Harrassowitz: 412-16.

Sedov, A. (1996) "Qana' (Yemen) and the Archaeological Evidence." In *Tradition and Archaeology: Early Maritime Contacts in the Indian Ocean: Proceedings of the International Seminar, Techno-archaeological Perspectives of Seafaring in the Indian Ocean, 4th cent. B.C.-15th cent. A.D., New Delhi, February 28-March 4, 1994*. H. P. Ray and J.-F. Salles (ed.) New Delhi: Manohar Publishers and Distributors: 11-35.

-----. (2007) "The Port of Qana' and the incense Trade." In *Food for the Gods: New Light on the Ancient Incense Trade*. D. Peacock and D. Williams (eds.). Oxford: Oxbow; Oakville: David Brown Books: 71-111.

Seland, E. H. (2010) *Ports and Political Power in the* Periplus: *Complex Societies and Maritime Trade on the Indian Ocean in the First Century AD*. Oxford: Archaeopress.

Severin, T., Rehren, T., and Schleicher, H. (2011) "Early metal smelting in Aksum, Ethiopia: copper or iron?" *European Journal of Mineralogy* 23: 981-92.

Shinnie, P. L. (1967) *Meroe: A Civilization of the Sudan*. New York: F. A. Praeger.

-----. (1978) "The Nilotic Sudan and Ethiopia, c. 660 BC to c. AD 600." In *The Cambridge History of Africa. Volume 2: from c. 500 BC to AD 500*. J. D. Fage (ed.). Cambridge: Cambridge University Press: 210-71.

-----. (1996) *Ancient Nubia*. London and New York: Kegan Paul International.

Shinnie, P. L. and Anderson, J. R. (2004) "The Excavations." In *The Capital of Kush 2: Meroë Excavations 1973-1984*. Wiesbaden: Harrassowitz Verlag: 5-102.

Shinnie, P.L. and Bradley, R. J. (1980). *The Capital of Kush 1*. Berlin: Akademie-Verlag.

Shinnie, P. L., Kirwan, L. P., Jakobielski, S., and Leclant, J. (1982) "Discussion: Ethiopia and the Nile Valley." In *Meroitic Studies: Proceedings of the Third International Meroitic Conference, Toronto 1977*. N. B. Millet and A. L. Kelly (eds.). Berlin: Akademie-Verlag: 55-7.

Shinnie, P. L. and Robertson, J. H. (1993) "'The end of Meroë'—a comment on the paper by Patrice Lenoble & Nigm el Din Mohamed Sharif." *Antiquity* 67: 895-9.

Sidebotham, S. E. (1986) *Roman Economic Policy in the Erythra Thalassa, 30 B.C.-A.D. 217*. Leiden: E.J. Brill.

-----. (1996) "Roman Interests in the Red Sea and Indian Ocean." In *The Indian Ocean in Antiquity*. J. Reade (ed.). London and New York: Kegan Paul International in association with the British Museum: 287-308.

-----. (2011) *Berenike and the Ancient Maritime Spice Route*. Berkeley: University of California Press.

Sidebotham, S. E., Hense, M., and Nouwens, H. M. (2008) *The Red Land: The Illustrated Archaeology of Egypt's Eastern Desert*. Cairo and New York: American University in Cairo Press.

Sima, A. (2003) "Ag'azi." In *Encyclopaedia Aethiopica*. S. Uhlig (ed.). Wiesbaden: Harrassowitz: Vol. 1: 144-5.

Sinor, D. (1990) "The Establishment and Dissolution of the Türk Empire." In *The Cambridge History of Early Inner Asia*. D. Sinor (ed.). Cambridge: Cambridge University Press: 285-316.

Skeat, T. C. (1977) "A Letter from the King of the Blemmyes to the King of the Noubades." *Journal of Egyptian Archaeology* 63: 159-70.

Smidt, W. (2010) "Taka." In *Encyclopaedia Aethiopica*. S. Uhlig (ed.). Wiesbaden: Harrassowitz: Vol. 4: 821-2.

Smith, S. T. (2003) *Wretched Kush: Ethnic Identities and Boundaries in Egypt's Nubian Empire*. London and New York: Routledge.

Snowden, F. M. (1970) *Blacks in Antiquity: Ethiopians in the Greco-Roman Experience*. Cambridge, Massachusetts: Belknap Press of Harvard University Press.

Spalinger, A. J. (2005) *War in Ancient Egypt: The New Kingdom*. Oxford: Blackwell.

Spaudling, J. (1995) "Medieval Christian Nubia and the Islamic World: A Reconsideration of the Baqt Treaty." *The International Journal of African Historical Studies* 28 (3): 577-94.

Tadesse Tamrat (1988) "Processes of Ethnic Interaction and Integration in Ethiopian History: The Case of the Agaw." *Journal of African History* 29: 5-18.

El Tayeb, M. (2002) *Genesis of the Makurian Culture in the Light of Archaeological Sources*. Lille: Université Charles-de-Gaulle-Lille III.

Thelwall, R. and Schadeberg, T. C. (1983) "The Linguistic Settlement of the Nuba Mountains." *Sprache und Geschichte in Afrika* 5: 219-31.

Tomber, R. (2005) "Aksumite and other Imported Ceramics from Early Historic Kamrej." *Journal of Indian Ocean Archaeology* 2: 99-102.

Top. Chr.=Cosmas Indicopleustes (1968-73) *Topographie chrétienne*. W. Wolska-Conus (ed. and transl.). 3 vols. Paris: Éditions du Cerf.

Török, L. (1985) "The date of the end of Meroe." *Meroitic Newsletter* 24: 6-22.

-----. (1988) *Late Antique Nubia: History and archaeology of the southern neighbour of Egypt in the 4th-6th c. A. D.* Budapest: Archaeological Institute of The Hungarian Academy of Sciences.

-----. (1989) "Kush and the external world." In *Studia Meroitica 1984: Proceedings of the Fifth Conference for Meroitic Studies, Rome 1984*. S. Donadoni and S. Wenig (eds.). Berlin: Akademie-Verlag: 49-215.

-----. (1997) *The Kingdom of Kush: Handbook of the Napatan-Meroitic Civilization*. Leiden and New York: Brill.

-----. (1999) "The End of Meroe." In *Recent Research in Kushite History and Archaeology: Proceedings of the 8th International Conference for Meroitic Studies*. D. A. Welsby (ed.). London: British Museum: 133-56.

-----. (2002) *The Image of the Ordered World in Ancient Nubian Art: The Construction of the Kushite Mind, 800 BC-300 AD*. Leiden and Boston: Brill.

-----. (2009) *Between Two Worlds: The Frontier Region between Ancient Nubia and Egypt, 3700 BC-AD 500*. Leiden and Boston: Brill.

-----. (2011) "From El Hobagi to Ballana and Back." In *La pioche et la plume: autour du Soudan, du Liban et de la Jordanie: hommages archéologiques à Patrice Lenoble*. V. Rondot, F. Alpi, and F. Villeneuve (dir.). Paris: Presses de l'université Paris-Sorbonne: 515-30.

Trigger, B. G. (1969) "The Myth of Meroe and the African iron Age." *African Historical Studies* 2 (1): 23-50.

Trimingham, J. S. (1949) *Islam in the Sudan*. London and New York: Oxford University Press.

Tucker, A. N. and Bryan, M. A. (1956) *The Non-Bantu Languages of North-eastern Africa*. London and New York: Published for the International African Institute by the Oxford University Press.

Van der Veen, M. and Morales, J. (2011) "Summer Crops—From Trade to Innovation." In Van der Veen, M. *Consumption, Trade and Innovation: Exploring the Botanical Remains from the Roman and Islamic Ports at Quseir al-Qadim, Egypt*. Frankfurt am Main: Africa Magna Verlag: 75-119.

Wainwright, G. A. (1942a) "Cosmas and the Gold Trade of Fazoqli." *Man* 42: 52-8.

-----. (1942b) "Early Records of iron in Abyssinia." *Man* 42: 82-8.

Ward, C. (2006) "Boat-building and its social context in early Egypt: interpretations from the First Dynasty boat-grave cemetery at Abydos." *Antiquity* 80:118-29.

Weinandy, T. G. (2007) *Athanasius: A Theological Introduction*. Aldershot and Burlington: Ashgate.

Welsby, D. A. (1996) *The Kingdom of Kush: The Napatan and Meroitic Empires*. London: Published for the Trustees of the British Museum by British Museum Press.

-----. (1998) *Soba II: Renewed excavations within the metropolis of the Kingdom of Alwa in Central Sudan*. London: British Museum Press.

-----. (1999) "Meroitic Soba." In *Studien zum antiken Sudan: Akten der 7. internationalen Tagung für meroitische Forschungen vom 14. bis 19. September 1992 in Gosen/bei Berlin*. S. Wenig (ed.). Wiesbaden: Harrassowtiz Verlag: 663-77.

-----. (2002) *The Medieval Kingdoms of Nubia: Pagans, Christians and Muslims along the Middle Nile*. London: British Museum Press.

Wendrich, W. Z. (1998) "Fringes are Anchored in Warp and Weft: The Relations between Berenike, Shenshef, and the Nile Valley." In *Life on the Fringe: Living in the Southern Egyptian Deserts during the Roman and Early-Byzantine Periods*. O. E. Kaper (ed.). Leiden: Research School CNWS, School of Asian, African, and Amerindian Studies: 243-51.

Whitehouse, D. (1997) *Roman Glass in the Corning Museum of Glass*. Vol. 1. Corning, New York: Corning Museum of Glass.

Wild, J. P., Wild, F. C., and Clapham, A. J. (2005) "Roman Cotton Revisited." In *Vestidos, textiles y tintes: estudios sobre la producción de bienes de consumo en la antigüedad: actas del II Symposium Internacional sobre Textiles y Tintes del Mediterráno en el Mundo Antiguo, Atenas, 24 al 26 de noviembre, 2005*. C. Alfaro Giner and L. Karali (eds.). Valencia: University of Valencia: 143-7.

Wild, J. P., Wild, F. C., and Clapham, A. J. (2007) "Irrigation and the spread of cotton growing in Roman times." *Archaeological Textiles Newsletter* 44: 16-18.

Williams, R. (1987) *Arius: Heresy and Tradition*. London: Darton, Longman, and Todd.

Winnicki, J. K. (2009) *Late Egypt and her Neighbours: Foreign Population in Egypt in the First Millennium BC*. Warsaw: Warsaw University, Faculty of Law and Administration, Chair of Roman and Antique Law; Institute of Archaeology, Department of Papyrology.

Wright, D. R. (1999) "'What Do You Mean There Were No Tribes in Africa?': Thoughts on Boundaries—and Related Matters—in Precolonial Africa." *History in Africa* 26: 409-26.

Young, J. (1999) "Along Ethiopia's western frontier: Gambella and Benishangul in transition." *Journal of Modern African Studies* 37 (2): 321-46.

Zarins, J. (1990) "Obsidian and the Red Sea Trade: Prehistoric Aspects." In *South Asian Archaeology 1987: Proceedings of the Ninth International Conference of the Association of South Asian Archaeologists in Western Europe, held in the Fondazione Giorgio*

Cini, Island of San Giorgio Maggiore, Venice. M. Taddei (ed.). Rome: Istituto Italiano per il Medio ed Estremo Oriente: 507-41.

Zarroug, M. A. (1991) *The Kingdom of Alwa*. Calgary: University of Calgary Press.

Zibelius, K. (1972) *Afrikanische Orts- und Völkernamen in hieroglyphischen und hieratischen Texten*. Wiesbaden: Dr. Ludwig Reichert.

Zibelius-Chen, K. (2006) "The Chronology of Nubian Kingdoms from Dyn. 25 to the End of the Kingdom of Meroe." In *Ancient Egyptian Chronology*. E. Hornung, R. Krauss, and D. A. Warburton (eds.). Leiden and Boston: Brill: 284-303.

Zwettler, M. J. (1996) "The "era of NBT" and "YMNT": two proposals (1)." *Arabian Archaeology and Epigraphy* 7 (1): 95-107.

-----. (2000) "*Ma'add* in Late-Ancient Arabian Epigraphy and Other Pre-Islamic Sources." *Wiener Zeitschrift für die Kunde des Morgenlandes* 90: 223-309.

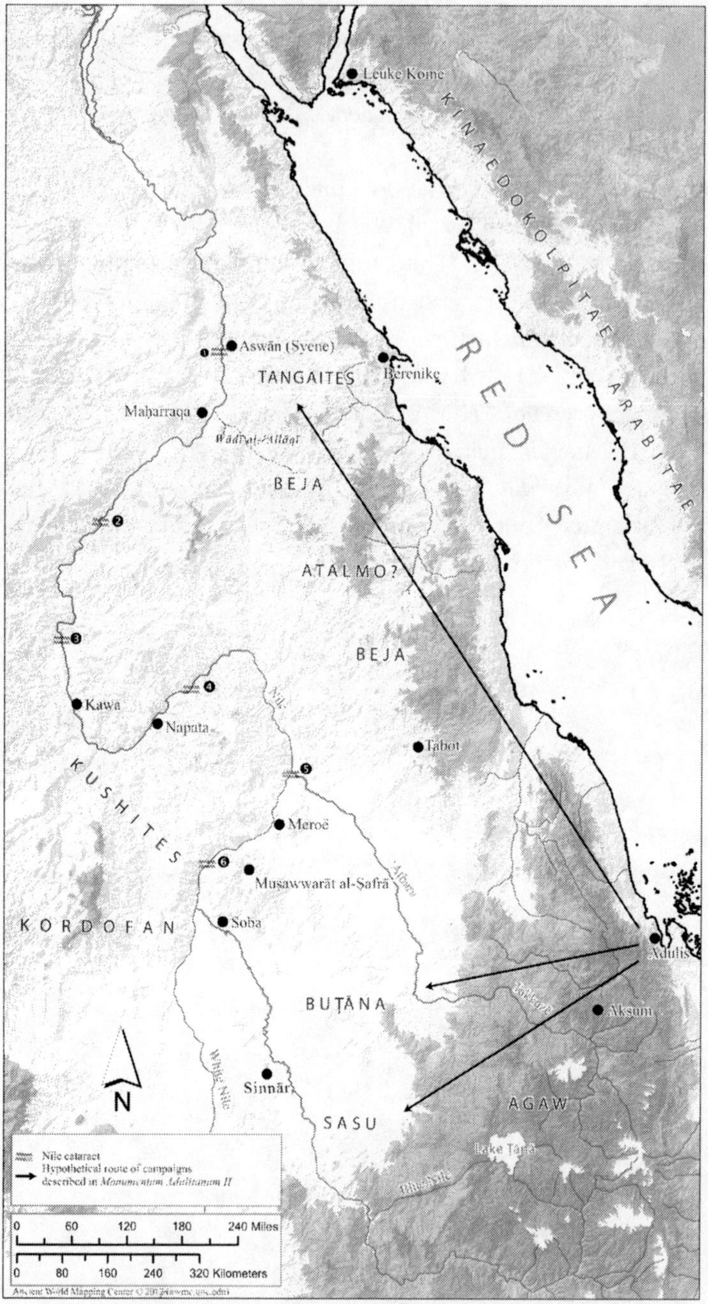

Map 1. Northeast Africa in the third century CE

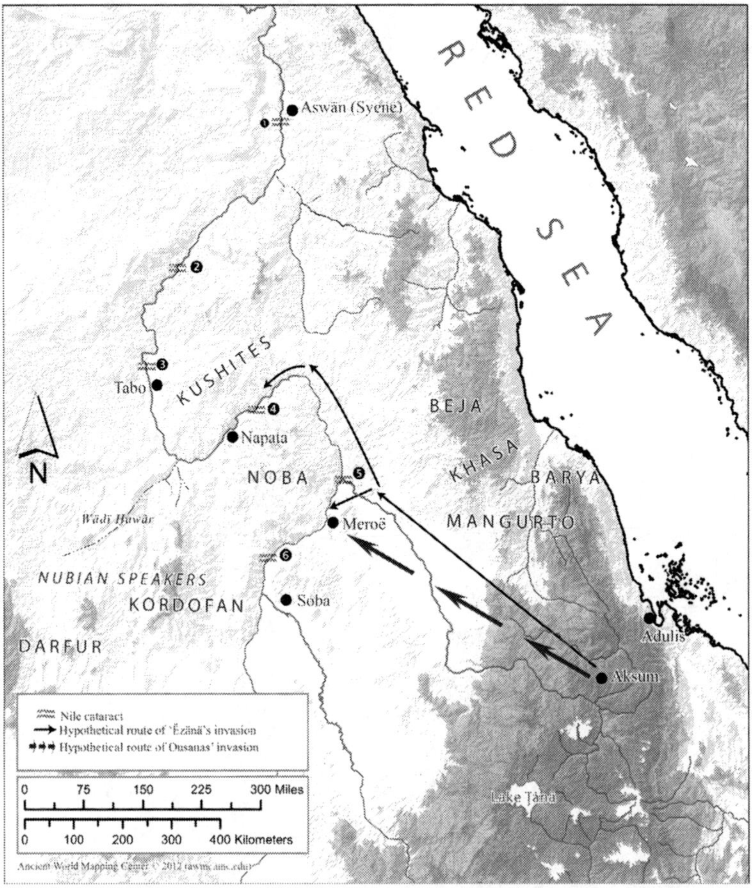

Map 2. Northeast Africa in the fourth century CE

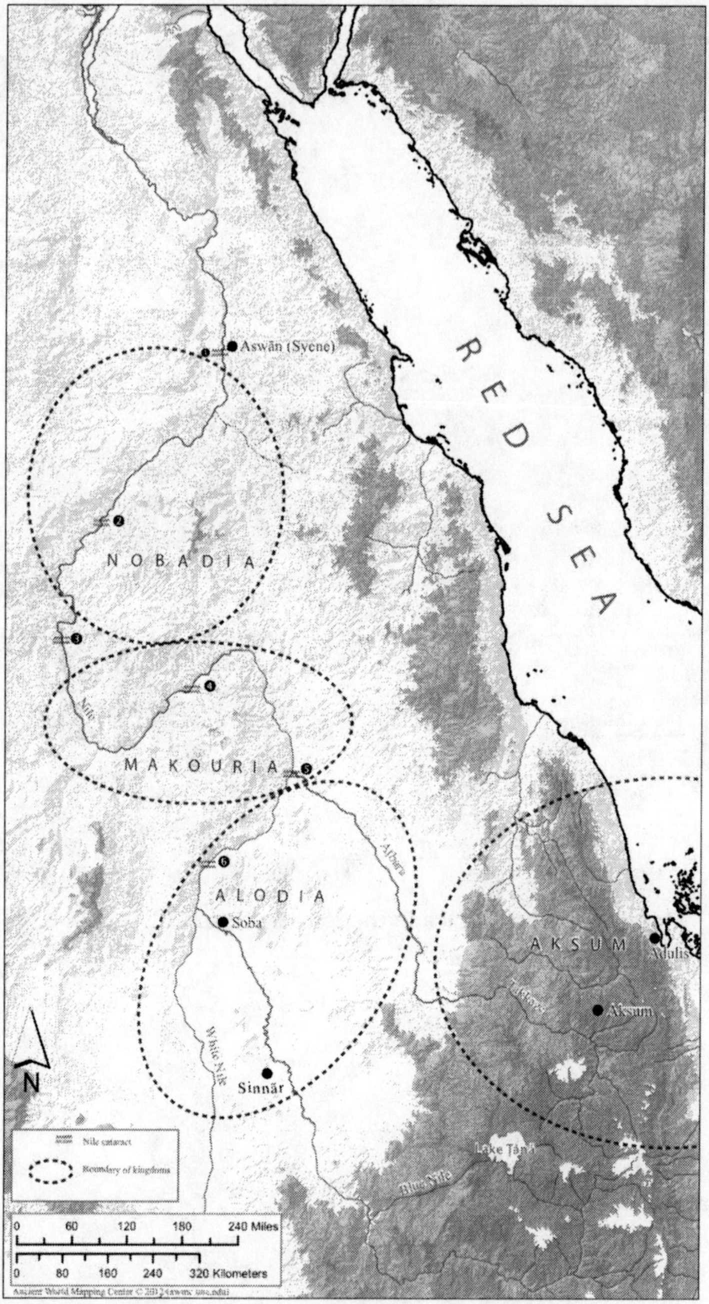

Map 3. Northeast Africa in the sixth century CE

Index

'Abrehā: 149.
Adras: 47.
Adulis: 13, 26, 27, 28, 34, 38, 42, 54.
Aedesius: 89, 94.
Agaw: 54, 56, 170, n. 219.
Aithiopika: 140, 141, 171.
Alara: 18, n. 24.
Alodia: 13, 116, 125, 152, 155, 161, 162.
Alwa: 114, 115, 116, 121, n. 458, n. 489, n. 518.
aphthartodocetism: 161, 162.
Arabitae: 41, 64, n. 150.
Ares (see Maḫrem)
Arianism: 90, 91.
army, Aksumite: 13, 41, 48, 61, 67, 77, 78, 85, 95, 99, 106, 108, 116, 116, 120, 121, 124, 125, 133, 137, 145, 149, 158, n. 304, n. 529.
Aswān (=Syene): 48, 141, 152.
Atalmo: 45, 47, 103.
'Aṭbara River: 32, 104, 108, 116, 119, 121, 124, 128, n. 351.
Atiadites: 95, 97, 98, 100, 103.
Attabitē: 47.
Banī 'Āmir: 47, 97, 103, n. 183.
Barya: 95, 97, 98, 102, 103, 105, 120, 131, 132, 135, 163, 165.
Bayūḍa: 83, n. 345, n. 346.
Beja (see also Blemmyes): 45, 45, 50, 52, 59, 62, 69, 75, 79, 81, 87, 97, 101, 103, 105, 125, 135, 140, 150, 157, 159, n. 96, n. 173, n. 183, n. 244, n. 385, n. 455, n. 510, n. 534, n. 538, n. 539.
Berenike: 27, 50, 64, 158, 160, n. 79, n. 199, n. 203.
Blemmyes: 45, 62, 65, 105, 140, 142, 156, 158, 159, n. 96, n. 173, n. 242, n. 336, n. 510, n. 614, n. 659, n. 671.
Buṭāna: 30, 58, 118, n. 105, n. 238.
camel: 107, 113, n. 254, n. 464, n. 480.
cattle: 24, 62, 98, 126, 127, n. 540, n. 547.

Christian Topography: 37, 39, 41, 54, 55, 68, n. 142, n. 181, n. 222, n. 304, n. 657.
Christianity: 42, 77, 88, 89, 91, 93, 95, 100, 110, 126, 130, 155, 162, n. 154, n. 203, n. 242, n. 385, n. 426, n. 657.
coins, Aksumite: 70, 139, 152, 157.
Constantine: 71, 93, 140, n. 381, n. 613.
Constantius II: 91, 91, 92, 96, n. 381.
Constantius Chlorus: n. 242.
copper: 107, 108, 111, 129, 134, n. 466.
Cosmas Indicopleustes: 13, 37, 38, 41, 42, 45, 47, 53, 55, 61, 68, 152, n. 138, n. 139, n. 142, n. 181, n. 220, n. 221, n. 222, n. 304, n. 657.
cotton: 27, 107, 108, 111, 129, 134, n. 79, n. 96, n. 467, n. 468.
Dāne'ēl: 163, 165.
Daro: 114, 115, 117, 121.
Di'mat: 17, 19, 20, 22, 30, 32, n. 23, n. 31, n. 32, n. 33, n. 40, n. 41, n. 51, n. 142, n. 277.
Diocletian: 48, 64, n. 189, n. 613.
Dodekaschoinos: 48, 64, n. 187, n. 189, n. 659.
Dongola Reach: 83, n. 514.
Eastern Desert: 14, 17, 28, 37, 45, 49, 50, 59, 60, 62, 64, 65, 81, 157, n. 96, n. 125, n. 173, n. 176.
    ware: 33, 105, 159, n. 125, n. 197.
Egypt
    Ptolemaic: 25, n. 66, n. 264.
    Roman: 13, 27, 32, 34, 37, 46, 48, 52, 59, 60, 63, 64, 65, 153, 159, n. 187, n. 225.
'Ella 'Amīdā (see Ousanas)
Eritrea: 15, 18, 23, 26, 27, 31, 35, 43, 47, 60, 118, n. 3, n. 32, n. 51, n. 142, n. 411.
Ethiopian Highlands: 12, 13, 29, 30, 35, 37, 44, 45, 51, 52, 57, 59, 65, 69, 80, 98, 153, 159, 167, n. 142, n. 219, n. 364, n. 522.
Ethiosemitic: 21, 47, 69, 98, n. 30, n. 467, n. 484.
Eusebius: 140, n. 599.
'Ēzānā: 11, 12, 13, 14, 40, 42, 44, 47, 52, 54, 59, 67, 71, 73, 75, 76, 79, 80, 82, 85, 85, 86, 87, 88, 89, 91, 92, 94, 95, 97, 98, 99, 101, 103, 104, 106, 106, 106, 108, 109, 110, 112, 114, 115, 116, 119, 121, 123, 125, 125,

127, 129, 132, 133, 134, 134, 136, 137, 138, 138, 140, 143, 145, 146, 149, 150, 151, 154, 157, 160, 165, 168, n. 145, n. 154, n. 211, n. 219, n. 246, n. 263, n. 270, n. 279, n. 283, n. 364, n. 385, n. 400, n. 404, n. 409, n. 426, n. 432, n. 433, n. 445, n. 454, n. 467, n. 485, n. 538, n. 539, n. 548, n. 552, n. 554, n. 567, n. 614.
Fertoti: 114, 116, 118, 121, 146.
fīdal: 21, 52, 69, 130, n. 535, n. 554.
Frumentius: 89, 91, 93, 96, 164, n. 381, n. 382, n. 400.
Gadarā: 43, 68.
Gash Delta: 16, 30, 81, 171.
George of Cappadocia: 91, 91, 96.
gold: 54, 55, 70, 73, 80, 107, 112, 152, 160, 170, n. 234, n. 263, n. 264, n. 470, n. 641.
    mines: 62.
Ḥājiz Group: 30, 104, n. 445.
Ḥarsiyotef: 81, n. 337.
Heliodorus: 140, 141, 171, n. 605, n. 610, n. 612.
Hiera Sykaminos (see Maḥarraqa)
Ḥimyar: 43, 52, 69, 77, 101, 149, 150, 151, 154, 158, n. 142, n. 269, n. 409, n. 432, n. 464, n. 628, n. 629, n. 636, n. 671, n. 678.
Hittites: 169, n. 709.
El Hobagi: 109, 144, n. 460.
Horn of Africa: 14, 18, 25, 37, 78, 98, 125, 167, 168, 170, n. 3, n. 13, n. 23, n. 27, n. 30, n. 58, n. 221.
incense: 16, 170, n. 221, n. 715, n. 716.
India: 25, 37, 62, 89, 139, 140, 156, 167, n. 3, n. 10, n. 66, n. 79, n. 96, n. 139, n. 382, n. 468, n. 614.
Indian Ocean: 15, 25, 27, n. 66.
iron: 27, 55, 107, 108, 111, 129, 134, n. 224, n. 472, n. 473, n. 474, n. 476, n. 548.
ivory: 34.
Jabal Qaylī: 30.
John of Ephesus: 14, 150, 161, 162, n. 657, n. 681, n. 682, n. 686.
Julian of Halicarnassus: 161.
Justin I: 158, 159.
Justinian: 162, n. 657.

Kālēb: 12, 22, 40, 43, 77, 111, 129, 131, 138, 147, 149, 150, 151, 154, 157, 158, 159, 161, n. 50, n. 142, n. 148, n. 269, n. 432, n. 449, n. 464, n. 465, n. 485, n. 628, n. 630, n. 636, n. 650, n. 671.
Karib'īl Watar Yuhan'im: 43.
Kasalā: 105, 108, 118, 163, 165.
Kāsū: 18, 53, 88, 101, 109, 114.
Kawa: 120, 121, 137.
Kerma: 16, 111.
Kordofan: 82, n. 649.
al-Kurrū: 144, n. 620.
Kyeneion: 34.
Longinus: 161, 162.
Ma'dīkarib Ya'fur: 149.
Maḥarraqa: 48.
Maḥrem: 42, 73, 88, 125.
Makouria: 155, n. 329, n. 514.
Mangurto: 95, 97, 98, 102, 103, 105, 120, n. 432, n. 445.
Marsā Gawāsīs: 16.
Medjayū: 81.
Meroë: 14, 18, 29, 31, 33, 44, 49, 63, 67, 72, 73*ff.*, 73, 74, 75, 77, 78, 78, 80, 82, 84, 92, 92, 97, 109, 112, 116, 119, 121, 124, 136, 138, 139, 140, 141, 143, 144, 145, 146, n. 96, n. 106, n. 211, n. 240, n. 290, n. 364, n. 454, n. 458, n. 468, n. 473, n. 474, n. 518, n. 547, n. 620, n. 659.
Meroitic: 18, 21, 31, 49, 82, 109, 119, 136, 168, n. 43, n. 189, n. 342, n. 351, n. 416, n. 578, n. 649, n. 659.
Metete: 81, n. 337.
Muṣawwarāt al-Ṣafrā': 58, 132, 140, n. 240.
musnad: 19, 21, 52, 69, 80, 85, 86, 129, 130, 132, 150, 156, 168, n. 32, n. 285, n. 535, n. 552, n. 564.
Mycenaeans: 169, n. 709.
Najrān: 43.
Napata: 18, 83, 119, 138, n. 24, n. 473, n. 591.
Nastaseñ: 127, 135, n. 491.
Nile Valley: 11*ff.*, 14*ff.*, 18, 22, 26, 48, 50, 58, 60, 67, 82, 97, 109, 118, 134, 167, n. 10, n. 125, n. 173, n. 351, n. 445, n. 468, n. 480.
    middle: 12, 15, 30, 83, 86, 99, 105, 143, 167.

Nobades: 84, 156, 158, 159, n. 189, n. 657, n. 671.
Nobatia: 162.
Nubia, Lower: 48, 84, 144, 152, 156, n. 78, n. 189, n. 254, n. 473, n. 659.
Nubian language: 12, 82, 84, 105, 119, n. 96, n. 189, n. 342, n. 351, n. 353, n. 416, n. 489.
obsidian: 14, n. 7, n. 712.
Ousanas: 11, 12, 13, 14, 60, 61, 67, 70, 76, 76, 78, 80, 80, 82, 85, 86, 88, 90, 93, 99, 101, 106, 129, 132, 133, 138, 140, 143, 145, 146, 150, 151, 154, 160, n. 285, n. 315, n. 337, n. 341.
Periplus of the Erythraean Sea: 25, 26, 33, 34, 60, 75, 125, n. 67, n. 68, n. 69, n. 71, n. 86, n. 97, n. 100, n. 126, n. 530.
Phonen: 156.
pottery: 16, 23, 27, 32, 34, 37, 61, 104, 151, n. 7, n. 10, n. 53, n. 75, n. 125, n. 351, n. 454, n. 709.
Procopius: 48, 61, n. 142, n. 189, n. 253, n. 357, n. 630, n. 636.
Ptolemaic Period: 23, 40, n. 58.
Ptolemaïs Theron: 26, 33.
Ptolemy III: 38, n. 58.
Punt: 16, 168, n. 15, n. 272.
Qāni': 28, 151.
Red Sea: 7, 12, 13, 15, 22, 25, 26, 41, 41, 43, 50, 60, 64, 65, 68, 149, 154, 167, 168, 170, n. 7, n. 10, n. 27, n. 58, n. 78, n. 96, n. 110, n. 142, n. 242.
roads, Aksumite: 59, 61, 64, 132, 133, 135.
Roman Empire: 25, 30, 51, 84, 90, 146, 167, n. 66, n. 242.
Rufinus of Aquileia: 89, 94, 104, n. 242, n. 375, n. 398.
Saba': 19, 20, 43, 69, 101, 149, 150, 151, 154, n. 29, n. 41, n. 149, n. 678.
Sāsānids: 85, 141, n. 357.
Sasu: 52, 53, 55, 58, 63, 64, 80, 152, 170, n. 221.
Śe'āzānā: 91, 91, 93, 125, n. 385.
Sembrouthes: 43, 68, n. 274.
sheep: 62, 98, 122, 127.
Silko: 156, n. 659.
Sinnār: 34, n. 241.
slaves: 98, 125, n. 142, n. 416, n. 533.

SNM 24841: 73, 74, 75, 76, 78, 80, 86, 97, 99, 121, 124, 136, 145, n. 304, n. 364.
Soba: 32, 117, 152, 161, 163, 171, n. 454.
Somalia: 25, 152, 159, n. 3, n. 15, n. 222.
Soqotra: 28, n. 220, n. 653.
Sri Lanka: 28.
Sumūyafa' 'Ashwa': 149, n. 629.
Syene (see Aswān)
Tabito: 114, 116, 118, 121, 146.
Tabo: 137, n. 473.
Tabot: 28, 33, 37, 61, 171.
Tasanay: 31.
Tekkazē River: 34.
Teqorideamani: 44.
temples: 20, 31, 73, 120, 124, n. 106, n. 528.
    Kushite: 81, 136, 137.
    Noba: 107, 108, 110, 122, 138, 156, n. 454.
Tihāma: 22, 41, 43, 149, 150, 154, n. 164, n. 432.
trade: 11, 13, 15, 24, 25, 26, 30, 32, 34, 37, 49, 54, 55, 60, 61, 64, 125, 139, 143, 152, 167, 167, 168, 170, 171, n. 7, n. 66, n. 75, n. 225, n. 226, n. 246, n. 329, n. 466, n. 468, n. 533, n. 641, n. 716.
Wādī al-'Allāqī: 62, n. 264.
Wa'zeb: 12, 129, 147, 149, 160, n. 630, n. 678.
Wāzēbā: 76, 90, 93, n. 315, n. 341.
Yemen: 12, 16, 19, 22, 28, 41, 77, 151, 154, n. 27, n. 142, n. 149, n. 276, n. 432, n. 464, n. 653.
Yūsuf 'As'ar Yath'ar: 149, 152, 158.
Ẓafār: 43, 69, 77, 149, 154, n. 142, n. 464, n. 485.
zebu: 15, n. 10.

CPSIA information can be obtained at www.ICGtesting.com
Printed in the USA
LVOW132040100613

337905LV00001B/2/P

9 780814 760666